THE SHREDDED CHEF

120 RECIPES FOR BUILDING MUSCLE, GETTING LEAN, AND STAYING HEALTHY

Michael Matthews

oculus

ISBN-978-1478213659

Cover Designed by: Damon Freeman

Typesetting by Kiersten Lief

Published by: Waterbury Publishers, Inc.

www.oculuspublishers.com

Visit the author's website:

www.muscleforlife.com

ABOUT THE AUTHOR

Hi,

I'm Mike and I've been training for nearly a decade now.

I believe that every person can achieve the body of his or her dreams, and I work hard to give everyone that chance by providing workable, proven advice grounded in science, not a desire to sell phony magazines, workout products, or supplements.

Through my work, I've helped thousands of people achieve their health and fitness goals, and I share everything I know in my books.

So if you're looking to get in shape and look great, then I think I can help you. I hope you enjoy my books and I'd love to hear from you at my site, www.muscleforlife.com.

Sincerely,

Mike

CONTENTS

Never be bored with a poultry dish again! This section has chicken and turkey recipes for getting big, for getting ripped, and it has 5 of my favorite marinades!

In this section, you'll find the following recipes:

Chicken & Turkey Recipes for Getting Lean   81

BEEF   111

It's hard to beat beef when it comes to building muscle, and in this section, you'll learn some of my favorite dishes! This section has beef recipes for getting big and for getting ripped.

In this section, you'll find the following recipes:

Pork tenderloin is a great source of lean protein, and it can be prepared in many ways!

In this section, you'll find the following recipes:

FISH & SEAFOOD   159

Fish is one of the healthiest sources of protein you can eat and perfect for getting lean.

In this section, you'll find the following recipes:

PASTA & GRAINS   185

Whole grains are a great source of slow-burning carbohydrates and fiber.

In this section, you'll find the following recipes:

Delicious salads with tasty, low-calorie dressings are a great addition to every diet.

In this section, you'll find the following recipes:

Great side dishes are a perfect way to add some excitement and variety of taste to your meals.

In this section, you'll find the following recipes:

PROTEIN SHAKES   249

Protein shakes are a great way to meet daily nutrition requirements, and are especially good for post-workout meals.

In this section, you'll find the following recipes:

PROTEIN BARS AND SNACKS   259

Learn how to make your own healthy protein bars using high-quality ingredients, plus a few other yummy snacks!

In this section, you'll find the following recipes:

DESSERTS   283

Everyone likes a tasty indulgence now and then, so I haven't forgotten the sweets.

In this section, you'll find the following recipes:

BONUS SPREADSHEET   295

Chances are you'd like to use the recipes in this book to plan out your meals. This handy spreadsheet will help! In it you'll find a list of every recipe in the book along with their calories, protein, carbs, and fats!

BUILD MUSCLE AND LOSE FAT BY EATING TASTY, NUTRITIOUS FOOD

I used to hate cooking because I sucked at it.

Literally everything I made tasted horrible—and it took way too long.

To make things worse, I'm into weight lifting and had to eat a lot of that crappy food every week.

When I was eating to gain muscle, I couldn't really enjoy it because I didn't know how to make tasty meals that gave me enough calories and macronutrients (protein, carbs, and fats). I basically felt like a farm animal hitting the daily trough of chicken, eggs, oatmeal, brown rice, and potatoes.

When I was dieting to lose weight, well, I cringe when I think of the bland, plain chicken breasts and vegetables that I used to force down every day for months (I became quite a connoisseur of hot sauce, but eventually even that couldn't redeem the food). I would get excited over the banana I got to have with my afternoon shake. My buddies joked that I had the palate of a Rottweiler.

Finally, after years of desensitizing myself to food, I decided to figure out how to cook fast, healthy meals that tasted good and also met my nutritional needs. I wanted to look forward to hearty, nutritious meals when eating to gain muscle, and I wanted to enjoy some of what I got to eat while losing weight.

This book is a compilation of recipes that fit the bill. Every recipe in this book is designed to help you build lean muscle or lose fat while actually getting healthier (because who cares if you look great but feel like crap?).

And they all TASTE GOOD.

So why buy this book?

Because following a diet, whether to get bigger or lose fat, is SO much more pleasurable when you can enjoy your meals. I think this book will become a good friend.

WHAT MAKES
THE SHREDDED CHEF
DIFFERENT?

As you probably know, you *must* eat properly to see good results from working out. You can grind away on the treadmill and pound weights until the cows come home and still see little to no results if you don't know how to support those activities with the right nutrition.

Muscles can't grow unless the body has the right nutrients to repair the damage caused by lifting weights. Eat too little, and you can not only fail to make gains, but you can actually lose muscle.

Your body can't lose fat unless you make it operate at just the right deficit of calories. Eat just a few hundred too many calories per day, and you'll find yourself stuck in the miserable rut of feeling like you're "on a diet" without losing any weight.

That being said, many diet plans out there exist in a vacuum. That is, they assume that eating conditions will always remain the same. They don't take into account the fact that most people can't stomach the same handful of food options every day, or that being severely restricted in one's diet can lead to all-out splurging, which then leads to the dreaded weight yo-yo.

What's needed is *balance*—a diet that allows for a variety of foods and that allows you to indulge now and again. It also has to be simple and practical so as to fit in with the craziness of our daily lives. And last but not least, it needs to enhance your overall health by incorporating healthy carbs and fats instead of the junk found in most people's fridges.

Well, that's what *The Shredded Chef* is all about. If you follow the advice given in this book, you'll not only find it easy to follow diets to gain muscle or lose fat, but you'll also be able to actually enjoy them.

As you'll see, most of the recipes are sorted into two categories: recipes for getting big and recipes for getting lean.

Recipes for getting big are going to be higher-calorie meals with a fair amount of carbs and fats, and they'll help you reach your daily calorie needs for building muscle.

Recipes for getting lean are lower-calorie meals with few carbs and fats, which is vital for dieting successfully.

You can, of course, eat any of the recipes whether you're trying to build muscle or lose weight. You simply have to ensure whatever you eat fits within your dietary plan.

So yes, this is a cookbook, but it's also going to teach you a bit about how to use these recipes to get bigger, leaner, and stronger...*and* healthier. And with 120 recipes, I think you'll get quite a lot of use out of this book.

HOW TO EAT RIGHT WITHOUT OBSESSING OVER EVERY CALORIE

I have good news.

You can look and feel great without breaking out a calculator every time you eat.

Getting proper nutrition is a precise science, but it doesn't have to be agonizing. In fact, I recommend a more laid-back approach. If you make planning or tracking meals too complicated, you'll have trouble sticking with it.

That being said, in order to lose fat, you must keep your body burning more energy than you're feeding it, and the energy potential of food is measured in calories. Eat too many calories—give your body more potential energy than it needs—and it has no incentive to burn fat.

In order to gain muscle, your body needs a surplus of energy to repair and rebuild itself (along with plenty of protein). Thus, you need to eat slightly more than your body burns to get bigger.

In this chapter I'm going to share some simple rules that you can follow to eat right. Just by following these rules, you'll find that you can lose or gain weight when you want to and that you'll feel healthy and vital.

1. MAKE SURE YOU EAT ENOUGH

A calorie is a measurement of the potential energy found in food, and your body burns quite a bit of energy every day. Everything from the beating of your heart to the digestion of your food requires energy, and your body has to get it from the food you eat.

Thus, it's important that you feed your body enough, and that's especially true when you work out. If you underfeed your body, don't be surprised if you don't have the energy to train hard or if you feel generally exhausted.

If you exercise at least three times per week, use the following formula to ensure you're feeding your body enough to repair itself.

- Eat 1 gram of protein per pound of body weight per day.

- Eat 1.5 grams of carbs per pound of body weight per day.

- Eat 1 gram of healthy fats per 4 pounds of body weight per day.

That's where you start. For a 130 lb. woman, it would look like this:

- 130 grams of protein per day

- 195 grams of carbs per day

- 32 grams of fat per day

That's about 1,600 calories per day, which should work for making slow, steady muscle and strength gains without any fat added along the way (which really should be the goal of "maintenance"—not staying exactly the same).

If your priority is to gain muscle, then you need to add about 500 calories per day to your "maintenance" diet. The easiest way to do this is to bump up your carbs by about 50 grams per day, and your fats by about 30 grams per day.

If you're trying to lose fat, then you need to subtract about 500 calories per day from your maintenance diet. To do this, drop your carbs by about 90 grams per day, your protein by about 10 grams per day.

It's also important that you consume high-quality calories. Junk food calories, such as white bread, pastas, chips, juice and soda, will make you look and feel like crap, while good calories, such as fruits, vegetables, whole grains, and lean proteins, will keep you in tip-top shape.

2. EAT ENOUGH PROTEIN

If you work out, you need more protein than someone who doesn't work out. Why? Because exercise causes muscle damage.

With every rep you perform, you're causing "micro-tears" in your muscle fibers, and your body needs protein to fully repair this damage.

The body doesn't just repair them to their previous state, however; it builds them bigger and stronger so it can better handle the stress of exercise.

So, in order to get the most out of your workouts, you need to eat enough protein. And that doesn't mean just eating a lot after working out. It means eating enough every day, which will require you to eat some with every meal you have (and as a general rule, eating .75 – 1 gram of protein per pound of body weight is a good target if you exercise regularly).

By doing this, you can ensure your body has the amino acids it needs to build muscle and repair tissue. If you fail to feed your body enough protein, it will fall behind in the muscle breakdown and repair cycle, and you can actually get smaller and weaker despite exercise.

There are two main sources of protein out there: whole food protein and supplement protein.

Whole food protein is, as you guessed, protein that comes from natural food sources, such as beef, chicken, fish, etc. The best forms of whole food protein are chicken, turkey, lean red meat, fish, eggs, and milk.

If you're vegetarian, your best options are eggs, low-fat cottage cheese (Organic Valley is my favorite brand), low-fat European style (Greek) yogurt (0% Fage is my favorite), tempeh, tofu, quinoa, almonds, rice, and beans.

While we're on the subject of vegetarianism, some people claim that you must carefully combine your proteins if you're vegetarian or vegan to ensure your body is getting "complete" proteins (all of the amino acids needed to build tissue). This theory and the faulty research it was based on was thoroughly debunked as a myth by the American Dietetic Association, yet it still hangs around. While it's true that some sources of vegetable protein are lower in certain amino acids than other forms of protein, there is no scientific evidence to prove that they lack them altogether.

Protein supplements are powdered or liquid foods that contain protein from various sources, such as whey (a liquid remaining after milk has been curdled and strained in the process of making cheese), egg, and soy—the three most common sources of supplement protein. There are also great plant-based supplements out there that are a blend of high-quality protein sources such as quinoa, brown rice, peas, hemp, and fruit.

You don't NEED protein supplements to eat well, but it can be impractical for some to try to get all their protein from whole foods considering the fact that you will be eating protein 4 – 6 times per day.

Now, there are a few things you should know about eating protein. First is the subject of how much protein you can absorb in one sitting. Studies relating to this are very contradictory and disputed, mainly because it's a complex subject. Your genetics, metabolism, digestive tract health, lifestyle, and amount of lean mass are all important factors. But in the spirit of keeping things simple, here's what we know: you can eat and properly use a lot of protein in each meal. How much, exactly? Well, your body should have no trouble absorbing upwards of 100 grams in one sitting.

That said, there aren't any benefits of eating this way (I find gorging quite uncomfortable, actually), but it's good to know in case you miss a meal and need to make it up by loading protein into a later meal.

Another thing to know about protein is that different proteins digest at different speeds, and some are better utilized by the body than others. Beef protein, for example, is digested quickly, and 70 – 80% of what's eaten is utilized by the body (the exact number varies based on what study you read, but they all fall between 70 – 80%). Whey protein is also digested quickly and its "net protein utilization" (NPU) is in the low 90% range. Egg protein digests much slower than whey and beef, and its NPU also falls in the same range.

NPU and digestion speeds are important to know because you want to rely on high-NPU proteins to meet your daily protein requirement, and you want a quick-digesting protein for your post-workout meal, and a slow-digesting protein for your final meal before you go to bed (to help you get through the fasting that occurs during sleep).

I could give you charts and tables of the NPU rates of various proteins, but I'm going to keep it simple. In order to meet your daily protein requirements, here are your choices:

Whole Food Proteins

Lean meats (beef, pork, chicken, and turkey)

Fish

Eggs

Vegetarian sources noted above

Protein Supplements

Egg

Whey

Casein

In case you're wondering why I left soy protein off the list of recommended supplements, it's because it's just a bad protein source. To start, most soy protein supplements use genetically modified soybeans (which is a very dangerous trend encroaching further and further into the world of agriculture), and studies have shown that too much soy can increase estrogen levels and inhibit your body's testosterone production (due to a plant estrogen found in soybeans). Just stay away from it.

3. EAT HEALTHY FATS

Fats are the densest energy source available to your body. Each gram of fat contains over twice the calories of a gram of carbohydrate or protein. Healthy fats, such as those found in olive oil, avocados, flax seed oil, many nuts, and other foods, are actually an important component for overall good health. Fats help your body absorb the other nutrients that you give it; they nourish the nervous system, help maintain cell structures, regulate hormone levels, and more.

Saturated fats are a form of fat found mainly in animal products such as meat, dairy products, and egg yolks. Some plant foods, such as coconut oil, palm oil, and palm kernel oil, are also high in saturated fats. While it's commonly believed that eating saturated fat harms your health, the opposite is actually true. Recent studies have shown that including saturated fats in your diet can reduce your risk of heart disease.

Trans fats are scientifically modified saturated fats that have been engineered to give foods longer shelf lives. Many cheap, packaged foods are full of trans fats (such as run-of-the-mill popcorn, yogurt, and peanut butter) as are many frozen foods (such as frozen pizza, packaged pastries, cakes, etc.). And fried foods are often fried in trans fats. These fats are bad news, and eating too much of them can lead to all kinds of diseases and complications. They have no nutritional value for the body and thus should be avoided altogether.

Most people eat more fat than is necessary, thus adding lots of unnecessary calories to their daily intake. Getting enough healthy fats every day is pretty simple. Here's how it works:

- Keep your intake of saturated fats relatively low (below 10% of your total calories). Saturated fat is found in foods like meat, dairy products, eggs, coconut oil, bacon fat, and lard. If a fat is solid at room temperature, it's a saturated fat.

- Completely avoid trans fats. Trans fats are found in processed foods such as cookies, cakes, fries, and doughnuts. Any food that contains "hydrogenated oil" or "partially hydrogenated oil" likely contains trans fats, so just don't eat it. (Sure, having a cheat here and there that contains trans fats won't harm anything, but you definitely don't want to eat them regularly.)

- Get at least half of your daily fat from unsaturated fats such as olive oil, nuts, peanut oil, avocados, flax seed oil, safflower oil, or sesame oil. If a fat is liquid at room temperature, it's an unsaturated fat.

By simply sticking to the recipes in this book, you'll avoid unhealthy fats and include healthy fats without even trying.

4. EAT GOOD CARBS

The carbohydrate is probably the most misunderstood, maligned, and feared macro-nutrient. Thanks to the scores of bogus diet plans and suggestions out there, many people equate eating carbs with getting fat. While eating TOO MANY carbs can make you fat (just as eating too much protein or fat can), carbs are hardly your enemy. They play an essential role in not only muscle growth but in overall body function.

Regardless of what type of carbohydrate you eat—broccoli or apple pie—the body breaks it down into two substances: glucose and glycogen. Glucose is commonly referred to as "blood sugar," and it's an energy source used by your cells to do the many things they do. Glycogen is a substance stored in the liver and muscles that can be easily converted to glucose for immediate energy. When you lift weights intensely, your muscles burn up their glycogen stores to cope with the overload.

Now, why is broccoli good for you but apple pie isn't? Because your body reacts very differently to broccoli than to apple pie. You've probably heard the terms "simple" and "complex" carbs before and wondered what they meant. You might have also heard of the glycemic index and wondered what it was all about.

These things are actually pretty simple. The glycemic index is a numeric system of ranking how quickly carbohydrates are converted into glucose in the body. Carbs are ranked on a scale of 0 to 100 depending how they affect blood sugar levels once eaten. A GI rating of 55 and under is considered "low GI," 56 to 69 is medium, and 70 and above is high on the index. A "simple" carb is one that converts very quickly (is high on the glycemic index), such as table sugar, honey, and watermelon, while a "complex" carb is one that converts slowly (is low on the glycemic index), such as broccoli, apple, and whole-grain bread.

It's very important to know where the carbs you eat fall on the index, because studies have linked regular consumption of high-GI carbs to increased risk for heart disease, diabetes, and obesity.

The amount of carbohydrates that you should eat every day depends on what you're trying to accomplish. Building muscle requires that you eat a substantial amount of carbs, while dieting to lose weight requires that you reduce carbs.

Regardless of how many carbs you need to eat per day, there's a simple rule to follow regarding high-, medium- and low-glycemic carbs.

Eat carbs in the medium–high range of the glycemic index (60 – 90 is a good rule of thumb) about 30 minutes before you exercise, and again within 30 minutes of finishing your workout.

The reason you want some carbs before training is that you need the energy for your training. The reason you want them after is that your muscles' glycogen stores are heavily depleted, and by replacing glycogen quickly, you actually help your body maintain an anabolic state and not lose muscle tissue.

My favorite pre- and post-workout carbs are bananas and rice milk, but other good choices are baked potato, instant oatmeal, and fruits that are above 60 on the glycemic index, such as cantaloupe, pineapple, watermelon, dates, apricots, and figs. Some people recommend eating foods high in table sugar (sucrose) after working out because it's high on the GI, but I stay away from processed sugar as much as possible.

All other carbs you eat should be in the middle or at the low end of the glycemic index (60 and below is a good rule of thumb). It really is that simple. If you follow this rule, you'll avoid many problems that others suffer from due to the energy highs and lows that come with eating high-GI carbs that burn the body out.

Below is a list of common snack foods with corresponding average GI scores. The GI scores vary a bit from brand to brand, but not by much. Generally speaking, it's best to stay away from these types of carbs.

(The following information is sourced from the University of Sydney, the University of Harvard, and Livestrong.com.)

FOOD	GI
White bread bagel	72
Corn chips	63

Pretzels	83
Candy bar	62 – 78
Wheat or corn cracker	67 – 87
Rye cracker	64
Rice cake	78
Popcorn	72
White rice	64
Pizza	80
Raisins	64
Whole wheat bread	71
White bread	70
Baguette	95
English muffin (white bread)	77
Baked potato	85
Muesli	66

So, forget stuff like sugar, white bread, processed, low-quality whole wheat bread, bagels, junk cereals, muffins, white pasta, crackers, waffles, rice cakes, corn flakes, and white rice. I wouldn't even recommend eating these things often as pre- or post-workout carbs because they're just not good for your body.

Even certain fruits, such as watermelon and dates, are bad snack foods because of where they fall on the glycemic index. If you're unsure about a carb you like, look it up to see where it falls on the glycemic index. If it's above 60, just leave it out of your meals that aren't immediately before or after working out.

5. EAT YOUR FRUITS AND VEGGIES

Your body requires many different things to function optimally. It can't look and feel great on protein and carbs alone. You need calcium to ensure your muscles can contract and relax properly. You need fiber to help move food through the digestive tract. You need iron to carry oxygen to your cells and create energy.

There are many other "little helpers" that your body needs to perform its many physiological processes, and fruits and vegetables contain many vital nutrients that you can't get from vitamin supplements. By eating 3 – 5 servings of both fruits and vegetables per day, you enjoy the many benefits that these nutrients give to your body, such as lowering your risk of cancer, heart disease, diabetes, and many other diseases.

This isn't hard to do, either. A medium-sized piece of fruit is one serving, as is half a cup of berries. A cup of greens is a serving of vegetables, as is half a cup of other vegetables.

Fruit *juices*, however, are another story. While they may seem like an easy way to get in your daily fruits, they are actually not much more than tasty sugar water. Not only do most fruit juices have sugar added, but the juice has also been separated from the fruit's fibrous pulp, which slows down the metabolism of the sugars. Without that, the juice becomes a very high-glycemic drink. You're better off drinking water and eating whole fruit.

The exception to this is creating juice using a juicer or blender to grind up the entire piece of fruit, removing nothing. This, of course, is no different than chewing up the fruit in your mouth.

Fruits widely recognized as the healthiest are apples, bananas, blueberries, oranges, grapefruit, strawberries, and pineapples.

Vegetables often recommended as the healthiest are asparagus, broccoli, spinach, sweet potatoes, tomatoes, carrots, onions, and eggplant.

6. PLAN AND PROPORTION YOUR MEALS PROPERLY

Many people's meal plans are engineered for getting fat. They skip breakfast, eat a junk food lunch, come home famished, have a big dinner with some dessert, and then have a snack like chips or popcorn while watching TV at night.

A much better strategy is to eat smaller meals every 3 – 4 hours, and include protein with each (as this fills you up and makes you feel satisfied).

Much of your daily carbohydrates should come before and after training, when your body needs them most. I eat about 10 – 15% of my daily carbs before training, and about 30 – 40% after, in my post-workout meal.

It's also important when dieting to lose weight to not eat carbs within several hours of going to bed. This advice has been kicking around the health and fitness world for quite some time, but usually with the wrong explanation.

There's no scientific evidence that eating carbs at night or before bed will lead to gaining fat, but it can *hinder* fat loss. How?

The insulin created by the body to process and absorb carbs eaten stops the use of fat as an energy source. Your body naturally burns the most fat while sleeping, and so going to sleep with elevated insulin levels interferes with fat loss.

Related to this is the fact that studies have indicated that the production and processing of insulin interferes with the production and processing of growth hormone, which has powerful fat-burning properties. Your body naturally produces much of its growth hormone while sleeping, so again, if your body is flushed with insulin when you go to sleep, your growth hormone production may suffer, which in turn may rob you of its fat-burning and muscle-building benefits.

So, as a general rule, when you're dieting to lose weight, don't eat any carbs within 4 – 5 hours of bedtime. You should only consume lean proteins after dinner. I follow this rule when bulking too, not because I'm worried about fat burning (you don't burn fat when bulking), but because I don't want to stunt my growth hormone production.

You can spread your fats throughout the day. I like to start my day with 1 – 2 tablespoons of a 3-6-9 blend (a combination of essential fatty acids, which are fats vital for the proper function of every cell, tissue, gland, and organ in your body), but you don't have to get one if you don't want to. You can simply stick to the sources of healthy fat given earlier.

7. DRINK A LOT OF WATER

The human body is about 60% water in adult males and about 70% in adult females. Muscles are about 70% water. That alone tells you how important staying hydrated is to maintaining good health and proper body function. Your body's ability to digest, transport, and absorb nutrients from food is dependent upon proper fluid intake. Water helps prevent injuries in the gym by cushioning joints and other soft-tissue areas. When your body is dehydrated, literally every physiological process is negatively affected.

I really can't stress enough the importance of drinking clean, pure water. It has zero calories, so it will never cause you to gain weight regardless of how much you drink. (You can actually harm your body by drinking too much water, but this would require that you drink several gallons per day.)

The Institute of Medicine reported in 2004 that women should consume about 91 ounces of water—or three-quarters of a gallon—per day, and men should consume about 125 ounces per day (a gallon is 128 ounces).

Now, keep in mind that those numbers include the water found in food. The average person gets about 80% of their water from drinking it and other beverages, and about 20% from the food they eat.

I've been drinking 1 – 2 gallons of water per day for years now, which is more than the IOM baseline recommendation, but I sweat a fair amount due to exercise and I live in Florida, which surely makes my needs higher. I fill a one-gallon jug at the start of my day and simply make sure that I finish it by dinner time. By the time I go to bed, I'll have drank a few more glasses.

Make sure the water you drink is filtered, purified water and not tap water. There's a big difference between drinking clean, alkaline water that your body can fully utilize and drinking polluted, acidic junk from the tap or bottle (which is the case with certain brands such as Dasani and Aquafina).

8. CUT BACK ON THE SODIUM

The average American's diet is so over-saturated with sodium it makes my head spin.

The Institute of Medicine recommends 1,500 milligrams of sodium per day as the adequate intake level for most adults. According to the CDC, the average American aged 2 and up eats *3,436 milligrams* of sodium per day.

Too much sodium in the body causes water retention (which gives you that puffy, soft look) and it can lead to high blood pressure and heart disease.

Frozen and canned foods are full of sodium, as are cured meats like bacon and sausage (one slice of bacon contains *1,000 milligrams* of sodium!).

Whenever possible, I chose low- or no-sodium ingredients for the recipes in this book. When you need to add salt, I recommend sea salt or Himalayan rock salt (sounds like fancy BS, but it's actually great stuff) because it has many naturally occurring minerals, whereas run-of-the-mill table salt has been "chemically cleaned" to remove "impurities," which includes these vital elements.

9. CHEAT CORRECTLY

Many people struggling with diets talk about "cheat days." The idea is that if you're good during the week, you can go buck wild on the weekends and somehow not gain fat. Well, unless you have a very fast metabolism, that's not how it works. If you follow a strict diet and exercise, you can expect to lose 1 – 2 pounds per week. If you get too crazy, you can gain it right back over a weekend.

So don't think cheat DAYS, think cheat MEALS—meals where you eat more or less anything you want (and all other meals of the week follow your meal plan). When done once or twice per week, a cheat meal is not only satisfying, but it can actually help you lose fat.

How?

Well, first there's the psychological boost, which keeps you happy and motivated, which ultimately makes sticking to your diet easier.

But there's also a physiological boost.

Studies on overfeeding (the scientific term for binging on food) show that doing so can boost your metabolic rate by anywhere from 3 – 10%. While this sounds good, it actually doesn't mean much when you consider that you would need to eat anywhere from a few hundred to a few thousand extra calories in a day to achieve this effect.

More important are the effects cheating has on a hormone called leptin, which regulates hunger, your metabolic rate, appetite, motivation, and libido, as well as serving other functions in your body.

When you're in a caloric deficit and lose body fat, your leptin levels drop. This, in turn, causes your metabolism to slow down, your appetite to increase, your motivation to wane, and your mood to sour.

On the other hand, when you give your body more energy (calories) than it needs, leptin levels are boosted, which can then have positive effects on fat oxidation, thyroid activity, mood, and even testosterone levels.

So if it's a leptin boost that you really want, how do you best achieve it?

Eating carbohydrates is the most effective way. Second to that is eating protein (high-protein meals also raise your metabolic rate). Dietary fats aren't very effective at increasing leptin levels, and alcohol actually inhibits it.

So, if your weight is stuck and you're irritable and demotivated, a nice kick of leptin might be all you need to get the scales moving again.

Have a nice cheat meal full of protein and carbs, and feel good about it.

(I would recommend, however, that you don't go too overboard with your cheat meals—don't eat 2,000 calories of junk food and desserts and think it won't do anything.)

How many cheat meals you should eat per week depends on what you're trying to accomplish.

When you're eating to stay lean and gain muscle slowly, two cheat meals per week is totally fine. When you're dieting to lose weight, you can have one cheat meal per week.

THE BOTTOM LINE

You may find this chapter a bit hard to swallow (no pun intended). Some people have a really hard time giving up their unhealthy eating habits (sugar and junk food can be pretty addictive). That being said, consider the following benefits of following the advice in this chapter:

1. If this is a completely new way of eating for you, I *guarantee* you'll feel better than you have in a *long* time. You won't have energy highs and lows. You won't feel lethargic. You won't have that mental fogginess that comes with being stuffed full of unhealthy food every day.

2. You will appreciate "bad" food so much more when you only have it once or twice per week. You'd be surprised how much better a dessert tastes when you haven't had one in a week. (You may also be surprised that junk food that you loved in the past no longer tastes good.)

3. You will actually come to enjoy healthy foods. I *promise*. Even if they don't taste good to you at first, just groove in the routine, and soon you'll crave brown rice and fruit instead of doughnuts and bread. Your body will adapt.

This chapter teaches you all there really is to eating properly so you can build muscle or lose weight on demand, all while staying healthy.

LET'S GET COOKING

Getting lean, while still feeding your muscles and body what they need, can be tough. That's why I wrote this book, and I'm confident that you'll be able to find the right recipes to fit your needs.

Nothing in this book is fancy or hard to make, yet many of the recipes are quite delicious. I'm sure that you'll find some new staples for your diet in this book.

For most of these recipes all you'll need is a couple pots and pans, and maybe a blender. The instructions are easy to follow, the prep times are minimal, and the ingredients are easy to find. Cooking doesn't get much simpler than this.

I recommend that you pick out a week's worth of recipes and then go shopping for the ingredients. Many of the recipes use the same ingredients, which will save you money and time.

So, let's get started!

BREAKFAST

For many years now, a staple in weight-loss plans and maintenance advice has been to make sure you eat a nice, big breakfast every day.

This is backed by observational research in which eating breakfast is associated with lower body weight in large populations, but it perfectly illustrates how bad advice can become so prevalent in this industry.

Observational research, which can't establish causation, suggests that something may be the case (skipping breakfast seems to be negatively associated with body weight), but indicates that more rigorous research is needed to see if there truly is a connection and why.

The media, however, jumps on such studies as cold, hard proof and starts running stories with headlines announcing "breakthrough" discoveries. Big health and fitness magazines and websites pick up on those stories for new content, trainers and gym-goers read it and spread it, and on it goes.

The side of the breakfast story you're not told is that research has shown that people who skip breakfast are more likely to eat junk food and tend to eat more in general. It wasn't the breakfast skipping that was causing the problem; it was the candy, soda, and excess calories. Breakfast eaters merely tend to maintain better overall dietary habits—no big surprise that they tend to be thinner as well.

So, eat breakfast if you like it (I do), especially if you find yourself very hungry when you wake up. But don't be afraid to delay it a couple of hours or skip it altogether and eat your first meal at lunch if that works better for you. (If you would like to know more about why fasting like this doesn't get in the way of muscle building or weight loss, and why it's actually healthy for you, read my book Muscle Myths.

If you're pressed for time in the mornings, you can make some of the recipes in this section in advance and just keep them in the fridge. Or you can make quick meals like oatmeal or egg scrambles. And if you have a little time, and so desire, treat yourself to something like pancakes (one of my favorite cheat foods!).

BREAKFAST RECIPES FOR GETTING BIG

FRENCH MUSCLE TOAST

Servings: 2 (2 pieces per serving)

Prep Time: 5 mins

Cooking Time: 5 – 10 mins

(Per Serving)

Calories: 445

Protein: 44 grams

Carbohydrates: 50 grams

Fat: 9 grams

1/2 cup skimmed milk

2 large eggs

2 egg whites

2 scoops vanilla whey protein powder

1/2 teaspoon ground cinnamon

4 slices whole grain bread

FOR THE TOPPING:

1 banana, mashed

1 tablespoon strawberry preserves

1 tablespoon water

> Mix the skimmed milk, eggs, and egg whites together in a bowl. Then mix in the protein powder and cinnamon and beat until completely mixed.

> Soak a slice of bread in the mixture until soggy (I like to let it sit for 30 seconds or so).

> Coat a pan with cooking spray and heat on medium-high heat.

> Put one or two slices of bread into the pan and cook for 2 minutes or until golden brown. Then flip the slices and cook the other side for another 1 – 2 minutes or until fully cooked. The bread should no longer be soggy but firm instead.

> While cooking the bread, mix up the fruit and water in a bowl. Top off each slice of bread with a dollop.

HIGH PROTEIN BANANA OATCAKES

Servings: 2 (2 oatcakes per serving)

Prep Time: 5 mins

Cooking Time: 10 mins

(Per Serving)

Calories: 351

Protein: 31 grams

Carbohydrates: 45 grams

Fat: 6 grams

1 cup old-fashioned oats

6 egg whites

1 ripe banana

1 cup low-fat cottage cheese

1/2 teaspoon ground cinnamon

1 teaspoon stevia or other sugar alternative

> Blend everything together until it's a smooth batter.
> Coat a pan with cooking spray and wipe away the excess with a paper towel. Save this for wiping the pan after cooking each pancake. Heat the pan on medium-low heat.

> Spoon about 1/2 cup of batter into the pan and cook for 1 – 2 minutes or until golden brown. Flip the pancake and cook for 30 seconds to 1 minute or until golden brown and firm. Put the pancake on a plate and wipe the pan with the paper towel.

> Repeat step 3 with the rest of the batter.

APPLE CINNAMON OATMEAL

Servings: 4

Prep Time: 5 mins

Cooking Time: 2 – 3 mins

(Per Serving)

Calories: 263

Protein: 29 grams

Carbohydrates: 30 grams

Fat: 3 grams

1 1/2 cups quick cooking oats

1/3 cup nonfat dry milk powder (optional)

1/4 cup dried apples, diced

4 scoops chocolate whey protein powder

1 tablespoon brown sugar

1 tablespoon stevia or other sugar alternative

3/4 teaspoon ground cinnamon

1/4 teaspoon salt

1/8 teaspoon ground cloves

1/2 cup water (per serving)

> Mix all of the ingredients except the water in a large airtight container and store, good for up to 6 months.

> To prepare the oatmeal: Shake the container well to ensure the ingredients are well mixed. In a saucepan, bring 1/2 cup of water to a boil. Measure out and stir in 1/2 cup of the mixture, cook and stir for 1 minute over medium heat. Remove from the heat and cover, let sit for 1 minute or longer depending on desired consistency.

QUICK AND EASY PEANUT BUTTER OATMEAL

Servings: 1

Prep Time: 2 – 3 mins

Cooking Time: 5 – 7 mins

(Per Serving)

Calories: 423

Protein: 41 grams

Carbohydrates: 35 grams

Fat: 14 grams

1/2 cup old-fashioned oats

1/4 teaspoon salt

2 teaspoons ground flax seed (available at Holland & Barratt)

2 egg whites

2/3 cup water

1 tablespoon peanut butter

ground cinnamon, to taste

1 scoop chocolate whey protein powder

> Place oats in a deep microwave safe bowl. Stir in the salt and flaxseed. In a separate bowl, whisk together the egg whites and water, then pour over the oatmeal and stir gently until just combined.

> Microwave on medium for 4 – 6 minutes.

> Remove from microwave and stir in the peanut butter, cinnamon, and protein powder.

BAKED RAISIN OATMEAL

Servings: 1

Prep Time: 3 – 4 mins

Cooking Time: 35 – 40 mins

(Per Serving)

Calories: 399

Protein: 38 grams

Carbohydrates: 42 grams

Fat: 8 grams

1 teaspoon vegetable oil

1/2 teaspoon stevia or other sugar alternative

2 egg whites

2 tablespoons skimmed milk

1/8 teaspoon salt

1/4 teaspoon baking powder

1/2 cup quick cooking oats

1 scoop chocolate or vanilla whey protein powder

1 tablespoon raisins

1/2 teaspoon brown sugar

1/8 teaspoon ground cinnamon

> In a large mixing bowl, beat together the oil and stevia, slowly mix in the egg whites, skimmed milk, salt, baking powder, oats, protein powder, and raisins. Top with the brown sugar and cinnamon and place in refrigerator overnight.

> Heat the oven to 350 °F/180 °C/Gas Mark 4, bake until firm, around 35 minutes.

SWEET POTATO PROTEIN PANCAKES

Servings: 1 (2 pancakes per serving)

Prep Time: 10 mins

Cooking Time: 5 mins

(Per Serving)

Calories: 358

Protein: 24 grams

Carbohydrates: 59 grams

Fat: 3 grams

1 medium-sized sweet potato

1/2 cup old-fashioned oats

1 large egg

4 egg whites

1/2 teaspoon vanilla extract

1/2 teaspoon ground cinnamon

1/4 cup fat-free plain yogurt

> Puncture the sweet potato several times with a fork. Wrap it in a paper towel and microwave it for 5 minutes on high. Run it under cool water and then remove the skin with a knife.

> Blend the oats until they are a powder and dump into a bowl. Blend the sweet potato until smooth and place it into the bowl with the oats. Stir in the egg, egg whites, vanilla extract, cinnamon, and yogurt. Mix well until it forms a smooth batter.

> Coat a pan with cooking spray and wipe away the excess with a paper towel. Save this for wiping the pan after cooking each pancake. Heat the pan on medium-low heat.

> Spoon about 1/2 cup of batter into the pan and cook for 1 – 2 minutes or until golden brown. Flip the pancake and cook for 30 seconds to 1 minute or until golden brown and firm. Put the pancake on a plate and wipe the pan with the paper towel.

> Repeat step 4 with the rest of the batter.

TURKEY BACON & VEGGIE OMELETTE

Servings: 1

Prep Time: 5 – 10 mins

Cooking Time: 5 – 6 mins

(Per Serving)

Calories: 283

Protein: 35 grams

Carbohydrates: 8 grams

Fat: 12 grams

1/2 cup fresh mushrooms, sliced

3 spears asparagus, cut into 2-inch pieces

1/3 cup of scallions/spring onions, chopped

5 egg whites

1 large egg

2 slices turkey bacon, cooked and cut into small slices

1 tablespoon low-fat Parmesan cheese, shredded

> Place a large skillet over medium heat, lightly coat in oil and, once hot, add the mushrooms, asparagus, and scallions/spring onions. Cook, stirring occasionally until the asparagus is fairly soft, about 4 minutes.

> Whisk the eggs and pour over the vegetables, reduce heat to medium-low.

> While the omelette cooks, lift the edge to allow all of the uncooked egg to flow underneath. Once most of the egg is cooked, add the turkey bacon and cheese on top and let melt to desired consistency, fold the omelette in half and remove from heat.

SWEET POTATO & SAUSAGE FRITTATA

Servings: 1

Prep Time: 5 mins

Cooking Time: 15 – 20 mins

(Per Serving)

Calories: 425

Protein: 43 grams

Carbohydrates: 29 grams

Fat: 17 grams

1 medium-sized sweet potato, cut into small cubes

1 breakfast turkey or chicken sausage, chopped

1 egg

6 egg whites

1/4 cup low-fat cheddar cheese, shredded

salt and ground black pepper, to taste

1/8 cup tomato, chopped and seeded

1/8 cup scallions/spring onions, thinly sliced

> Preheat the oven to 350 °F/180 °C/Gas Mark 4.

> Coat a medium-sized oven-proof pan in cooking spray and place over medium heat. Put the potatoes in the pan and cover them for about 5

minutes. Add the sausage and cover, cook for another 4 – 5 minutes, stirring occasionally (you want to cook the sweet potatoes until slightly tender).

> Beat the eggs, cheese, salt, and pepper in a large mixing bowl with a whisk.

> Pour the egg mixture over the sweet potato and sausage and cook for about 5 – 6 minutes, or until the eggs are golden brown on the bottom.

> Transfer the pan to the oven for about 5 minutes, or until top is golden brown. Top with the tomatoes and scallions.

> Top with the tomatoes and scallions/spring onions.

BREAKFAST PITA WRAP

Servings: 1

Prep Time: 5 mins

Cooking Time: 8 – 10 mins

(Per Serving)

Calories: 452

Protein: 31 grams

Carbohydrates: 49 grams

Fat: 20 grams

4 white mushrooms, sliced

1 tablespoon onion, chopped

1 tablespoon red bell pepper, chopped

pinch of ground black pepper

1 large egg

3 egg whites

1/2 small tomato, seeded and chopped

3 tablespoons skimmed milk

1 whole grain pitta (choose the brand with the lowest fat and sodium), halved and toasted

1/2 avocado, sliced

> Coat a pan with cooking spray and cook the mushrooms, onion, and bell pepper on medium heat. Cook for 3 – 4 minutes. Add black pepper.

> Mix the egg, egg whites, tomato, and skimmed milk in a bowl and beat until frothy.

> Pour the egg mixture into the pan and cook for 3 – 4 minutes, stirring until firm.

> Fill each pitta half with half of the egg mixture and half the avocado.

BREAKFAST RECIPES FOR GETTING LEAN

LEAN AND MEAN ZUCCHINI/COURGETTE HASH

Servings: 1

Prep Time: 5 mins

Cooking Time: 10 mins

(Per Serving)

Calories: 202

Protein: 15 grams

Carbohydrates: 11 grams

Fat: 11 grams

2 large eggs

1 cup zucchini/courgette, grated

1/4 cup onion, diced

1/4 teaspoon garlic powder

1/4 teaspoon onion powder

salt and ground black pepper, to taste

> Mix all the ingredients together in a bowl.
> Heat a pan on high and then lower to medium heat.
> Spray some cooking spray into the pan and spoon the mixture into it. Cook about 5 minutes and flip. Cook another 5 minutes.

SIMPLE SPINACH SCRAMBLE

Servings: 1

Prep Time: 2 – 3 mins

Cooking Time: 5 mins

(Per Serving)

Calories: 275

Protein: 36 grams

Carbohydrates: 9 grams

Fat: 10 grams

1 cup spinach (fresh or frozen)

1/4 cup onion, chopped

1/4 cup red bell pepper, chopped

6 egg whites

2 large eggs

salt and ground black pepper, to taste

> Clean the spinach off and throw it into a pan while still wet. Cook on medium heat and season with salt and pepper.
> Once the spinach is wilted, add the onion and bell pepper and cook until the onions are translucent and the pepper chunks are soft.
> Add the eggs and scramble until cooked. Top with salt and pepper.

ZUCCHINI/COURGETTE FRITTATA

Servings: 1

Prep Time: 5 mins

Cooking Time: 10 – 12 mins

(Per Serving)

Calories: 214

Protein: 31 grams

Carbohydrates: 8 grams

Fat: 7 grams

1/4 cup onion, chopped

1/2 cup zucchini/courgettes, shredded

6 egg whites

1 large egg

salt and ground black pepper, to taste

1 tablespoon low-fat cheddar cheese, shredded

> Preheat the oven to 350 °F/180 °C/Gas Mark 4.
> Coat an 8-inch/20 cm oven-proof skillet in cooking spray and place over medium heat. Add the onion and zucchini/courgette and sauté for 2 – 3 minutes.

> In a large mixing bowl, whisk together the eggs. Pour over the top of vegetables, sprinkle with salt and pepper. Cook until almost set, about 6 – 7 minutes. Sprinkle the cheese on top and transfer to the oven. Bake for 4 – 5 minutes or until the cheese is melted.

VEGGIE EGG & CHEESE SCRAMBLE

Servings: 1

Prep Time: 5 mins

Cooking Time: 5 mins

(Per Serving)

Calories: 235

Protein: 33 grams

Carbohydrates: 11 grams

Fat: 8 grams

1/4 cup mushrooms, chopped

1/4 cup green bell peppers, chopped

1/4 cup onions, chopped

6 egg whites

1 large egg

2 tablespoons skimmed milk

1/4 cup tomato, chopped and seeded

1 tablespoon low-fat Cheddar cheese, shredded

salt and ground black pepper, to taste

> Coat a skillet or frying pan in cooking spray and place over medium-high heat. Add the mushrooms, peppers, and onions; continue to sauté until onions are translucent.

> In a large mixing bowl, whisk together the eggs and skimmed milk. Add the egg mixture to the vegetables and stir. Add the tomatoes and continue to stir. Cook until the eggs are almost done, then sprinkle on the cheese, salt, and pepper.

TASTY TURKEY &
SPINACH OMELETTE

Servings: 1

Prep Time: 5 mins

Cooking Time: 10 mins

(Per Serving)

Calories: 315

Protein: 49 grams

Carbohydrates: 13 grams

Fat: 8 grams

1/2 cup onions, chopped

1/2 cup mushrooms, sliced

3 ounces/85 grams deli turkey slices, chopped

6 egg whites

1 large egg

1 slice fat-free cheese

1 cup spinach

> Lightly coat a non-stick pan with cooking spray and place over medium heat. Add the onion, mushrooms, and turkey and cook for about 5 minutes. Once cooked, transfer to a plate and set aside.

> Mix the egg and egg whites in a bowl and pour the mixture into the pan.

> After a couple of minutes, you should see bubbles. Gently lift the edges of the omelette with a spatula to let the uncooked part of the eggs flow toward the edges and cook. Continue cooking for 2 – 3 minutes or until the centre of the omelette starts to look dry.

> Place the slice of fat-free cheese in the middle of the omelette and spread the turkey mixture and spinach on top (in the centre of the omelette). Using a spatula gently fold one edge of the omelette over.

> Let the omelette cook for another two minutes or until the cheese melts to your desired consistency. Slide the omelette out of the skillet and onto a plate.

BREAKFAST BAKING

When you think of getting ripped, you don't think of muffins, biscuits, and bread. And rightly so—pre-made foods like these are full of unhealthy carbs, sugar, and fats, and they're usually full of sodium too. But boy, do they taste good. What are we to do?

Simple. Make your own, and make them healthy. These recipes are tweaked to do your body good with whole-grain flour, protein powder, flaxseed oil, and egg whites.

BANANA MASH
MUSCLE MUFFINS

Servings: 3 (1 muffin per serving)

Prep Time: 10 mins

Cooking Time: 15 – 20 mins

(Per Serving)

Calories: 271

Protein: 17 grams

Carbohydrates: 32 grams

Fat: 11 grams

3/4 cup old-fashioned oats

1/4 cup oat bran

1 tablespoon whole grain flour

1/2 teaspoon ground cinnamon

1/2 scoop chocolate whey protein powder

1/4 teaspoon baking soda

6 egg whites

1/2 teaspoon stevia or other sugar alternative

1 tablespoon flaxseed oil (available in Tesco and Holland & Barratt)

1 large ripe banana, mashed

2 tablespoons walnuts, chopped

> Preheat the oven to 400 °F/200 °C/Gas Mark 6.

> In a large bowl, combine the first six ingredients. In a separate bowl, beat the eggs, stevia, and oil. Stir the dry ingredients in until just moistened. Fold in the mashed bananas and nuts, careful not to mix too much.

> Lightly coat a non-stick muffin pan with cooking spray and pour in the mixture (each cup should only be 3/4 full). Bake for about 15 – 18 minutes, until the tops are golden and a toothpick inserted into the middle comes out clean. Let them sit for a few minutes before removing them from the pan.

MAPLE WALNUT PROTEIN MUFFINS

Servings: 12

Prep Time: 10 mins

Cooking Time: 15 – 20 mins

(Per Serving)

Calories: 179

Protein: 16 grams

Carbohydrates: 13 grams

Fat: 8 grams

3 egg whites

3 tablespoons walnut oil or unsalted butter, softened

1/4 cup maple syrup

1/2 cup skimmed milk

1/2 cup whole grain flour

1/4 cup wheat germ

1/4 cup oat bran

6 scoops chocolate whey protein powder

2 teaspoons baking powder

1 teaspoon baking soda

1/2 cup chopped walnuts

> Preheat the oven to 350 °F/180 °C/Gas Mark 4.

> In a large mixing bowl, add the egg whites, oil, maple syrup, and skimmed milk and mix well. In a separate bowl, mix together the flour, wheat germ, oat bran, protein powder, baking powder, and baking soda. Combine the dry and wet ingredients, stir only until the dry ingredients are moistened. Gently stir in the nuts.

> Lightly coat a non-stick muffin pan with cooking spray and pour in the mixture (each cup should only be 3/4 full). Bake for 20 – 25 minutes or until toasty brown and a toothpick inserted into the middle comes out clean. Let them sit for a few minutes before removing them from the pan.

MIXED BERRY MUFFINS

Servings: 10 (1 muffin per serving)

Prep Time: 5 mins

Cooking Time: 15 – 20 mins

(Per Serving)

Calories: 165

Protein: 18 grams

Carbohydrates: 19 grams

Fat: 2 grams

1 cup old-fashioned oats, finely blended

1 cup fat-free cottage cheese

1 tablespoon vanilla extract

8 egg whites

14 pitted dates

1/2 lemon, juiced

1/4 cup ground flaxseed (available in Holland & Barratt)

1/2 teaspoon cinnamon

4 scoops chocolate or vanilla whey protein powder

3/4 cup fresh or frozen mixed berries

> Preheat the oven to 400 °F/200 °C/Gas Mark 6.

> Blend all the ingredients except the berries until it's a smooth batter. Gently fold the berries into the batter.

> Lightly coat a non-stick muffin pan with cooking spray and pour the batter evenly in the 10 cups (each cup should only be 3/4 full). Bake for about 16 minutes or until cooked. The tops should be golden and a toothpick inserted into the middle should come out clean. Let them sit for a few minutes before removing them from the pan.

SWEET POTATO MUFFINS

Servings: 8 (1 muffin per serving)

Prep Time: 5 mins

Cooking Time: 20 mins

(Per Serving)

Calories: 110

Protein: 15 grams

Carbohydrates: 11 grams

Fat: 1 gram

2 medium sized sweet potatoes, cooked and peeled

1/2 cup old-fashioned oats

4 scoops chocolate or vanilla protein powder

1 tablespoon stevia or other sugar alternative

2 egg whites

1/2 teaspoon cinnamon

1/2 teaspoon vanilla extract

1 teaspoon baking powder

> Preheat the oven to 350 °F/180 °C/Gas Mark 4.
> In a blender or food processor, add all of the ingredients. Blend until smooth.

> Lightly coat a non-stick muffin pan with cooking spray and pour in the mixture (each cup should only be 3/4 full). Bake for about 20 minutes or until cooked. The tops should be golden and a toothpick inserted into the middle should come out clean. Let them sit for a few minutes before removing from the pan.

CHICKEN & TURKEY

Like anyone who is into working out, I've come to love chicken and turkey. They're relatively cheap, super lean, full of protein, and they can be made to taste many different ways (and turkey can replace ground beef in many different recipes like meat loaf, chili, spaghetti sauce, hamburgers, and meatballs).

Turkey and chicken also make great "fast food." You can cook up a whole batch and keep it in the fridge. When you're in a hurry, grab about 5 ounces and an apple, and there's a quick meal.

CHICKEN & TURKEY RECIPES FOR GETTING BIG

MEXICAN MEATLOAF

Servings: 8

Prep Time: 5 – 10 mins

Cooking Time: 50 mins – 1 hr

(Per Serving)

Calories: 285

Protein: 32 grams

Carbohydrates: 36 grams

Fat: 3 grams

1 pound/450 grams lean ground turkey

1 pound/450 grams lean ground chicken

1 (15 ounce/425 grams) can black beans, rinsed and drained

1 (15 ounce/425 grams) can whole kernel corn, drained and rinsed

1/2 (4 ounce/115 grams) can fire-roasted diced green chillies

1 cup mild chunky salsa

1 (1 ounce/28 grams) package dry taco seasoning mix

3/4 cup plain bread crumbs

3 egg whites

1 (28 ounce/800 grams) can enchilada sauce, divided

salt and ground black pepper to taste

> Preheat the oven to 400 °F/200 °C/Gas Mark 6. Coat a 9 x 13 inch/23 cm x 33 cm baking dish with cooking spray.

> In a large mixing bowl, combine the ground turkey, ground chicken, black beans, corn, green chillies, salsa, taco seasoning, bread crumbs, and egg whites and mix thoroughly.

> Form the mixture into a loaf shape and place inside the prepared baking dish, top with half of the enchilada sauce and place in the oven for 45 minutes.

> Remove from the oven and top with the remaining enchilada sauce, return to the oven and bake until the meatloaf is no longer pink inside, about 10 – 15 minutes. A thermometer inserted into the centre should read at least 160 °F/70 °C.

CHUNKY CHICKEN QUESADILLAS

Servings: 2

Prep Time: Under 5 mins

Cooking Time: 15 mins

(Per Serving)

Calories: 293

Protein: 28 grams

Carbohydrates: 31 grams

Fat: 6 grams

1 boneless, skinless chicken breast (6 ounces/170 grams), rinsed, dried, trimmed of fat

1 tablespoon fat-free sour cream

2 (8 inch/20 cm) whole wheat tortillas

1/3 cup salsa

1 cup lettuce, shredded

1/3 cup low-fat cheddar cheese, shredded

> Coat a medium-sized skillet with cooking spray and place over medium heat. Place chicken on the skillet and cook for 3 – 5 minutes per side, or until cooked through. Remove from heat and set aside.

> Spread the sour cream on one tortilla. Slice the chicken breast and spread on top. Cover with salsa and lettuce.

> Sprinkle the cheddar cheese on top and cover with the other tortilla.

> Coat a large pan with cooking spray and cook the quesadilla on low heat for about 3 minutes on each side. Turn carefully with a large spatula.

POLLO FAJITAS

Servings: 4 (1 fajita per serving)

Prep Time: 5 mins

Cooking Time: 10 mins

(Per Serving)

Calories: 371

Protein: 45 grams

Carbohydrates: 31 grams

Fat: 8 grams

4 boneless, skinless chicken breasts (6 ounces/170 grams each), rinsed, dried, trimmed of fat, and cut into strips

1 tablespoon Worcestershire sauce

1 tablespoon apple cider vinegar

1 tablespoon low-sodium soy sauce

1 teaspoon chilli powder

1 clove garlic, minced

1 dash hot sauce (Tabasco is good to use)

1 tablespoon vegetable oil

1 medium onion, thinly sliced

1 green bell pepper, sliced

salt and ground black pepper, to taste

4 (8 inch/20cm) whole wheat tortillas

1/2 lemon, juiced

> In a medium-sized mixing bowl, add the Worcestershire sauce, vinegar, soy sauce, chilli powder, garlic, and hot sauce. Add the chicken strips to the sauce and lightly mix to coat. Cover and let marinate at room temperature for 30 minutes (can also be refrigerated for several hours)

> Place the oil in a large skillet over high heat. Once the oil is hot, add the chicken strip mixture to the pan and sauté for 5 – 6 minutes. Add the onion and green pepper, season with salt and pepper, and continue to sauté for another 3 – 4 minutes, or until chicken is fully cooked.

> Warm the tortillas on a pan or in the microwave. Top tortillas with the fajita mixture, sprinkle with lemon juice.

AUSSIE CHICKEN

Servings: 4

Prep Time: 30 mins (including marinating)

Cooking Time: 25 – 30 mins

(Per Serving)

Calories: 437

Protein: 48 grams

Carbohydrates: 20 grams

Fat: 19 grams

4 boneless, skinless chicken breasts (6 ounces/170 grams each), rinsed, dried, trimmed of fat and pounded to 1/2-inch/1 1/4 cm thickness

2 teaspoons seasoning salt

6 slices bacon, cut in half

1/4 cup yellow mustard

1/4 cup honey

1/8 cup mayonnaise

1 tablespoon dried onion flakes

1 tablespoon vegetable oil

1 cup fresh mushrooms, sliced

1/2 cup reduced fat Monterey Jack cheese/mature cheddar cheese, shredded

2 tablespoons fresh parsley, chopped

> After prepping your chicken breasts, rub with the seasoning salt, cover and refrigerate for 30 minutes.

> Preheat the oven to 350 °F/180 °C/Gas Mark 4.

> Cook the bacon in a large skillet over medium-high heat until crisp, set aside.

> In a medium-sized mixing bowl, mix together the mustard, honey, mayonnaise, and dried onion flakes.

> Heat the oil in a large skillet over medium heat. Add the chicken to the skillet and cook for 3 – 5 minutes per side, or until browned. Transfer the chicken to a 9 x 13 inch/ 23 cm x 33 cm baking dish. Top with the honey mustard sauce, then a layer of mushrooms and bacon. Sprinkle the shredded cheese on top.

> Bake for 15 minutes, or until cheese is melted and chicken juices run clear. Top with the parsley.

GREEK PITTA PIZZA

Servings: 1

Prep Time: 5 mins

Cooking Time: 5 – 10 mins

(Per Serving)

Calories: 472

Protein: 49 grams

Carbohydrates: 36 grams

Fat: 15 grams

1 boneless, skinless chicken breast (6 ounces/170 grams), rinsed, dried, trimmed of fat

1 whole grain pitta bread

1/2 tablespoon extra-virgin olive oil

2 tablespoons olives, sliced

1 teaspoon red wine vinegar

1/2 clove garlic, minced

1/4 teaspoon dried oregano

1/4 teaspoon dried basil

salt and ground black pepper, to taste

1/4 cup fresh spinach

2 tablespoons low-fat feta cheese, crumbled

1/2 small tomato, chopped and seeded

> Coat a medium-sized skillet with cooking spray and place over medium heat. Place chicken on the skillet and cook for 3 – 5 minutes per side or until cooked through. Remove from heat and set aside.

> Prepare your pizza by brushing the pitta with the oil. Place on a baking sheet and grill 4 inches/10 cm from the heat for 2 minutes. Meanwhile, get a mixing bowl and add the olives, vinegar, garlic, oregano, basil, salt, pepper, and any remaining oil. Mix well.

> Spread the mixture over the pitta. Chop the chicken breast into slices. Top the pitta with the spinach, feta, tomato, and chopped chicken. Grill for about 3 more minutes, or until the cheese is desired consistency.

HARVEST CHICKEN STEW

Servings: 6

Prep Time: 15 mins

Cooking Time: 1 hr – 1 hr 10 mins

(Per Serving)

Calories: 342

Protein: 45 grams

Carbohydrates: 35 grams

Fat: 3 grams

6 boneless, skinless chicken breasts (6 ounces each/170 grams), rinsed, dried, trimmed of fat, and cut into cubes

4 cups peeled eggplant/aubergine, cut into 1-inch/2.5 cm cubes

4 cups small red potatoes, cut into 1/8-inch/0.5 cm slices

4 medium carrots, sliced

3 medium onions, cut into quarters

3 1/2 cups low-sodium chicken broth/chicken stock

3/4 cup fresh parsley, chopped

2 tablespoons fresh thyme leaves, chopped

1/4 teaspoon salt

1/4 teaspoon ground black pepper

1/2 cup cold water

2 tablespoons whole grain flour

> Preheat the oven to 350 °F/180 °C/Gas Mark 4.
> Add the chicken, eggplant/aubergine, potatoes, carrots, onions, broth, parsley, thyme, salt, and pepper to an ovenproof Dutch oven/large ovenproof casserole dish with lid, cover and bake 50 minutes.
> Place the cold water and flour in a tightly covered container or sealable bag and shake. Add the flour mixture and the remaining ingredients to the stew and stir well. Cover and place back in oven for about 20 minutes longer, or until the potatoes are tender and chicken is fully cooked.

CHICKEN & TURKEY RECIPES FOR GETTING LEAN

SUPER-FAST CHICKEN SALAD SANDWICH

Servings: 2

Prep Time: 5 mins

(Per Serving)

Calories: 299

Protein: 30 grams

Carbohydrates: 30 grams

Fat: 7 grams

6 oz/170 grams of cooked chicken, chopped into chunks

1 celery stick, finely chopped

1 tablespoon onion, finely chopped

1 tablespoon pine nuts

1 heaping teaspoon spicy brown mustard

1 heaping teaspoon fat-free sour cream

1 heaping teaspoon fat-free plain yogurt

pinch of ground black pepper

4 slices whole grain bread

2 leaves lettuce

> In a bowl, mix the celery, onion, pine nuts, mustard, sour cream, yogurt, and pepper. Mix in the chicken.

> Spread half of the mixture on a slice of bread. Top with a lettuce leaf and then with another slice of bread. Repeat with the rest of the mixture to make a second sandwich.

PINEAPPLE CHICKEN

Servings: 2

Prep Time: 3 – 5 mins

Cooking Time: 10 mins

(Per Serving)

Calories: 342

Protein: 40 grams

Carbohydrates: 35 grams

Fat: 5 grams

2 boneless, skinless chicken breasts (6 ounces/170 grams each), rinsed, dried, trimmed of fat, and cut into small cubes

1 teaspoon extra-virgin olive oil

1/4 cup sweet Spanish or red onion, finely chopped

pinch of ground black pepper

1 tablespoon orange juice

1 can (8 ounces/225 grams) pineapple chunks

1 banana, sliced

1 teaspoon maple syrup

> Put the oil in a pan and cook the onion on medium-high heat. Add the dash of pepper and cook for 1 minute, until the onion is slightly translucent.

> Put the chicken, orange juice, and pineapple with juice into the pan. Bring to a boil and reduce to medium heat.

> Add the banana and syrup and cook for 1 – 2 minutes.

> Stir it up and reduce the heat to low. Cover it and let it simmer for about 5 – 7 minutes, or until chicken is cooked through.

CHICKEN YAKITORI

Servings: 4

Prep Time: 5 mins

Cooking Time: 10 – 15 mins

(Per Serving)

Calories: 253

Protein: 41 grams

Carbohydrates: 8 grams

Fat: 2 grams

4 boneless, skinless chicken breasts (6 ounces/170 grams each), rinsed, dried, trimmed of fat, cut into 2-inch/5 cm cubes

1/2 cup low-sodium soy sauce

1/2 cup sherry or white cooking wine

1/2 cup low-sodium chicken broth/chicken stock

1/3 teaspoon ground ginger

1 pinch garlic powder

1 bunch scallions/spring onions, chopped

> Place a small saucepan over medium-high heat. Add the soy sauce, sherry, chicken broth/stock, ginger, garlic powder, and scallions/spring onions. Bring to a boil and immediately remove from heat, set aside.

> Preheat the oven grill. Start threading the chicken onto metal or bamboo skewers (if using wood, I recommend soaking in water for 30 minutes to prevent them catching on fire). Coat a grill pan with cooking spray and place chicken skewers on pan. Brush each skewer with the sherry sauce.

> Place the pan under the grill for 3 minutes, until browned. Remove from the oven, turn the chicken over and spoon a little more sauce onto each one. Return to the grill until the chicken is cooked through and nicely browned.

HONEY GLAZED CHICKEN

Servings: 4

Prep Time: 5 – 10 mins

Cooking Time: 25 – 30 mins

(Per Serving)

Calories: 199

Protein: 40 grams

Carbohydrates: 10 grams

Fat: 1 gram

4 boneless, skinless chicken breasts (6 ounces each/170 grams), rinsed, dried, trimmed of fat

2 tablespoons orange juice

2 tablespoons honey

1 tablespoon lemon juice

1/8 teaspoon salt

> Preheat oven to 375 °F/190 °C/Gas Mark 5.
> Coat a 9 x 13 inch baking dish with cooking spray, add the chicken. In a small mixing bowl, mix together the orange juice, honey, lemon juice, and salt. Baste each piece of chicken.
> Cover the dish with foil and bake for 10 minutes. Remove the foil and flip the chicken. Bake another 10 – 15 minutes, until the chicken is cooked through and the juices run clear.

MUSCLE MEATBALLS

Servings: 4 (4 meatballs per serving)

Prep Time: 10 mins

Cooking Time: 20 – 25 mins

(Per Serving)

Calories: 266

Protein: 46 grams

Carbohydrates: 11 grams

Fat: 5 grams

1 1/2 pounds/680 grams extra-lean ground turkey breast

2 egg whites

1/2 cup toasted wheat germ

1/4 cup quick cooking oats

1 tablespoon whole flaxseeds (available at Holland & Barratt)

1 tablespoon Parmesan cheese, grated

1/2 teaspoon all-purpose seasoning

1/4 teaspoon ground black pepper

> Preheat the oven to 400 °F/200 °C/Gas Mark 6. Coat a large baking dish with cooking spray.

> Mix all of the ingredients in a bowl.

> Make 16 meatballs and place them in the baking dish.

> Bake for 7 minutes and turn the meatballs. Bake for 8 – 13 minutes longer, or until no longer pink in the centre.

ANTIPASTO CHICKEN

Servings: 4

Prep Time: 5 mins

Cooking Time: 20 – 25 mins

(Per Serving)

Calories: 248

Protein: 43 grams

Carbohydrates: 8 grams

Fat: 6 grams

4 boneless, skinless chicken breasts (6 ounces/170 grams each), rinsed, dried, trimmed of fat

1 teaspoon garlic-pepper blend

1 jar (6 ounces/170 grams) marinated artichoke hearts, undrained

1 small red bell pepper, chopped

2 medium tomatoes, chopped

1 can (2 1/4 ounces/65 grams) ripe olives, drained and sliced

1 tablespoon fresh basil, chopped

> Coat a 12-inch/30 cm skillet in cooking spray and place over medium heat. Sprinkle the chicken breasts with the garlic-pepper blend and place in skillet.

> Cook for about 3 – 5 minutes, flip, and cook another 3 – 5 minutes, until brown.

> In a medium-sized mixing bowl, mix together the remaining ingredients (depending on the artichoke hearts you get, they may need to be cut in half). Spoon the mixture over the chicken and continue to sauté, about 10 minutes longer, or until the chicken is cooked through.

THAI BASIL CHICKEN

Servings: 4

Prep Time: 5 mins

Cooking Time: 10 – 15 mins

(Per Serving)

Calories: 191

Protein: 41 grams

Carbohydrates: 2 grams

Fat: 3 grams

4 boneless, skinless chicken breasts (6 ounces/170 grams each), rinsed, dried, trimmed of fat

3 cloves garlic, finely chopped

2 jalapeño peppers, seeded and finely chopped

1 tablespoon fish sauce

1 teaspoon stevia or other sugar alternative

1/4 cup fresh basil, chopped

1 tablespoon fresh mint, chopped

1 tablespoon unsalted dry-roasted peanuts, chopped

> Cut each chicken breast into about 8 strips, set aside.

> Coat a 12-inch/30 cm skillet in cooking spray and heat over medium-high heat. Add the garlic and peppers and sauté, stirring constantly until garlic is just golden.

> Add the chicken strips and cook 8 – 10 minutes, stirring frequently, until chicken is cooked through. Add the fish sauce and stevia and sauté 30 seconds. Remove from heat and sprinkle on the basil, mint, and peanuts.

INDIAN CURRY CHICKEN

Servings: 4

Prep Time: 10 mins

Cooking Time: 20 – 25 mins

(Per Serving)

Calories: 247

Protein: 46 grams

Carbohydrates: 9 grams

Fat: 3 grams

4 boneless, skinless chicken breasts (6 ounces/170 grams each), rinsed, dried, trimmed of fat, cut into 1-inch/2.5 cm cubes

1 small onion, chopped

1 clove garlic, minced

3 tablespoons curry powder

1 teaspoon paprika

1 bay leaf

1 teaspoon ground cinnamon

1/2 teaspoon fresh ginger root, grated

salt and ground black pepper, to taste

1 tablespoon tomato paste

1 cup fat-free plain Greek yogurt

1/2 cup water

1/2 lemon, juiced

1/2 teaspoon Indian chilli powder

> Coat a 12-inch/30 cm skillet with cooking spray and place over medium heat. Sauté the onion until translucent, then stir in the garlic, curry powder, paprika, bay leaf, cinnamon, ginger, salt, and pepper.

> Continue stirring for 2 minutes, then add in the chicken, tomato paste, yogurt, and water. Bring to a boil, then reduce heat and simmer for 10 minutes. Remove the bay leaf, stir in the lemon juice and chilli powder. Simmer 5 more minutes, or until chicken is cooked through.

SIMPLE ITALIAN CHICKEN

Servings: 4

Prep Time: 5 mins

Cooking Time: 20 – 25 mins

(Per Serving)

Calories: 281

Protein: 40 grams

Carbohydrates: 5 grams

Fat: 12 grams

4 boneless, skinless chicken breasts (6 ounces/170 grams each), rinsed, dried, trimmed of fat

2 tablespoons extra-virgin olive oil

2 teaspoons garlic, crushed

1/4 cup seasoned bread crumbs

1/4 cup low-fat Parmesan cheese, grated

> Preheat the oven to 425 °F/220 °C/Gas Mark 7.

> Warm the olive oil and garlic in the microwave to blend the flavours. In a separate bowl, combine the bread crumbs and Parmesan cheese. Dredge the chicken breasts in the oil mixture, letting the excess run off, then coat in the bread crumb mixture.

> Place the coated chicken breasts into a shallow baking dish and place in the oven for 10 minutes, flip and cook for another 10 – 15 minutes, until the chicken is no longer pink in the centre and the juices run clear.

GRILLED GINGER CHICKEN

Servings: 4

Prep Time: 5 mins

Cooking Time: 10 – 15 mins

(Per Serving)

Calories: 247

Protein: 41 grams

Carbohydrates: 5 grams

Fat: 9 grams

4 boneless, skinless chicken breasts (6 ounces/170 grams each), rinsed, dried, trimmed of fat

1/4 cup canola oil/vegetable oil or extra virgin olive oil

1/4 cup low-sodium soy sauce

3 lemons, juiced

1/4 teaspoon garlic powder

1 teaspoon onion salt

1 tablespoon ground ginger

> In a small mixing bowl, combine the oil, soy sauce, lemon juice, garlic powder, onion salt, and ground ginger. Place the chicken in a ziplock bag and pour the marinade in. Seal tightly and place in refrigerator to marinate for at least 4 hours.

> Grill over direct medium heat for about 4 – 5 minutes, turn and cook for another 4 – 5 minutes, or until chicken is cooked through.

CHICKEN & VEGETABLE STIR-FRY

Servings: 4

Prep Time: 5 mins

Cooking Time: 15 mins

(Per Serving)

Calories: 200

Protein: 42 grams

Carbohydrates: 6 grams

Fat: 2 grams

4 boneless, skinless chicken breasts (6 ounces/170 grams each), rinsed, dried, trimmed of fat, cut into thin strips

2 tablespoons red wine

1 tablespoon low-sodium soy sauce

1/2 teaspoon cornstarch/cornflour

1 teaspoon stevia or other sugar alternative

1 teaspoon salt

2 cups broccoli florets

1 red bell pepper, seeded and chopped

1/2 cup yellow onion, sliced

> In a small mixing bowl, combine the red wine, soy sauce, cornstarch, stevia, and salt. Mix well to dissolve the cornstarch/cornflour.

> Coat a 12-inch/30 cm skillet in cooking spray and place over medium-high heat. Add the broccoli, bell pepper, and onion. Sauté until the vegetables are tender and onions are browned. Add the chicken and stir-fry for 2 – 3 more minutes, until chicken is browned.

> Pour the sauce over the chicken and vegetables and continue to stir-fry until sauce is thickened and chicken is cooked through, about 2 – 4 minutes.

CHICKEN STROGANOFF

Servings: 4

Prep Time: 5 mins

Cooking Time: 15 – 20 mins

(Per Serving)

Calories: 245

Protein: 50 grams

Carbohydrates: 11 grams

Fat: 3 grams

4 boneless, skinless chicken breasts (6 ounces/170 grams each), rinsed, dried, trimmed of fat, sliced

salt and ground black pepper, to taste

1 medium onion, chopped

2 tablespoons garlic, minced

2 tablespoons dried tarragon

2 1/2 cups fresh mushrooms, sliced

3/4 cup low-sodium chicken broth/stock

1/2 container (8 ounce/225 grams) fat-free sour cream

> Coat a 12-inch/30 cm skillet with cooking spray and place over medium-high heat. Add salt and pepper to your chicken breast and

place into skillet. Cook until golden on one side, about 2 minutes, turn and repeat.

> Push the chicken pieces to one side of the skillet. Add the onion to the other side and sauté until softened. Stir in the garlic, tarragon, and mushrooms and cook for 2 more minutes.

> Add the chicken broth/stock and stir, lower the heat to medium-low. Add the sour cream and mix the chicken in well with the rest of the sauce. Simmer for 5 minutes, stirring occasionally, until sauce slightly thickens.

5 DELICIOUS CHICKEN MARINADES

Below are five quick and easy marinades for chicken for changing up the tastes of any of the chicken recipes. To prepare each, simply put the ingredients in a bowl and mix.

The best way to marinate chicken is to put the marinade and chicken into a large ziplop sandwich bag and let it sit overnight in the fridge. These amounts are for 1 – 2 cups of marinade, good for 3 – 5 chicken breasts.

TERIYAKI

You can do this one in two ways. If you want to make it really easy, you can make a nice zesty teriyaki marinade by using 1/2 cup Italian dressing and 1/2 cup teriyaki sauce.

If you want to make teriyaki marinade from scratch it's as follows:

1/2 cup soy sauce

1/2 cup water

1/8 cup Worcestershire sauce

1 1/2 tablespoons distilled white vinegar

1 1/2 tablespoons vegetable oil

1 1/2 tablespoons onion powder

1 teaspoon garlic powder

1/2 teaspoon ginger powder

stevia to taste

PINEAPPLE

1 cup crushed pineapple

1/3 cup soy sauce

1/3 cup honey

1/4 cup cider vinegar

2 cloves garlic, minced

1 teaspoon ginger powder

1/4 teaspoon powdered cloves

CARNE ASADA

1/4 cups red wine vinegar

2 tablespoons olive oil

2 tablespoons steak sauce

1 clove garlic, minced

1 teaspoon sage

1 teaspoon savoury

1/2 teaspoon salt

1/2 teaspoon dry mustard

1/2 teaspoon paprika

LEMON-WINE

2 tablespoons olive oil

1/4 cup white wine

2 tablespoons fresh lemon juice

2 tablespoons brown sugar

1 tablespoon fresh thyme

1 tablespoon fresh rosemary

2 cloves garlic, minced

2 teaspoons lemon zest

JALAPEÑO LIME

1/2 cup orange juice concentrate

1/3 cup chopped onion

1/4 cup lime juice

2 tablespoons honey

1/2 seeded and diced jalapeño pepper

1 teaspoon ground cumin

1 teaspoon grated lime peel

1/4 teaspoon garlic salt

1 clove garlic, minced

BEEF

It's hard to beat beef when it comes to muscle-building proteins, with every ounce giving you six grams of protein. It's high in creatine (an amino acid that helps with muscle repair and also boosts strength) and high in iron (which promotes healthy blood), and it contains a spectrum of other nutrients, such as vitamin B12, zinc, and antioxidants.

How lean do you want your beef? 80% lean or fattier is too fatty (ground chuck, for instance, has more fat per ounce than protein, which makes sticking to a reasonable diet tough). Look for the "extra lean" or "select" category of meats, which have 15% fat or less. As long as you don't overcook these meats, they can taste great. I love making hamburgers from 95% lean beef with a nice red color. Some of the leanest cuts of beef are tenderloin, eye of round, top loin, sirloin tip, and bottom round.

I also highly recommend that you spend a little extra money to get hormone-free, cage-free, grass-fed beef. Run-of-the-mill meats come from cows that have been pumped full of antibiotics and steroids and fed with genetically modified crops covered in pesticides. Traces of all these chemicals make their way into your system when you eat the meat, and they can interfere with your body's natural balance of hormones.

Additionally, when an animal was raised in a cage, the food it produces is inferior to its free-roaming counterparts. Cage-free chickens produce healthier eggs higher in omega-3 fatty acids, and meat from free-roaming cows has significantly higher amounts of vitamin E and conjugated linoleic acid (a fat that promotes the growth of muscle and the reduction of fat) than meat from cattle cooped up in a pen.

The bottom line is that lean beef is an awesome testosterone-boosting, muscle-building source of protein, and you should absolutely include it in your diet.

BEEF RECIPES FOR GETTING BIG

KOREAN BBQ BEEF

Servings: 4

Prep Time: 5 mins

Cooking Time: Under 5 mins

(Per Serving)

Calories: 307

Protein: 39 grams

Carbohydrates: 6 grams

Fat: 13 grams

1 1/2 pounds/680 grams lean flank steak or minute steak thinly sliced

1/3 cup low-sodium soy sauce

1 tablespoon stevia or other sugar alternative

1/4 cup scallions/spring onions, chopped

2 tablespoons minced garlic

2 tablespoons sesame seeds

1 tablespoon sesame oil

1/2 teaspoon ground black pepper

> In a small mixing bowl, combine the soy sauce, stevia, scallions/spring onions, garlic, sesame seeds, sesame oil, and ground black pepper. Mix well.

> Place the beef in a large ziplock bag or container, pour the soy sauce marinade over it and seal. Refrigerate for at least 1 hour.

> Lightly coat a large skillet in cooking spray and place over high heat. Add the beef and sauté until cooked through, 1 – 2 minutes per side.

MIKE'S SAVOURY BURGERS

Servings: 4

Prep Time: Under 5 mins

Cooking Time: 10 – 15 mins

(Per Serving)

Calories: 395

Protein: 41 grams

Carbohydrates: 32 grams

Fat: 12 grams

1 1/2 pounds/680 grams extra-lean ground beef or chuck steak

4 tablespoons Dijon mustard

salt and ground black pepper, to taste

1/2 cup low-carb ketchup (available in Tescos and health food stores)

1/2 cup low-fat mayo

1 tablespoon red wine vinegar

2 teaspoons Worcestershire sauce

4 whole grain hamburger buns, toasted

4 sandwich slice pickles or gherkins, halved

> Preheat a grill over high heat.

> In a large mixing bowl, combine the beef, mustard, salt, and pepper. Shape into 4 equal sized patties and grill, 5 – 6 minutes per side for medium cooked.

> Meanwhile, in a large mixing bowl, mix together the ketchup, mayo, vinegar, and Worcestershire sauce.

> Toast the buns by cutting in half and placing under the grill cut side down, for about 20 seconds. They should be light golden brown. Top each burger with pickles and sauce.

BEEF LO MEIN

Servings: 1

Prep Time: 5 – 10 mins

Cooking Time: 10 – 15 mins

(Per Serving)

Calories: 526

Protein: 49 grams

Carbohydrates: 45 grams

Fat: 15 grams

6 ounces/170 grams extra lean beef, sliced into 1-inch/2.5 cm strips

1 teaspoon sesame oil

1/4 cup fresh snow pea pods, trimmed

1/4 cup broccoli florets

1/4 cup carrots, shredded

1 scallion/spring onion, chopped

1/8 teaspoon red pepper flakes

1/2 garlic clove, minced

2 tablespoons low-sodium soy sauce

1/2 teaspoon fresh ginger, grated

2 ounces/55 grams whole grain noodles, cooked

1 teaspoon sesame seeds, toasted

> Heat the oil in a wok or large skillet over medium-high heat. Add the beef and stir-fry for 4 – 6 minutes or until browned. Remove from pan and set aside.

> Add the snow peas, broccoli, carrots, scallions/spring onions, red pepper flakes, and garlic and stir-fry for 2 – 3 minutes. Add the soy sauce, ginger, cooked noodles, and beef. Mix together well and stir-fry until hot.

> Remove from heat and sprinkle with sesame seeds.

STEAK SOFT TACOS

Servings: 4 (2 tacos per serving)

Prep Time: 10 mins

Cooking Time: 10 mins

(Per Serving)

Calories: 431

Protein: 34 grams

Carbohydrates: 56 grams

Fat: 10 grams

12 ounces/350 grams extra-lean strip sirloin steak, thinly sliced

1/2 teaspoon ground cumin

1 teaspoon chilli powder

3 cloves garlic, minced

2 cups cooked black beans, drained

1 cup salsa

8 (6 inch/15 cm) whole wheat tortillas

1 cup tomato, finely chopped

1/2 cup onion, finely chopped

1 cup shredded lettuce

8 teaspoons low-fat cheddar cheese, shredded

> Place the beef in a large mixing bowl, add the cumin, chilli powder, and garlic and toss to coat.

> Coat a large skillet in cooking spray and place over medium-high heat. Add the steak and stir-fry for 4 – 6 minutes. Add the beans and salsa and stir-fry until cooked to your satisfaction, then remove from heat.

> Meanwhile, warm the tortillas in a pan or the microwave. Top each tortilla with 1/8 of the steak mixture and toppings.

MOIST MEATLOAF

Servings: 6

Prep Time: 5 – 10 mins

Cooking Time: 50 mins – 1 hr

(Per Serving)

Calories: 252

Protein: 35 grams

Carbohydrates: 11 grams

Fat: 7 grams

2 pounds/900 grams extra-lean ground beef or minced chuck steak

1 teaspoon salt

1/2 teaspoon ground black pepper

1 egg

1 cup stuffing mix

1/2 cup skimmed milk

1/3 cup steak sauce

1 onion, diced

1/2 medium green bell pepper, diced

> Preheat oven to 350 °F/180 °C/Gas Mark 4. Lightly coat an 8.5 x 4.5 inch/22 cm x 11.25 cm loaf pan.

> In a large mixing bowl, add the ground beef, salt, pepper, egg, and stuffing mix and thoroughly mix. Stir in the skimmed milk, 3 tablespoons of the steak sauce, onion, and bell pepper.

> Transfer the mixture to the baking pan and form into a loaf. Baste the top with the remaining steak sauce. Transfer to oven and bake for 1 hour.

BEEF STROGANOFF

Servings: 4

Prep Time: 10 mins

Cooking Time: 1 hr – 1 hr 10 mins

(Per Serving)

Calories: 322

Protein: 30 grams

Carbohydrates: 9 grams

Fat: 19 grams

1 pound/450 grams lean beef sirloin or rump, sliced into strips

1/4 teaspoon salt

1/4 teaspoon ground black pepper

4 tablespoons unsalted butter

1/2 medium yellow onion, sliced

2 tablespoons cornstarch/cornflour

1/2 (10.5 ounce/300 grams) can condensed beef broth or stock

1/2 teaspoon Dijon mustard

1 clove garlic, minced

1/2 tablespoon Worcestershire sauce

1 (4 ounce/115 grams) can sliced mushrooms, drained

3 tablespoons fat-free sour cream

3 tablespoons fat-free cream cheese

3 tablespoons white wine

> Season the meat with the salt and pepper. Melt the butter in a large skillet over medium heat. Add the beef and brown on all sides. Push to one side of the pan.

> Add the onions and cook for 3 – 5 minutes, until tender. Push the onions over to the side with the beef. Mix the cornstarch/cornflour with 2 tablespoons of beef broth/stock then pour into the skillet, mix with the juices in the pan to dissolve.

> Pour in the remaining beef broth/stock. Bring to a boil, stirring frequently. Lower the heat and stir in the mustard, garlic, and Worcestershire sauce. Cover with a tight fitting lid and simmer for 45 minutes to an hour, until the meat is cooked to your satisfaction.

> 5 minutes before the beef is done, stir in the mushrooms, sour cream, cream, cream cheese and white wine. Stir well and let the beef finish cooking in the sauce.

SUPREMELY SPICY CHILLI

Servings: 12

Prep Time: 15 mins

Cooking Time: 2 hrs, until meat is soft

(Per Serving)

Calories: 474

Protein: 44 grams

Carbohydrates: 38 grams

Fat: 15 grams

2 pounds/900 grams extra-lean minced beef

1 pound/450 grams boneless chuck steak, trimmed of fat, and cut into 1/4-inch/ 0.5 cm cubes

1 pound/450 grams lean Italian sausage

2 tablespoons unsalted butter

1 tablespoon canola oil/vegetable oil or extra virgin olive oil

2 red bell peppers, diced

2 jalapeño peppers, finely chopped

3 Anaheim chillies, roasted, peeled, and chopped

3 poblano chillies, roasted, peeled, and chopped

2 yellow onions, diced

4 tablespoons minced garlic

2 teaspoons granulated onion

2 teaspoons granulated garlic

3 tablespoons chilli powder

2 teaspoons hot paprika

2 teaspoons ground cumin

2 teaspoons cayenne pepper

2 teaspoons ground coriander

2 teaspoons salt

2 teaspoons ground black pepper

1 cup tomato paste

2 cups tomato sauce

12 ounces/340 ml lager beer

1 cup low-sodium chicken stock

2 (15.5 ounce/440 grams) cans pinto beans, with juice

2 (15.5 ounce/440 grams) cans kidney beans, with juice

1 bunch scallions/spring onions, thinly sliced

> Place a large stock pot or Dutch oven over high heat, add the butter and oil. Once butter has melted, add the bell pepper, jalapeño, chillies, and onion and cook until tender, about 5 minutes.

> Add the chuck cubes and brown on all sides. Mix in the ground beef, sausage, and minced garlic, gently stir, trying not to break up the ground meat too much. Cook until meat is browned and cooked through, about 7 – 10 minutes.

> Stir in the granulated onions, granulated garlic, chilli powder, paprika, cumin, cayenne, coriander, salt, and pepper and let cook for 1 minute. Stir in the tomato paste and sauce and let cook for 2 minutes. Pour in the beer, chicken stock, and beans. Thoroughly mix together, lower heat to medium-low and simmer for 2 hours, stirring occasionally. Serve with scallions/spring onions on top.

BEEF RECIPES FOR
GETTING LEAN

PEAR-CRANBERRY BEEF TENDERLOIN/FILLET

Servings: 4

Prep Time: 10 mins

Cooking Time: 15 – 20 mins

(Per Serving)

Calories: 237

Protein: 25 grams

Carbohydrates: 21 grams

Fat: 5 grams

4 beef tenderloin/fillet steaks, about 1-inch/2.5 cm thick and trimmed of fat (4 ounces/115 grams each)

1/2 large red onion, thinly sliced

2 cloves garlic, finely chopped

2 tablespoons dry red wine or grape juice

2 firm ripe pears, peeled and diced

1/2 cup fresh or frozen cranberries

2 tablespoons brown sugar

1/2 teaspoon pumpkin pie spice/all spice mixture

> Spray a 12-inch/30 cm skillet with cooking spray and place over medium-high heat. Add the onion, garlic, and wine. Sauté for about 3 minutes, until onion is tender but not brown.

> Add the pears, cranberries, brown sugar, and pumpkin pie spice. Reduce heat to medium-low. Simmer uncovered for about 10 minutes, stirring frequently, until the cranberries burst. Transfer chutney to bowl and set aside.

> Bring the heat back up to medium and add the beef to the skillet. Cook for about 4 minutes on each side for medium cooked. Serve with the chutney.

SPICED PEPPER BEEF

Servings: 4

Prep Time: 5 mins

Cooking Time: 15 – 20 mins

(Per Serving)

Calories: 165

Protein: 24 grams

Carbohydrates: 4 grams

Fat: 5 grams

4 beef tenderloin/sirloin steaks, about 1-inch/2.5 cm thick and trimmed of fat (4 ounces/115 grams each)

3 tablespoons low-carb ketchup (available in Tescos)

3 tablespoons water

3/4 teaspoon low-sodium soy sauce

1/2 medium green bell pepper, cut into thin strips

1 small onion, thinly sliced

coarsely ground black pepper, to taste

> Place beef between two pieces of parchment paper or plastic wrap, pound with the flat side of a tenderiser or rolling pin to tenderise.
> In a small mixing bowl, combine the ketchup, water, and soy sauce and beat with a whisk until thoroughly blended.

> Coat a 10-inch/25 cm skillet with cooking spray and place over medium-high heat. Cook beef in the skillet for 3 minutes, turning once. Add the bell peppers and onion and sauté. Add the ketchup mixture and reduce heat to low. Cover, let simmer for 12 minutes, or until the meat is cooked to your liking.

> Remove meat from pan and set aside. Bring the heat back up and add the ground pepper into the sauce left in the skillet, stir, then bring to a boil. Boil for 2 minutes, stirring frequently until sauce is slightly thickened. Spoon sauce over beef and serve.

BEEF TERIYAKI

Servings: 4

Prep Time: 5 mins (2 hrs for marination)

Cooking Time: 10 mins

(Per Serving)

Calories: 193

Protein: 25 grams

Carbohydrates: 11 grams

Fat: 5 grams

4 sirloin steaks, trimmed of fat (6 ounces/170 grams each)

1/3 cup low-sodium soy sauce

2 tablespoons molasses

2 teaspoons Dijon mustard

3 cloves garlic, minced

2 teaspoons ground ginger

salt and ground black pepper, to taste

> In a small mixing bowl, add the soy sauce, molasses, Dijon mustard, garlic, and ginger. Whisk together until mixed.
> Place the steaks in a large ziplock bag, sprinkle with salt and pepper, and pour in the marinade. Refrigerate for at least 2 hours, shaking occasionally.

> Heat a grill pan over high heat. Lightly coat with cooking spray and once the grill is hot, add the steak and grill 4 minutes undisturbed, flip and grill another 4 – 6 minutes, depending on how you prefer your steak cooked.

GORGONZOLA FILLET WITH BALSAMIC ONIONS

Servings: 4

Prep Time: 2 – 3 mins

Cooking Time: 15 – 20 mins

(Per Serving)

Calories: 276

Protein: 37 grams

Carbohydrates: 7 grams

Fat: 9 grams

4 extra-lean beef fillets (6 ounces/170 grams each)

3/4 teaspoon salt

3/4 teaspoon ground black pepper

1 large red onion, thinly sliced

1/4 cup balsamic vinegar

2 tablespoons crumbled Gorgonzola or blue cheese

> Preheat oven to 375 °F/190 °C/Gas Mark 5. Rub fillets evenly with 1/2 teaspoon of the salt and pepper, set aside.

> Coat a baking sheet in cooking spray. Place onions in a mixing bowl, add the vinegar, remaining salt, and pepper, toss to coat well. Transfer the onions to the baking sheet and spray with a light coating of cooking spray.

> Place onions in oven and bake for 20 minutes, or until onions are tender. Stir occasionally to prevent burning. Remove from oven and set aside.

> Meanwhile, coat a large skillet in cooking spray and place over medium-high heat. Add the fillets and cook for 5 – 7 minutes on each side or cooked to your liking. Top steaks evenly with cheese and onions.

SALISBURY STEAK

Servings: 5

Prep Time: 5 – 10 mins

Cooking Time: 15 mins

(Per Serving)

Calories: 199

Protein: 25 grams

Carbohydrates: 12 grams

Fat: 5 grams

1 pound/450 grams extra-lean ground round or chuck

3 cups fresh mushrooms, sliced

1/4 cup plain bread crumbs

2 egg whites

1/4 cup skim milk

1/4 teaspoon dried thyme leaves

3 tablespoons low-carb ketchup

1 jar (12 ounces/340 grams) fat-free beef gravy

> Finely chop 1 cup of the mushrooms and set the other 2 cups aside. In a medium-sized mixing bowl, combine the finely chopped mushrooms, ground beef, bread crumbs, egg whites, skim milk, thyme, and 1 tablespoon of the ketchup.

> Mix together very well. Shape the mixture into 5 oval patties, about 1/2-inch/1.25 cm thick.

> Coat a 12-inch/30 cm skillet in cooking spray and heat over medium-high heat. Add the patties and cook for about 2 – 3 minutes, flip and continue cooking for another 2 – 3 minutes, until brown.

> Add the remaining 2 cups of mushrooms, 2 tablespoons of ketchup, and gravy. Bring to a boil, then reduce heat to low. Cover and let simmer for 5 – 10 minutes, until patties are cooked to your liking.

ADOBO SIRLOIN

Servings: 4

Prep Time: 5 mins (2 hrs for marination)

Cooking Time: 10 – 15 mins

(Per Serving)

Calories: 213

Protein: 37 grams

Carbohydrates: 4 grams

Fat: 7 grams

4 extra-lean sirloin steaks (6 ounces/17 grams each)

1 lime, juiced

1 tablespoon garlic, minced

1 teaspoon dried oregano

1 teaspoon ground cumin

2 tablespoons adobo sauce from canned peppers (available in Sainsburys)

2 tablespoons canned chipotle peppers in adobo sauce, finely chopped

salt and ground black pepper, to taste

> In a small mixing bowl, combine the lime juice, garlic, oregano, cumin, and adobo sauce. Add chipotle peppers and mix well.

> Sprinkle some salt and pepper onto the meat, place into a ziplock bag and pour the adobo marinade over top. Place in refrigerator for at least 2 hours, shaking occasionally.

> Preheat a grill over high heat. Lightly coat the grill in cooking spray and once hot, place the steaks on the grill. Grill for 4 – 5 minutes on each side, until steaks are cooked to your liking.

THAI BEEF KEBABS

Servings: 4 (2 skewers per serving)

Prep Time: 5 – 10 mins (2 hrs for marination)

Cooking Time: 10 mins

(Per Serving)

Calories: 159

Protein: 24 grams

Carbohydrates: 2 grams

Fat: 5 grams

1 pound/450 grams beef tenderloin/sirloin, cut into 2-inch/5 cm cubes

2 tablespoons lemon juice

1 tablespoon low-sodium soy sauce

1 tablespoon garlic, minced

1 teaspoon red pepper flakes

1 teaspoon ground black pepper

> In a medium-sized mixing bowl, combine the lemon juice, soy sauce, garlic, red pepper flakes, and black pepper. Place the cubed beef into a ziplock bag and pour the marinade over. Place in refrigerator for at least 2 hours, shaking occasionally.

> Preheat the grill on high heat. Thread the beef evenly onto 8 skewers and place on the fully heated grill. Turn the steak every minute or two to brown all sides.

PORK

Pork is often criticized for its high fat content (especially ribs and bacon), but pork tenderloin is a good source of protein due to its high protein, low fat content, and versatility in terms of preparation. It's also a good source of B vitamins, niacin, and various minerals such as magnesium, iron, and zinc.

Whether dieting to lose weight or eating to gain muscle, pork can be a nice change from beef, chicken, and fish.

All of the recipes in this section of the book are suitable for both building muscle and losing weight due to being relatively low-calorie.

PLUM-MUSTARD
PORK CHOPS

Servings: 4

Prep Time: 5 mins

Cooking Time: 10 mins

(Per Serving)

Calories: 195

Protein: 32 grams

Carbohydrates: 7 grams

Fat: 4 grams

4 boneless pork chops, 1/2-inch/1.25 cm thick, trimmed of fat (5 ounces/140 grams each)

1/4 teaspoon salt

1/4 teaspoon ground black pepper

1/4 cup Chinese plum sauce or apricot jam

4 teaspoons yellow mustard

> Spray a 10-inch/25 cm non-stick skillet with cooking spray and place over medium-high heat. Rub the pork chops with the salt and pepper and place in skillet. Cook for 3 minutes on each side, until no longer pink in the centre.

> In a small mixing bowl, mix the plum sauce and mustard. Spoon on top of the pork and serve.

CAJUN PORK CHOPS

Servings: 4

Prep Time: 10 mins

Cooking Time: 15 – 20 mins

(Per Serving)

Calories: 194

Protein: 33 grams

Carbohydrates: 7 grams

Fat: 4 grams

4 boneless pork chops, 1/2-inch/1.25 cm thick, trimmed of fat (5 ounces/140 grams each)

2 teaspoons salt-free extra-spicy seasoning blend

1/2 medium onion, sliced

1 jalapeño peppers, seeded and finely chopped

1 can (14.5 ounces/410 grams) diced tomatoes, undrained

> Lay pork chops out and rub both sides with the spicy seasoning blend. Coat a 12-inch/30 cm non-stick skillet in cooking spray and place over medium-high heat.

> Add the onion and jalapeño and sauté for 2 minutes, until slightly tender, push the mixture to one side of the skillet. On the other side, add the pork chops. Cook for 3 minutes, turning once to brown on both sides.

> Add the tomatoes and bring to a boil, reduce heat and cover. Cook for 6 – 8 minutes, or until pork chops are no longer pink in centre.

ITALIAN BAKED PORK

Servings: 4

Prep Time: 2 – 5 mins

Cooking Time: 30 – 35 mins

(Per Serving)

Calories: 230

Protein: 39 grams

Carbohydrates: 0 grams

Fat: 8 grams

2 pork tenderloins, trimmed of excess fat (12 ounces/340 grams each)

1 tablespoon extra-virgin olive oil

1/2 teaspoon salt

1/4 teaspoon pepper

1/2 teaspoon fennel seed, crushed

1 clove garlic, finely chopped

> Preheat the oven to 375°F/190 °C/Gas Mark 5 and coat a baking dish in cooking spray.

> In a small mixing bowl, combine the oil and seasoning and mash together with the back of a spoon until it becomes a paste. Place the pork in the baking dish and apply the paste evenly.

> Place the pork in the oven and roast for 25 – 35 minutes or until cooked to your liking. I personally like this dish to have a slight amount of pink in the centre which is about 160 °F/70 °C on a meat thermometer.

SLOW COOKED BONE-IN PORK CHOPS

Servings: 4

Prep Time: 5 mins

Cooking Time: 4 – 5 mins, or until tender

(Per Serving)

Calories: 359

Protein: 32 grams

Carbohydrates: 13 grams

Fat: 20 grams

4 bone-in pork loin chops (8 ounces/225 grams each)

1 teaspoon garlic powder

1/2 teaspoon salt

1/2 teaspoon ground pepper

2 cups low-carb ketchup

2 tablespoons brown sugar

> Rub the pork chops with garlic powder, salt, and pepper. Press into the meat.
> Coat a large skillet in cooking spray and place over medium-high heat. Place chops in skillet and brown on both sides.

> In a small mixing bowl, mix together the ketchup and brown sugar. Pour half of the sauce in a 6 pint/3 litre slow cooker. Place the pork chops on top of the sauce and pour the remaining sauce over top. Cover and cook over low heat for 4 – 5 hours, or until meat falls off the bone. Top with a little sauce.

BREADED PARMESAN PORK CHOPS

Servings: 4

Prep Time: 5 mins

Cooking Time: 10 – 12 mins

(Per Serving)

Calories: 246

Protein: 41 grams

Carbohydrates: 9 grams

Fat: 5 grams

4 boneless pork chops, 1/2-inch/1.25 cm thick, trimmed of fat (6 ounces/170 grams each)

1/4 cup skimmed milk

1/4 cup fat-free Parmesan cheese, grated

1/4 cup seasoned bread crumbs

1/4 teaspoon salt

1/8 teaspoon pepper

1/4 teaspoon garlic powder

> Preheat the oven to 375 °F/190 °C/Gas mark 5.
> Set up the milk in one bowl and the cheese, bread crumbs, salt, pepper, and garlic powder in another. Dunk the pork chops in the milk, then coat in the bread crumb mixture.

> Coat a baking sheet in cooking spray and transfer breaded chops to the sheet. Place in oven and bake for 9 – 11 minutes on each side, or until they are cooked to your preference.

EASY ORANGE CHOPS

Servings: 4

Prep Time: Under 5 mins

Cooking Time: 20 – 25 mins

(Per Serving)

Calories: 229

Protein: 39 grams

Carbohydrates: 7 grams

Fat: 4 grams

4 boneless pork chops, 1/2-inch/1.25 cm thick, trimmed of fat (6 ounces/170 grams each)

salt and ground black pepper, to taste

1 can (11 ounces/310 grams) mandarin oranges, drained

1/2 teaspoon ground cloves

> Sprinkle some salt and pepper over the chops, press into the meat. Coat a large skillet in cooking spray and place over medium-high heat.
> Place the chops in the pan and brown on both sides. Pour the oranges over top and sprinkle with the cloves. Cover with a tight fitting lid and reduce to a simmer. Cook for 20 – 25 minutes, or until meat is cooked to your satisfaction.

FISH & SEAFOOD

Fish is a terrific, healthy source of protein. It's high in omega-3 fatty acids, which can help fight inflammation, heart disease, and arthritis, and even improve brain function. Some of my favorite fish are tuna, halibut, tilapia, mahi-mahi, and salmon.

When buying fish, ensure it doesn't smell fishy. Fresh fish has a nice, salty sea smell, not a stinky odor, despite what the merchant may say.

A quick tip for cooking fish: Fish takes about 8 – 10 minutes to cook per inch of thickness, measured at its thickest part.

TUNA WITH FRESH PESTO

Servings: 4

Prep Time: 5 mins

Cooking Time: 10 mins

(Per Serving)

Calories: 198

Protein: 23 grams

Carbohydrates: 3 grams

Fat: 10 grams

4 tuna, swordfish, or other firm fish steaks, 3/4-inch/1.5 cm thick (4 ounces/115 grams each)

3 teaspoons extra-virgin olive oil

1/2 teaspoon salt

1 cup loosely packed fresh coriander

1 cup loosely packed fresh Italian parsley (flat-leaf)

1/4 cup loosely packed fresh basil

4 medium scallions/spring onions, sliced

1 clove garlic, cut in half

2 tablespoons lime juice

1/4 cup low-sodium chicken broth/stock

1 tablespoon low-fat Parmesan cheese, grated

> Set oven to grill. Lay your tuna steaks out on a grill pan and brush with 1 teaspoon of the extra-virgin olive oil.

> Place dish in the oven and grill with tops 4 inches from heat, for about 4 minutes. Remove from oven, turn over and sprinkle with 1/4 teaspoon of the salt, return to oven for another 4 – 5 minutes, until fish flakes easily with a fork and is slightly pink in the centre.

> Meanwhile, combine the coriander, parsley, basil, scallions/spring onions, garlic, lime juice, 2 teaspoons oil, and 1/4 teaspoon salt in a food processor fitted with a metal blade attachment. Process for about 10 seconds, it should be finely chopped. With the food processor running, slowly add the chicken broth and process until almost smooth.

> Place in a mixing bowl and stir in the cheese, distribute evenly over each tuna steak.

LEMON-ROSEMARY SALMON STEAKS

Servings: 4

Prep Time: 5 mins marinating

Cooking Time: 15 – 20 mins

(Per Serving)

Calories: 273

Protein: 34 grams

Carbohydrates: 0 grams

Fat: 14 grams

4 salmon fillets (6 ounces/170 grams each)

1 tablespoon lemon juice

1/2 teaspoon dried rosemary

1 tablespoon extra-virgin olive oil

salt and ground black pepper, to taste

> Preheat the oven to 350°F/180 °C/Gas Mark 4. Combine lemon juice, rosemary, and olive oil in a medium baking dish.

> Season the salmon fillets with salt and pepper. Add them to the baking dish and turn to coat. Allow to marinate for 10 – 15 minutes.

> Cover with foil and bake for about 20 minutes, or until fish flakes easily with a fork.

SUN-DRIED SALMON FILLETS

Servings: 4

Prep Time: 5 mins

(Per Serving)

Calories: 298

Protein: 35 grams

Carbohydrates: 2 grams

Fat: 16 grams

4 wild Atlantic salmon fillets, cooked (6 ounces each)

1/4 cup sun-dried tomatoes, sliced

1 teaspoon dried parsley flakes

2 garlic cloves, minced

salt and ground black pepper, to taste

1 tablespoon extra-virgin olive oil

> Pulse the sun-dried tomatoes, parsley, and garlic in a food processor until a paste forms. Add salt and pepper, and drizzle in the oil.

> To serve, top each cooked salmon fillet with the sun-dried tomato mixture.

SALMON BURGERS

Servings: 2

Prep Time: Under 5 mins

Cooking Time: 5 mins

(Per Serving)

Calories: 273

Protein: 28 grams

Carbohydrates: 11 grams

Fat: 12 grams

1 can (16 ounces/450 grams) cooked salmon

1 egg

1/2 cup plain bread crumbs

1/2 small onion, diced

1 teaspoon Dijon mustard

1 tablespoon lemon juice

salt and ground black pepper, to taste

1 tablespoon extra-virgin olive oil

> Drain salmon. In a medium bowl, combine with the rest of the ingredients, except oil. Form into 4 patties.

> Heat oil in a large skillet over medium-high heat. Add salmon burgers and cook for 1 – 2 minutes per side, or until browned.

BISCUIT-COATED TILAPIA

Servings: 4

Prep Time: 5 – 10 mins

Cooking Time: 10 mins

(Per Serving)

Calories: 225

Protein: 25 grams

Carbohydrates: 10 grams

Fat: 10 grams

4 fresh tilapia filets, about 3/4-inch/1 1/2 cm thick (4 ounces/115 grams each) (available in Waitrose, Tesco and Sainsburys)

1/2 cup plain digestive biscuit crumbs

1 teaspoon lemon zest

1/4 teaspoon salt

1/4 teaspoon ground black pepper

1/4 cup skimmed milk

1 tablespoon canola oil/vegetable oil

2 tablespoons toasted pecans, chopped

> Position the oven rack to slightly above the middle point. Heat oven to 500 °F/260 °C/Gas mark 10. Cut the fish crosswise into 2-inch/5 cm wide pieces. In a small mixing bowl, add the digestive biscuits, lemon zest, salt, and pepper. Place the skimmed milk in a separate mixing bowl.

> Dunk the fish in the milk, then lightly coat with the cracker mix and transfer to a 13 x 9 inch/33 cm x 23 cm baking dish. Drizzle the oil and pecans over the fish and place in oven. Bake for about 10 minutes, or until fish flakes easily with a fork.

TUNA SALAD STUFFED PEPPERS

Servings: 4 (3 peppers per serving)

Prep Time: 5 – 10 mins

(Per Serving)

Calories: 152

Protein: 22 grams

Carbohydrates: 6 grams

Fat: 4 grams

2 cans (6 ounces/170 grams each) chunk tuna in oil, drained

1/2 teaspoon smoked paprika

1/2 teaspoon lemon zest

1 tablespoon lemon juice

1 tablespoon extra-virgin olive oil

salt and ground black pepper, to taste

1 jar (12) whole piquillo peppers

12 medium-sized whole basil leaves

> In a medium-sized mixing bowl, add the tuna and separate. Stir in the paprika, lemon zest, lemon juice, oil, salt, and pepper, and mix well.

> Dry the peppers and carefully split them open, rolling them out flat. Remove the seeds, then add a whole basil leaf, top with the tuna mixture and roll to close.

SAVOURY SOY AND WHITE WINE HALIBUT

Servings: 4

Prep Time: 10 mins & 1 hr marination

Cooking Time: 30 mins

(Per Serving)

Calories: 365

Protein: 47 grams

Carbohydrates: 16 grams

Fat: 12 grams

4 halibut fillets (6 ounces/170 grams each)

2 tablespoons extra-virgin olive oil

2 tablespoons low-sodium soy sauce

2 tablespoons lemon juice

2 tablespoons white wine

2 cloves garlic, minced

2 (quarter-sized) pieces fresh ginger, peeled and minced

salt and ground black pepper, to taste

3 medium leeks (white part only), thinly sliced

2 red bell peppers, seeded and thinly sliced

> In a medium-sized mixing bowl, add the olive oil, soy sauce, lemon juice, white wine, garlic, ginger, salt, and pepper, and mix well. Put the halibut in a ziplock bag and pour the marinade over top. Place in refrigerator for at least 1 hour, shaking occasionally.

> Preheat the grill. Remove the fish from the marinade and set aside. Place a large skillet over medium heat and pour in the marinade. Add the leeks and red pepper and cook for 15 minutes, or until tender.

> Meanwhile, place the fish on a baking pan and under the grill, 4 – 6 inches/ 10 – 15 cm from the heat. Cook 4 – 5 minutes, flip and cook another 4 minutes, or until flesh is opaque through and flakes easily. Top with vegetables and sauce.

CREAMY SCALLOP FETTUCCINE

Servings: 5 (1 1/2 cups per serving)

Prep Time: 10 – 15 mins

Cooking Time: 20 mins

(Per Serving)

Calories: 361

Protein: 32 grams

Carbohydrates: 47 grams

Fat: 4 grams

1 pound/450 grams large dry sea scallops

8 ounces/225 grams whole grain fettuccine

1 (8 ounce/225 ml) bottle clam juice (get lowest sodium you can find. Vimto is good available in Waitrose/Sainsburys)

1 cup skimmed milk

3 tablespoons cornstarch/cornflour

salt and ground black pepper, to taste

3 cups frozen peas, thawed

1/2 cup low-fat Parmesan cheese, grated

1/3 cup chives, chopped

1/2 teaspoon lemon zest

1 teaspoon lemon juice

> Cook pasta according to package directions.
> Meanwhile, dry the scallops with a paper towel and sprinkle with salt. Coat a large non-stick skillet with cooking spray and place over medium-high heat. Add the scallops and cook until golden brown, about 2 – 3 minutes per side. Remove from pan and set aside.
> Add the clam juice to the pan. In a medium sized mixing bowl, add the milk, cornstarch/cornflour, salt, and pepper, and whisk until smooth. Pour the milk mixture into the pan and whisk with the clam juice. Once the mixture is simmering, stir constantly, until sauce has thickened, about 1 – 2 minutes.
> Place the scallops and peas into the clam sauce and bring to a simmer. Add the fettuccine, chives, lemon zest, lemon juice, and most of the Parmesan, and mix together well. Remove from heat and top with a little extra cheese.

LEMON-GARLIC PRAWNS

Servings: 4

Prep Time: 10 mins

Cooking Time: 10 – 15 mins

(Per Serving)

Calories: 205

Protein: 30 grams

Carbohydrates: 15 grams

Fat: 4 grams

1 pound raw/450 grams jumbo prawns

2 red bell peppers, seeded and diced

2 pounds/900 grams asparagus, cut into 1-inch/2.5 cm pieces

2 teaspoons lemon zest

1/2 teaspoon salt

2 teaspoons extra-virgin olive oil

5 cloves garlic, minced

1 cup low-sodium chicken broth/chicken stock

1 teaspoon cornstarch/cornflour

2 tablespoons lemon juice

2 tablespoons fresh parsley, chopped

> Coat a large non-stick skillet with cooking spray and place over medium-high heat. Add the bell peppers, asparagus, lemon zest, and 1/4 teaspoon of the salt. Sauté until vegetables begin to soften, about 6 minutes. Transfer vegetables to a bowl, cover, and set aside.

> Add the oil and garlic to the pan and sauté for 30 seconds. Stir in the prawns. In a small bowl, add the broth and cornstarch/cornflour and whisk to combine. Pour in the broth mixture and remaining 1/4 teaspoon of salt and stir.

> Cook, stirring frequently, until the sauce thickens and the prawns are pink and cooked through, about 2 – 3 minutes. Remove from the heat, add the lemon juice and parsley, mix together, and serve the prawns over the vegetables.

SEARED WASAMI TUNA

Servings: 4

Prep Time: Under 5 mins

Cooking Time: 35 – 40 mins

(Per Serving)

Calories: 250

Protein: 43 grams

Carbohydrates: 15 grams

Fat: 3 grams

4 tuna steaks, about 3/4-inch/1 1/2 cm thick (6 ounces/170 grams each)

1 3/4 cup water

3 large ears of corn, shucked and kernels removed (about 2 cups)

1 teaspoon wasabi paste

salt, to taste

> In a small saucepan, add 1 3/4 cups water, 1 1/2 cups of corn, and salt. Bring to a boil over medium-high heat, then reduce heat and simmer until corn is very soft, about 20 minutes. Transfer cooked corn to a blender and blend until smooth. Pour into a small mixing bowl, add the wasabi paste, and mix thoroughly.

> Place the small saucepan back over medium heat and add the remaining 1/2 cup of corn and just enough water to cover. Cook for 10 minutes, or until corn is soft.

> Meanwhile, add salt to both sides of the tuna steaks and rub into meat. Coat a large nonstick skillet with cooking spray and place over medium-high heat. Once pan is hot, add the tuna and sear each side, about 3 minutes.

> Drain the corn, plate the fish and top with corn and wasabi sauce.

5 FAST & SIMPLE CANNED TUNA RECIPES

Canned tuna is a great fast food because it's high in protein, low in fat, and can be quickly prepared in many ways. Each of these recipes can be prepared in less than 15 minutes.

Below are five different ways to make quick and tasty canned tuna snacks. I recommend that you stick to the lowest-sodium brands packed in water.

TUNA SALAD STUFFED PITTA

Servings: 2

Calories: 184

Protein: 16 grams

Carbohydrates: 28 grams

Fat: 2 grams

3 ounces/85 grams canned tuna (drained)

1 hardboiled egg white

2 tablespoons diced celery

2 tablespoons raisins

1 tablespoon diced scallion/spring onion

2 teaspoons low-fat mayonnaise

1/2 teaspoon Dijon mustard

2 tablespoons diced pineapple

1 whole grain pitta

> In a medium-sized mixing bowl, add all of the ingredients except the pitta. Mix until well combined, divide into 2 equal portions. Cut the pitta in half, stuff each half with 1 portion of the tuna salad.

TUNA MELT

Servings: 1

Calories: 340

Protein: 38 grams

Carbohydrates: 32 grams

Fat: 7 grams

3 ounces/85 grams canned tuna (drained)

1 teaspoon low-fat mayo

dash of hot sauce (Tabasco is good, or even hotter if you want)

1/2 teaspoon lemon juice

2 slices whole grain bread

2 slices tomato

deli slice of low-fat cheddar cheese

salt and ground black pepper, to taste

> In a medium-sized mixing bowl, add the tuna, mayo, hot sauce, lemon juice, salt, and pepper. Mix until well combined. Place on whole grain bread, top with tomato slices, cheese, and remaining slice of bread. Melt the cheese in an oven or toaster oven.

SCHOOLYARD TUNA

Servings: 1

Calories: 349

Protein: 34 grams

Carbohydrates: 34 grams

Fat: 7 grams

3 ounces/85 grams canned tuna

1/4 cup low-fat cottage cheese

3 tablespoons sliced almonds

3 tablespoons raisins

2 tablespoons carrots, shredded

> In a medium-sized mixing bowl, add all of the ingredients and mix until well combined.

TUNA WITH PICO DE GALLO

Servings: 4

Calories: 150

Protein: 16 grams

Carbohydrates: 17 grams

Fat: 2 grams

6 ounces/170 grams canned tuna (drained)

2 diced tomatoes

1/4 cup chopped fresh coriander

2 tablespoons lime juice

1/4 cup diced red onion

1 diced small serrano chilli

4 pieces toasted whole grain bread

1/2 teaspoon salt

> In a medium-sized mixing bowl, add all of the ingredients except the bread. Mix until well combined, divide into 4 equal portions, and serve with piece of toasted whole grain bread.

SPICY TUNA

Servings: 1

Calories: 117

Protein: 22 grams

Carbohydrates: 4 grams

Fat: 1 gram

3 ounces/85 grams canned tuna

1 tablespoon diced pickled jalapeños

1 teaspoon hot sauce (Tabasco or hotter if you want)

4 tablespoons diced tomatoes

1/8 teaspoon cayenne pepper

salt and ground black pepper, to taste

> In a medium-sized mixing bowl, add all of the ingredients and mix until well combined.

PASTA & GRAINS

Carbohydrates are a vital source of energy for your body. They provide fuel in the form of glucose and glycogen and are the macronutrient that you manipulate most when trying to gain muscle or lose fat. When you're eating to gain muscle, the abundance of carbs in your diet not only increases your strength and endurance in the gym, but also gives you an overall sense of satiety and well-being. When you're eating to lose fat, your drastically lowered carb intake not only leads to dropped pounds, but also gives you that dry, hard look.

A good source of slow-burning, low-fat carbohydrates are whole grains such as wheat, brown rice, quinoa, oats, and barley. What are whole grains, exactly? They're grains that contain all the essential parts and naturally occurring nutrients of the entire grain seed. If the grain has been processed (cracked, crushed, rolled, chopped up, or cooked) and still has 100% of the original kernel, it's still a whole-grain product.

In contrast to whole grains are refined grains, which are grains that have been considerably modified from their natural state. Modifications include processes that remove essential parts of the grain, bleaching, and mixing back in a fraction of the nutrients removed.

So, stick to the whole grains and reap their many benefits, such as reduced risk of stroke, diabetes, and heart disease, healthier blood pressure levels, reduction of inflammation, and more.

As you'll see, the pasta recipes in this section always have some form of protein added because one serving of whole-grain pasta has only about 7 grams of protein.

As a note, the pasta measurements given are the dry weight. You'll need a scale to measure them exactly.

Also, I recommend lightly salting the pasta water and <u>not</u> adding oil to the water. Doing so actually makes it harder for the sauce to stick to the pasta.

CHICKEN CACCIATORE

Servings: 4

Prep Time: 5 mins

Cooking Time: 40 – 45 mins

(Per Serving)

Calories: 454

Protein: 45 grams

Carbohydrates: 48 grams

Fat: 7 grams

6 ounces/170 grams quinoa rotelle pasta (available in major supermarket chains)

4 boneless, skinless chicken breasts (6 ounces), rinsed, dried, trimmed of fat, cut into strips

1 tablespoon vegetable oil

1/2 medium onion, chopped

1/2 cup fresh mushrooms, thinly sliced

1 clove garlic, minced

1 can (28 ounces) of plum tomatoes, with juice

1/2 cup dry red wine

1 teaspoon dried oregano

1 bay leaf

1/2 cup fresh parsley, chopped

> Heat the oil in a large, deep skillet over medium-high heat. Add the chicken and brown on both sides. Add the onions, mushrooms, and garlic and sauté until vegetables are tender.
> Add the tomatoes, wine, oregano, and bay leaf and reduce heat to medium-low. Cover and simmer for 30 – 35 minutes, or until chicken is cooked through and sauce has thickened. Stir occasionally.
> Meanwhile, cook the pasta according to package directions.
> Add the cooked pasta and 1/4 cup of the pasta water to the chicken, cook for 1 – 2 minutes, mixing well so the sauce sticks to the pasta. Remove bay leaf and top with fresh parsley.

CHICKEN PESTO PASTA

Servings: 2

Prep Time: 5 mins

Cooking Time: 20 mins

(Per Serving)

Calories: 446

Protein: 32 grams

Carbohydrates: 43 grams

Fat: 16 grams

4 ounces/115 grams whole grain ziti or penne pasta

1 boneless, skinless chicken breast (6 ounces/170 grams), rinsed, dried, trimmed of fat, cut into small cubes

25 fresh basil leaves, finely chopped

1 teaspoon garlic, minced

1 tablespoon warm water

2 tablespoons crushed pine nuts

1 tablespoon extra-virgin olive oil

salt and ground black pepper, to taste

2 tablespoons Parmesan cheese, grated

> Bring a pot of lightly salted water to a boil, cook the pasta according to the package directions.

> In a large bowl, mix the basil, garlic, water, pine nuts, and oil.

> Turn on the stove to medium heat and coat your pan or skillet with cooking spray.

> Begin to cook the chicken in the pan. Once almost cooked, reduce the heat and stir in your salt, pepper, pesto, and Parmesan. Cook until chicken is no longer pink on inside, stir into cooked pasta.

CHICKEN FETTUCCINE WITH MUSHROOMS

Servings: 4

Prep Time: 5 – 10 mins

Cooking Time: 15 – 20 mins

(Per Serving)

Calories: 403

Protein: 34 grams

Carbohydrates: 38 grams

Fat: 12 grams

8 ounces/225 grams whole grain fettuccine

2 boneless, skinless chicken breasts (6 ounces/170 grams), rinsed, dried, trimmed of fat, cut into strips

2 tablespoons extra-virgin olive oil

3 cloves garlic, minced

2 ounces/55 grams (around 1 – 1 1/2 cups) shiitake mushrooms, stemmed and sliced

2 tablespoons lemon juice

2 teaspoons lemon zest

salt and ground black pepper, to taste

1/2 cup Parmesan cheese, grated

1/2 cup fresh basil, chopped

> Cook pasta according to package directions. When you drain the pasta, save 1/2 cup of the pasta water.
> Meanwhile, heat the oil in a large non-stick skillet over medium heat. Add the sliced chicken and cook for 3 – 4 minutes, add the garlic and mushrooms. Cook, stirring occasionally for 4 – 5 minutes or until the mushrooms are nice and tender. Stir in the lemon juice, lemon zest, salt, and pepper and remove from the heat.
> Add the pasta, 1/2 cup of pasta water, Parmesan, and basil to the skillet and toss.

PASTA SALAD
WITH CHICKEN

Servings: 6

Prep Time: 10 mins

Cooking Time: 20 – 25 mins

(Per Serving)

Calories: 381

Protein: 27 grams

Carbohydrates: 41 grams

Fat: 12 grams

1/2 box (8 ounces/225 grams) whole grain bow-tie/farfalle pasta

3 cups (about 3 breasts) cooked chicken breast, shredded

1 can (8 ounces/225 grams) chickpeas, drained and rinsed

1 can (2.25 ounces/65 grams) sliced black olives, drained

2 sticks of celery, chopped

2 cucumbers, peeled and cut into chunks

1/2 cup carrots, shredded

1/2 cup sweet Spanish onion, chopped

2 tablespoons Parmesan cheese, shredded

3 tablespoons extra-virgin olive oil

1/2 cup red wine vinegar

1/2 teaspoon Worcestershire sauce

1/2 teaspoon spicy brown mustard

1/2 heaped teaspoon minced garlic

2 tablespoons fresh Italian parsley, chopped

1 tablespoon fresh basil, chopped or 1 teaspoon dried basil

1/4 teaspoon ground black pepper

> Cook the pasta according to the package directions; drain. Run pasta under cold water for about 30 seconds or until completely cool, then transfer to a large mixing bowl.

> Add the remaining ingredients and mix thoroughly.

> Cover the bowl and place in the refrigerator overnight, or for at least 4 hours. Mix prior to serving.

BEEF LASAGNE

Servings: 4

Prep Time: 10 mins

Cooking Time: 50 mins – 1 hr

(Per Serving)

Calories: 279

Protein: 24 grams

Carbohydrates: 34 grams

Fat: 4 grams

6 no-boil lasagne sheets

1/2 pound/225 grams extra-lean ground or minced beef

1 teaspoon extra-virgin olive oil

1/2 small yellow onion, chopped

1/2 teaspoon dried oregano

pinch of ground black pepper

2 cups low-sodium tomato sauce/passata

1 cup fat-free ricotta cheese

1 tablespoon Parmesan cheese, grated

1 zucchini/courgette, thinly sliced

> Preheat the oven to 350 °F/180 °C/Gas mark 5.

> Heat oil in a large non-stick skillet over medium-high heat. Add the ground beef, onion, oregano, and pepper. Stir while breaking apart the beef, for about 6-8 minutes, or until the beef is fully cooked. Stir in the tomato sauce and bring to a boil, then remove from the heat.

> In a bowl, mix the ricotta and Parmesan.

> Now, to build the lasagne, take a 9 x 5 inch/23 cm x 13 cm baking dish and begin by layering 1/2 a cup of the sauce, 2 of the lasagne sheets, 1/2 cup of the cheese mix, another 1/2 cup of the sauce, and 1/2 of the zucchini/courgettes. Add the next 2 sheets and repeat 1/2 cup of cheese, 1/2 cup of sauce, and 1/2 of the zucchini/courgettes. Finish by topping the zucchini/courgettes with the remaining 1/2 cup of sauce and 2 lasagne sheets.

> Cover the dish with foil and bake in the oven for 30 minutes.

> Remove the foil, then bake for 15 minutes longer. Remove from the oven and let sit for at least 10 minutes before serving.

ASPARAGUS AND GOAT'S CHEESE PASTA

Servings: 4

Prep Time: 5 mins

Cooking Time: 20 mins

(Per Serving)

Calories: 389

Protein: 20 grams

Carbohydrates: 50 grams

Fat: 13 grams

1/2 pound/225 grams whole grain thin spaghetti

1 pound/450 grams asparagus, ends trimmed

1 tablespoon unsalted butter

2 tablespoons all-purpose flour

1 (14 ounce/400 grams) can low-sodium chicken broth/ chicken stock

4 ounces/115 grams goat's cheese

1 teaspoon lemon zest

pinch of ground black pepper

1/2 cup Parmesan cheese, grated

> Bring a large pot of lightly salted water to a boil and add the noodles, cook to package instructions.

> Meanwhile, heat a large pan of lightly salted water to boiling over high heat. Add the asparagus and blanch in the boiling water for 3 minutes, or until they turn bright green. Remove and rinse under cold water to stop the cooking.

> Heat a saucepan over medium-high heat, add the butter. Once the butter is melted whisk in the flour. Add the broth/stock and cook for 2 minutes, stirring constantly, until the sauce thickens. Mix in the goat's cheese and lemon zest.

> Add the spaghetti and asparagus to the pan and toss, covering the pasta in sauce. Serve with pepper and the Parmesan.

PORK TENDERLOIN STIR-FRY

Servings: 4

Prep Time: 5 mins

Cooking Time: 15 mins

(Per Serving)

Calories: 461

Protein: 36 grams

Carbohydrates: 62 grams

Fat: 8 grams

8 ounces/225 grams rice noodles

1 pound/450 grams pork tenderloin, trimmed

1/3 cup water

1/4 cup Shao Hsing rice wine or dry sherry

2 tablespoons low-sodium soy sauce

2 teaspoons cornstarch/cornflour

1 tablespoon peanut oil or canola oil/sesame oil/vegetable oil

1 medium onion, thinly sliced

1 pound bok choy/pak choy (about 1 medium head), trimmed and cut into long, thin strips

1 tablespoon minced garlic

1 tablespoon chilli-garlic sauce (Blue Dragon is widely available)

> Bring a large pot of lightly salted water to a boil and add noodles, cook according to package instructions. Drain, quickly rinse with cold water to stop from further cooking.

> While the pasta is boiling, slice the pork into thin rounds, then cut each round into matchsticks.

> In a small bowl whisk the water, rice wine (or sherry), soy sauce, and cornstarch/cornflour.

> Heat the oil in a Dutch oven/heatproof casserole dish over medium heat. Add the onion and cook for 2 – 3 minutes. Once the onions are softened, add the bok choy/pak choy and cook, stirring occasionally until it begins to soften, about 5 minutes. Add the pork, garlic, and chilli-garlic sauce. Stir occasionally until the pork is just cooked through, about 2 – 3 minutes.

> Take your cornstarch/cornflour mixture and give it a quick whisk, then add to the Dutch oven/heatproof casserole dish and bring to a boil. Stir frequently for 2 – 4 minutes until the sauce has thickened. Serve on top of the noodles.

SALADS

The Shredded Chef is all about eating healthy, high-quality proteins, carbs, and fats to maximize muscle growth and fat loss. Whole grains and animal proteins are a vital part of this, as are plant foods. Fruit and vegetables provide essential vitamins and minerals that support many physiological processes connected not only with building muscle and losing fat, but also with general health and vitality.

The one pitfall of salads is *dressing*. Pretty much every dressing you could buy in your local grocery store is full of sodium, unhealthy fats, and chemical additives. That's why I recommend making your own dressings from high-quality ingredients.

A little trick I learned for eating less dressing (important when dieting to lose weight) is to do the following: instead of spooning a bunch of dressing over your salad, keep it on the side. Dip your fork in it before each bite, and drizzle it over a few bites' worth of salad. You won't feel cheated in terms of taste and will be surprised at how much less dressing you use by doing this.

Delicious salads are a great way to get in some of your daily servings of fruit and vegetables. I eat a salad almost every day, regardless of whether I'm eating to gain muscle or lose fat.

This section starts with some recipes for a few healthy salad dressings (in case you don't want to make one of the full-blown recipes given) and then gets into some full-salad recipes.

RED WINE VINAIGRETTE DRESSING

Servings: 2

Calories: 124

Protein: 0 grams

Carbohydrates: 0 grams

Fat: 14 grams

2 tablespoons extra-virgin olive oil

2 tablespoons red wine vinegar

1/2 teaspoon Dijon mustard

1/4 teaspoon dried thyme

1/4 teaspoon minced garlic

pinch of ground black pepper

> Mix all the ingredients in a bowl (how's that for simple?).

BALSAMIC VINAIGRETTE

Servings: 2

Calories: 133

Protein: 0 grams

Carbohydrates: 2 grams

Fat: 14 grams

2 tablespoons extra-virgin olive oil

2 tablespoons balsamic vinegar

1/2 teaspoon fresh basil, chopped

1/2 teaspoon honey mustard (use the lowest sodium one you can find)

1/4 teaspoon minced garlic

pinch of ground black pepper

> Mix all the ingredients in a bowl.

CREAMY WHITE
VINEGAR DRESSING

Servings: 4

Calories: 11

Protein: 1 gram

Carbohydrates: 2 grams

Fat: 0 grams

1/4 cup fat-free plain yogurt

1 tablespoon fat-free sour cream

1 tablespoon fresh coriander, chopped

1 teaspoon white vinegar

1/4 teaspoon minced garlic

pinch of ground black or white pepper

> Mix all the ingredients in a bowl.

STEAK AND SWEET POTATO SALAD

Servings: 1

Prep Time: 5 – 6 mins

Cooking Time: 10 – 15 mins

(Per Serving)

Calories: 252

Protein: 28 grams

Carbohydrates: 22 grams

Fat: 5 grams

1 filet mignon, about 1-inch/2 1/2 cm thick (8 ounces/225 grams)

1/2 tablespoon ground black pepper

1 large sweet potato

4 medium white button mushrooms, stems trimmed and sliced

2 scallions/spring onions, thinly sliced

1 cup mixed baby salad leaves

> Coat the steak with pepper on all sides and press the pepper into the meat. Coat a small skillet in cooking spray and place over medium heat. Add the steak and cook until seared and nicely browned, about 4 minutes, flip and cook for another 5 minutes over medium. Remove from the pan and set aside to cool to room temperature.

> Meanwhile, puncture the sweet potato in a few places with a knife or fork and place in the microwave on high for 5 minutes, turn and heat for another 5 minutes.

> Add the baby salad leaves to a large salad bowl. Once the steak and potatoes have cooled, cut the steak into slices and the potato into chunks. Scatter the mushrooms and potatoes over the salad leaves, then add the steak and top with scallions/spring onions. Divide into 2 equal portions and top with dressing of your choice.

CLASSIC COBB SALAD

Servings: 2

Prep Time: 5 mins

(Per Serving)

Calories: 494

Protein: 54 grams

Carbohydrates: 20 grams

Fat: 23 grams

1 small head iceberg lettuce, chopped

2 boneless, skinless chicken breasts (6 ounces/170 grams each), cooked, and cut into small cubes

2 hard boiled eggs, chopped

2 medium tomatoes, chopped

1 avocado, sliced

1 cup carrots, grated

1/4 cup low-fat mild cheddar cheese, shredded

> Evenly divide the lettuce between two large bowls.
> Toss in the rest of the ingredients and serve with dressing of your choice.

SPINACH & SALMON SALAD

Servings: 2

Prep Time: 15 mins

Cooking Time: 15 – 20 mins

(Per Serving)

Calories: 395

Protein: 42 grams

Carbohydrates: 24 grams

Fat: 15 grams

2 salmon fillets (6 ounces/170 grams each), rinsed and dried

1 teaspoon fresh parsley, chopped, or 1 teaspoon dried parsley

1/2 medium lemon, juiced

1 teaspoon ground black pepper

1 teaspoon extra-virgin olive oil

1 clove garlic, minced

1/2 cup sweet Spanish onion, chopped

20 asparagus spears, with bottoms cut off

1/2 yellow bell pepper, cored, seeded, and cut into strips

1 tablespoon honey mustard (use the lowest sodium one you can find)

4 cups spinach leaves

10 grape or cherry tomatoes, halved

1/2 cup blueberries

1 tablespoon slivered almonds

> Choose a skillet that's large enough to allow the salmon to lay flat, you may need to cut the salmon in half to accommodate this.

> Place the salmon in the skillet skin side down, add the parsley, lemon juice, and black pepper. Cover with about 1 inch/ 2 1/2 cm of water, or enough to come just over the top of the fish.

> Turn the heat on medium and bring the water to a gentle simmer, let simmer for about 10 minutes, or until the fish is opaque. Remove from the heat and cover.

> In a non-stick skillet over medium-high heat, add the oil, garlic, and onion. Cook for about 3 minutes, or until lightly browned. Add the asparagus and bell pepper. Bring the heat down to medium and cook for 2 – 3 minutes longer, or until the veggies are slightly tender. Finish by stirring in the honey mustard and cooking for 30 seconds longer to caramelise.

> Now to prepare the salad, evenly divide your spinach, tomato, and blueberries between two plates. Carefully remove your salmon from the pan and gently scrape off the skin and fat. Top each plate with half of the salmon, lay your veggies on top and sprinkle with almonds.

QUICK & EASY PROTEIN SALAD

Servings: 1

Prep Time: 15 – 20 mins

(Per Serving)

Calories: 323

Protein: 28 grams

Carbohydrates: 29 grams

Fat: 13 grams

2 cups baby spring mix (small mixed salad leaves i.e. rocket, spinach etc)

2 scallions/spring onions, chopped

1/2 cucumber, halved and sliced

4 mushrooms, halved and sliced

1/4 medium avocado, diced

1/2 cup fat-free cottage cheese

1 hardboiled egg, diced

1 lemon, juiced

1 clove garlic, minced

3 tablespoons low-fat buttermilk

salt and ground black pepper, to taste

> Add the spring mix/baby leaves, scallions/spring onions, cucumber, mushrooms, avocado, cottage cheese, and hardboiled egg to a medium-sized mixing bowl and toss. Transfer to large plate.

> In a small mixing bowl, add the lemon juice, garlic, buttermilk, salt, and pepper and mix well. Pour dressing over salad.

TROPICAL CHICKEN SALAD

Servings: 1

Prep Time: 10 mins

(Per Serving)

Calories: 351

Protein: 42 grams

Carbohydrates: 20 grams

Fat: 13 grams

1 boneless, skinless chicken breast (6 ounces/170 grams), cooked, and cut into cubes

1/8 cup celery, diced

1/4 cup pineapple, cut into chunks

1/4 cup orange, cut into chunks

1 tablespoon pecans, chopped

1/4 cup seedless grapes, halved

2 cups romaine lettuce

salt and ground black pepper, to taste

> Combine all ingredients except for the lettuce in a large bowl.

> Gently mix until well combined and season with salt and pepper.

> Serve on top of the lettuce leaves.

SIDES

The following side dishes can be included with your meals, not only to add some excitement and variety of taste, but also to help you meet your nutritional requirements. Be creative, mix and match sides with main dishes, and you'll discover food combinations that you'll come back to time and time again.

GREEN BEANS ALMONDINE

Servings: 4

Prep Time: Under 5 mins

Cooking Time: 5 – 10 mins

(Per Serving)

Calories: 83

Protein: 4 grams

Carbohydrates: 10 grams

Fat: 5 grams

1 pound/450 grams fresh green beans, washed and trimmed

1/2 teaspoon extra-virgin olive oil

1/4 cup slivered almonds

salt and ground black pepper, to taste

> Bring a large pot of water to a boil on high heat. Add the green beans and boil for 2 – 4 minutes, or until tender.
> Drain the beans and place in a large bowl. Stir in the oil, salt, and pepper.
> Heat a non-stick skillet over medium-high heat. Coat the almonds in cooking spray and add to hot skillet. Stir frequently for 2 – 3 minutes, or until toasted. Reduce heat to medium and add the green bean mixture. Cook for another 2 minutes, stirring occasionally.

BAKED YELLOW
SQUASH

Servings: 4

Prep Time: 5 mins

Cooking Time: 15 – 20 mins

(Per Serving)

Calories: 75

Protein: 6 grams

Carbohydrates: 11 grams

Fat: 2 grams

1 teaspoon extra-virgin olive oil

2 egg whites

1/2 cup skimmed milk

2/3 cup low-carb bread crumbs

1 tablespoon Parmesan cheese, shredded

1/2 teaspoon onion powder

1/2 teaspoon paprika

1/2 teaspoon dried parsley

1/2 teaspoon garlic powder

1/4 teaspoon ground black pepper

2 large yellow squash, quarter-cut lengthwise, then cut in half widthwise

> Preheat the oven to 450°F.

> In medium-sized bowl, lightly whisk the egg whites and milk.

> In a different medium-sized bowl, add the bread crumbs, cheese, onion powder, paprika, parsley, garlic powder, and pepper. Mix well.

> Dunk the squash in the egg mixture and then coat in the bread crumb mixture.

> Coat a baking dish in the oil and add the squash cut side up. Place in the oven for 15 minutes, or until browned.

ROASTED GARLIC
TWICE-BAKED POTATO

Servings: 6

Prep Time: 5 mins

Cooking Time: 1 hr 20 – 30 mins

(Per Serving)

Calories: 216

Protein: 6 grams

Carbohydrates: 39 grams

Fat: 5 grams

6 medium-sized baking potatoes

1 whole garlic bulb

1 teaspoon extra-virgin olive oil

2 tablespoons unsalted butter, softened

1/2 cup skimmed milk

1/2 cup low-fat buttermilk/sour cream

1 1/2 teaspoons fresh rosemary, minced

1/2 teaspoon salt

1/2 teaspoon ground black pepper

dash of paprika

> Place the potatoes on a baking sheet and bake at 400 °F/200 °C/Gas mark 6 for 45 – 55 minutes, or until tender.

> Meanwhile, remove the outer papery skin from garlic, drizzle with oil and wrap in 2 sheets of heavy-duty foil. Add the garlic to the oven for 30 – 35 minutes or until softened. Let garlic and potatoes cool for about 10 minutes.

> Once cool enough to handle, cut a thin slice off the top of each potato and discard. Scoop out the pulp until just a thin shell remains, place the pulp in a large mixing bowl, add the softened butter and mash.

> Cut the top off of the garlic head, leaving the root intact, and squeeze the softened garlic into the bowl with the potatoes, add the milk, buttermilk/sour cream, rosemary, salt, and pepper and mix well.

> Spoon the potato mixture back into the shells and place back on the baking sheet. Bake at 425 °F/220 °C/Gas mark 7 for 20 – 25 minutes, or until heated through. Remove from oven and add a dash of paprika to each top.

SWEET POTATO CHIPS

Servings: 6

Prep Time: 5 mins

Cooking Time: 25 mins, or until crispy

(Per Serving)

Calories: 82

Protein: 1 gram

Carbohydrates: 12 grams

Fat: 4 grams

2 medium-sized sweet potatoes, peeled and thinly sliced

1 tablespoon extra-virgin olive oil

1/2 teaspoon salt

> Position one rack in the centre and one in the lower position of the oven and preheat oven to 400 °F/200 °C/Gas Mark 6.

> Place the sweet potatoes in a large bowl and drizzle olive oil over top, toss to coat well. Spread potatoes evenly over 2 baking sheets and place in oven. Bake, flipping once half way through, until centres are soft and edges are slightly crispy, about 22 – 25 minutes. Sprinkle salt over top.

MIKE'S DELICIOUS
BROWN RICE

Servings: 4

Prep Time: Under 5 mins

Cooking Time: 50 mins – 1 hr

(Per Serving)

Calories: 291

Protein: 8 grams

Carbohydrates: 42 grams

Fat: 10 grams

1 cup long-grain brown rice

2 cups low-sodium chicken broth/stock

1 / 2 cup carrot, shredded

1/2 cup zucchini/courgettes, shredded

3 tablespoons sunflower kernels (available in Holland & Barratt or other health shops)

3 tablespoons sliced almonds

1/4 teaspoon red pepper flakes

2 tablespoons fresh parsley, minced

> Add the rice to the chicken broth/stock and bring to a boil. Reduce heat to medium-low and cover with a tight fitting lid, let cook for 50 minutes.

> Remove rice from heat and let sit covered for 10 minutes.

> When the rice is almost finished, coat a large skillet in cooking spray and place over medium-high heat. Add the carrot and zucchini/courgettes and sauté for 2 minutes. Add the sunflower kernels, almonds, and red pepper flakes and cook until the almonds are browned.

> Add the rice and parsley, combine ingredients well, and sauté for 1 minute so flavours can mix.

MUSHROOM RISOTTO

Servings: 4

Prep Time: Under 5 mins

Cooking Time: 15 – 20

(Per Serving)

Calories: 255

Protein: 12 grams

Carbohydrates: 49 grams

Fat: 3 grams

1 cup Arborio rice

3 small onions, finely chopped

1 clove garlic, crushed

1 teaspoon fresh parsley, minced

salt and ground black pepper, to taste

1 1/2 cups fresh mushrooms, sliced

1 cup skimmed milk

1/4 cup fat-free half and half

3 cups low-sodium chicken broth/stock

1 teaspoon unsalted butter

1/2 cup low-fat Parmesan cheese, grated

> Coat a large skillet in cooking spray and place over medium-high heat. Add the onion and garlic and sauté until onion is tender. Remove the crushed garlic and stir in the parsley, salt, pepper, and mushrooms. Reduce heat to low and cook until mushrooms have softened.

> Add the milk and cream to the skillet, mix everything, then stir in the rice. Bring to a simmer, then stir in the chicken broth/stock one cup at a time, until it is absorbed by the rice.

> Once the rice is finished cooking, stir in the butter and cheese, let cheese melt for a minute, then remove from heat.

CRANBERRY QUINOA SALAD

Servings: 4

Prep Time: 5 mins

Cooking Time: 15 – 20 mins

(Per Serving)

Calories: 287

Protein: 8 grams

Carbohydrates: 51 grams

Fat: 7 grams

1 cup quinoa, rinsed

1 1/2 cups water

1/4 cup red bell pepper, chopped

1/4 cup yellow bell pepper, chopped

1 small red onion, finely chopped

1 1/2 teaspoons curry powder

1/4 cup fresh coriander, chopped

1 lime, juiced

1/4 cup sliced almonds, toasted

1/2 cup carrots, minced

1/2 cup dried cranberries

salt and ground black pepper, to taste

> Pour the water in a large saucepan, cover with a tight fitting lid, and place over high heat. Once water starts to boil, pour in the quinoa, reduce heat to low, and cover. Simmer until the water has been absorbed, about 15 – 20 minutes. Transfer the quinoa to a large mixing bowl and place in the refrigerator until cold.

> Once the quinoa is chilled, stir in the bell peppers, red onion, curry powder, coriander, lime juice, sliced almonds, carrots, cranberries, salt, and pepper.

COUSCOUS SALAD

Servings: 8

Prep Time: 5 – 10 mins

Cooking Time: 5 mins

(Per Serving)

Calories: 222

Protein: 8 grams

Carbohydrates: 40 grams

Fat: 3 grams

1 box (12 ounces/340 grams) couscous

8 leaves Bibb/butterhead lettuce

2 lemons, juiced

1/2 teaspoon lemon zest

2 tablespoons honey

1 tablespoon Dijon mustard

1 teaspoon extra-virgin olive oil

1 container (3.5 ounces/100 grams) low-fat feta cheese, crumbled

3 plum tomatoes, chopped

1 medium cucumber, peeled and cut into chunks

1/2 onion, finely chopped

1 can (2.25 ounces/65 grams) sliced black olives, drained and rinsed

1/4 teaspoon ground black pepper

1/2 cup fresh parsley, chopped

> Bring a pot of lightly salted water to a boil. Place your couscous in a separate bowl; add the boiling water and mix well. Cover and cook for about 5 minutes, or according to package instructions.

> Meanwhile, place the lettuce leaves on 8 separate plates.

> In a small bowl, add your lemon juice, lemon zest, honey, mustard, and oil. Whisk to combine the ingredients well.

> In a different bowl, combine the cooked couscous, cheese, tomatoes, cucumber, onion, olives, pepper, and parsley. Once mixed, stir in the lemon juice mixture.

> Top the lettuce with equal amounts of the couscous salad. This dish can be served warm or refrigerated and served chilled.

LEMON AND CORIANDER QUINOA

Servings: 6

Prep Time: Under 5 mins

Cooking Time: 5 – 7 mins

(Per Serving)

Calories: 109

Protein: 4 grams

Carbohydrates: 20 grams

Fat: 2 grams

1 cup quinoa, rinsed

1/4 cup fresh lemon juice

1/2 cup fresh coriander, chopped

> Prepare the quinoa according to package directions. Once cooked, add the lemon juice and fresh coriander. Mix well and serve.

CURRY POTATOES AND CAULIFLOWER

Servings: 4

Prep Time: Under 5 mins

Cooking Time: 25 mins

(Per Serving)

Calories: 234

Protein: 10 grams

Carbohydrates: 50 grams

Fat: 1 gram

1 cauliflower head (2 – 3 pounds/ 1 1/2 kg), cut into florets

1 pound/450 grams (around 3 medium) potatoes, peeled and cut into 1-inch/2 1/2 cm cubes

1 medium onion, chopped

2 cloves garlic, crushed

2 tablespoons garam masala or curry powder

1 cup low-sodium vegetable broth/stock

2 cups frozen peas

> Bring a pot of lightly salted water to a boil. Add the cauliflower and potatoes and cook for 4 – 5 minutes. Drain.

> Meanwhile, coat a Dutch Oven/heatproof dish in cooking spray and place over medium heat. Add chopped onion and garlic and cook 2 – 3 minutes, or until the onion are softened. Add the garam masala and stir for 1 minute.

> Add the cooked potatoes and cauliflower and stir well, coating in the onion mixture, add the vegetable broth/stock and use to deglaze (scrape the bottom of the Dutch Oven/heatproof dish and remove any stuck bits). Cover and let simmer for 10 minutes. Add the peas, mix well, and cover for another 5 – 7 minutes.

VEGETABLE SAUTÉ

Servings: 6

Prep Time: 5 mins

Cooking Time: 10 mins

(Per Serving)

Calories: 46

Protein: 2 grams

Carbohydrates: 5 grams

Fat: 3 grams

1 tablespoon extra-virgin olive oil

2 cloves garlic, crushed

2 medium zucchini/courgettes cut in half, then into sticks

2 cups cherry tomatoes, halved lengthwise

3 cups baby spinach

1 tablespoon fresh lemon juice

pinch of ground black pepper

> Heat the oil in a pan on medium-low heat. Add the garlic and cook for 1 minute, stir in the zucchini/courgettes and raise the heat to medium.

> Cook for 3 – 4 minutes, stir in the tomatoes, cook for another minute, then stir in the spinach. Cook for another 3 – 4 minutes, then stir in the lemon juice and black pepper.

BROWN RICE PILAFF

Servings: 4

Prep Time: 5 – 10 mins

Cooking Time: 40 – 45 mins

(Per Serving)

Calories: 210

Protein: 5 grams

Carbohydrates: 38 grams

Fat: 4 grams

Fat: 3 grams 1 tablespoon unsalted butter

1 shallot, chopped

1 cup long-grain brown rice, rinsed

salt and ground black pepper, to taste

2 cups low-sodium chicken broth/stock

1 clove garlic, smashed

2 sprigs fresh thyme

3 tablespoons fresh flat-leaf parsley, chopped

3 scallions/spring onions, thinly sliced

> Melt the butter in a large pan over medium heat. Add the shallot and cook for 1 – 2 minutes, until tender. Add the rice and stir well, coating

with the butter and shallot mixture. Cook for a few minutes, until the rice is glossy. Add salt and pepper.

> Stir in the chicken broth/stock, garlic, and thyme. Cover with a tight fitting lid and cook for 40 minutes. Remove from the heat and let sit for 10 minutes. Remove the thyme sprigs and garlic clove (optional). Fluff the rice with a spoon or fork and stir in the parsley and scallions/ spring onions.

HEALTHY SWEET POTATO CASSEROLE

Servings: 6

Prep Time: 10 – 15 mins

Cooking Time: 30 mins

(Per Serving)

Calories: 265

Protein: 7 grams

Carbohydrates: 56 grams

Fat: 2 grams

3 cups sweet potatoes, cooked and mashed

1/3 cup packed brown sugar

1/3 cup skimmed milk

2 tablespoons low-fat margarine, melted

1 teaspoon vanilla extract

1/2 teaspoon salt

2 egg whites

1/2 cup packed brown sugar

1/4 cup all-purpose flour

2 tablespoons low-fat margarine, chilled

> Preheat the oven to 350 °F/180 °C/Gas mark 4.

> Coat a 2-quart baking dish with cooking spray.

> In a large mixing bowl, add the mashed sweet potatoes, 1/3 cup brown sugar, skimmed milk, melted low-fat margarine, vanilla extract, salt, and egg whites. Mix well and transfer to the baking dish, spreading evenly.

> In a medium-sized mixing bowl, add the 1/2 cup brown sugar and flour. Slowly add in the 2 tablespoons chilled low-fat margarine and stir until the mixture has the consistency of coarse crumbs.

> Sprinkle the crumb mixture over the sweet potatoes and bake for 30 minutes.

SQUASH & BROCCOLI STIR-FRY

Servings: 6

Prep Time: 10 mins

Cooking Time: 10 – 15 mins

(Per Serving)

Calories: 82

Protein: 2 grams

Carbohydrates: 15 grams

Fat: 3 grams

1 pound/450 grams butternut squash, peeled, seeded and cut into 1/4-inch/ 1/2 cm slices

1 garlic clove, minced

1/4 teaspoon ground ginger

1 cup broccoli florets

1/2 cup celery, thinly sliced

1/2 cup onion, thinly sliced

2 teaspoons honey

1 tablespoon lemon juice

2 tablespoons sunflower kernels (Holland & Barratt or other health food shops)

> Coat a large skillet with cooking spray and place over medium-high heat. Add the squash, garlic, and ginger and stir-fry for 3 minutes. Add the broccoli, celery, and onion, and continue to stir-fry for 3 – 4 minutes or until all the vegetables are tender.

> Meanwhile, in a small bowl, combine the honey and lemon juice and mix well.

> Place the vegetables in a large serving dish and pour the honey mixture over, toss to coat. Sprinkle the sunflower kernels on top.

PROTEIN SHAKES

Protein shakes are a great way to help meet daily nutritional requirements, and are especially good for your post-workout meal due to fast absorption of the protein and high-glycemic carbs.

I recommend that you use a high-quality whey (I like Optimum Nutrition's Natural Whey) or egg (I like Healthy 'n Fit's 100% Egg Protein) protein powder because both taste pretty good and have no artificial sweeteners. Casein is also a good option for your before-bed protein due to its slow absorption rate (this helps you make it through the night with minimal catabolism).

I don't recommend weight-gainer proteins unless you need to occasionally slam down a post-workout meal fast and don't even have time to make a proper shake.

If you're going to be making several shakes per day (and most of us do), I recommend that you simply mix the powder with water and then get your carbs from fruit or other sources. The shake recipes given in this section require a blender and other ingredients, and are more suited for your post-workout meals (most of these contain 50+ grams of carbs), or as a meal replacement.

KIWI-BANANA-MANGO MONSTER SHAKE

Servings: 1

Prep Time: 15 mins

(Per Serving)

Calories: 459

Protein: 35 grams

Carbohydrates: 78 grams

Fat: 2 grams

1/2 medium kiwi, peeled and sliced

1/2 medium banana, sliced

1/2 medium mango, peeled and diced

1/2 cup fresh or canned pineapple, diced

1 scoop vanilla whey protein powder

1 cup skimmed milk

1/2 cup papaya, diced

1 lemon, juiced

1/2 tablespoon clover honey

1 packet (1 gram/0.03 oz) stevia or other sugar alternative

> Place all of your ingredients in a blender, blend on high until desired consistency.

CHOCOLATE ALMOND MOCHA SHAKE

Servings: 1

Prep Time: Under 5 mins

(Per Serving)

Calories: 397

Protein: 55 grams

Carbohydrates: 16 grams

Fat: 13 grams

1/2 cup skimmed milk

1 tablespoon instant coffee

10 unsalted almonds

1 tablespoon lecithin granules (try Tesco Supplements Range)

2 packets (2 grams/0.06 oz) stevia or other sugar alternative

2 scoops chocolate whey protein powder (Holland & Barratt)

1 cup crushed ice or 6 – 8 ice cubes

> Start blending all of your ingredients except the ice on high. Once mixed, turn the blender to medium and add your ice cubes until desired consistency.

POST-WORKOUT PEANUT BUTTER BLAST

Servings: 1

Prep Time: 5 mins

(Per Serving)

Calories: 810

Protein: 69 grams

Carbohydrates: 70 grams

Fat: 27 grams

1 1/2 cups skimmed milk

1 tablespoon vanilla extract

1 tablespoon flaxseed oil (available Holland & Barratt or Tesco Supplements)

1 teaspoon L-glutamine powder (available from Tesco Supplements)

1 tablespoon micronized creatine monohydrate (available from Tesco Supplements)

1 tablespoon peanut butter

1/4 cup old-fashioned oats

1 cup crushed ice or 6 − 8 ice cubes

2 scoops vanilla or chocolate whey protein powder (Holland & Barratt)

1 banana, frozen

> Start blending all of your ingredients except the banana and protein powder on high. Once mixed, turn the blender to medium and add your banana and protein powder, blend until desired consistency.

ORANGE JULIUS

Servings: 1

Prep Time: 5 mins

(Per Serving)

Calories: 453

Protein: 51 grams

Carbohydrates: 50 grams

Fat: 3 grams

2 scoops vanilla whey protein powder (Holland & Barratt)

1 cup orange juice

3/4 cup crushed ice or 4 – 6 ice cubes

1 tablespoon vanilla extract

1/2 medium banana

3 strawberries, frozen

2 packets (2 grams/0.06 oz) of stevia or other sugar alternative

> Place all ingredients in blender and blend on medium speed until desired consistency.

PROTEIN BARS & SNACKS

Meeting your daily caloric and nutritional requirements is going to mean eating "snack" meals in between your breakfasts, lunches, and dinners. You might have to change your definition of "snack," however.

When I say "snack," I don't mean crackers, cookies, muffins, cereal, doughnuts, chips, pretzels, ice cream, candy, or any other tempting little late-night nibbles. If you have any of these nutritionally bankrupt foods in your home, I recommend you throw them out right now. Yes, all of them, because at best they're "empty" calories and at worst, actually harmful to your muscle-building or fat-loss ambitions.

Instead, you should stock up on healthy snacks such as low-fat cottage cheese, fresh fruits and vegetables, low-fat or fat-free yogurt, nuts, and granola.

What about protein bars for snacks? Most protein bars sold in stores are better snacks than Snickers bars, but that's not saying much.

The problem with most protein bars is they contain a large amount of junk carbs such as sugar and high fructose corn syrup, and not much protein (and to make matters even worse, some companies selling these bars claim they have more protein than they do!). Most bars also contain artificial sweeteners such as sucralose or aspartame, chemicals to enhance the taste, and chemical preservatives. There's just too much junk in most to make them worth eating.

In this section of the book, I'm going to show you how to make your own delicious protein bars using healthy, high-quality ingredients, along with a few other yummy snacks.

CHOCOLATE PEANUT BUTTER PROTEIN BARS

Servings: 6 (1 bar per serving)

Prep Time: 5 mins

(Per Serving)

Calories: 278

Protein: 20 grams

Carbohydrates: 27 grams

Fat: 11 grams

3 cups old-fashioned oats

1/2 cup peanut butter

1 cup skimmed milk

4 scoops chocolate or vanilla whey protein powder (Holland & Barratt)

dash of cinnamon

1 tablespoon stevia or other sugar alternative

> Combine all of the ingredients except the stevia in a large bowl and mix until a sticky batter is formed. Coat a shallow baking dish in cooking spray and spread the mixture out over the dish.

> Evenly sprinkle the stevia over the mixture and place in the fridge overnight. Cut into 8 equal bars.

PROTEIN-PACKED YOGURT AND FRUIT

Servings: 1

Prep Time: Under 5 mins

(Per Serving)

Calories: 212

Protein: 22 grams

Carbohydrates: 32 grams

Fat: 1 gram

1 container (6 ounces/170 grams) fat-free plain yogurt

1 tablespoon vanilla whey protein powder (Holland & Barratt)

1 packet (1 gram/0.03 oz) stevia or other sugar alternative

splash of vanilla extract

1 cup fresh peaches, banana, or other fruit, chopped

> Mix the yogurt, protein powder, stevia, and vanilla extract in a medium bowl. Stir until fully combined.
> Top with fruit.

PROTEIN PUDDING BARS

Servings: 8 (1 bar per serving)

Prep Time: 5 mins

(Per Serving)

Calories: 284

Protein: 31 grams

Carbohydrates: 30 grams

Fat: 4 grams

8 scoops chocolate or vanilla whey protein powder

3 cups old-fashioned oats

1 package sugar-free fat-free Instant Whip (use same flavour as protein)

2 cups skimmed milk

> Combine all ingredients in a large bowl and mix until a sticky batter is formed. Coat a shallow baking dish in cooking spray and spread the mixture out over the dish.
> Place in the refrigerator overnight, cut into 8 equal bars once set.

STRAWBERRY BANANA PROTEIN BARS

Servings: 8 (1 bar per serving)

Prep Time: 5 – 10 mins

Cooking Time: 35 – 40 mins

(Per Serving)

Calories: 199

Protein: 22 grams

Carbohydrates: 16 grams

Fat: 5 grams

1 cup old-fashioned oats

6 scoops strawberry whey protein powder (Holland & Barratt)

1/2 cup fat-free dry milk powder

1/4 cup fat-free cream cheese

2 egg whites

1 1/2 bananas, mashed

1/4 cup water

2 tablespoons canola oil/vegetable oil

> Preheat the oven to 325 °F/160 °C/Gas mark 3.

> Spray a shallow baking dish with cooking spray. In a medium-sized mixing bowl, add the oatmeal, protein powder, and dry milk. In a separate medium-sized mixing bowl, combine the cream cheese, egg whites, bananas, water, and oil and beat with an electric hand mixer until thoroughly combined. Slowly add in the dry mixture and beat until fully combined.

> Pour the batter into the prepared baking dish and bake for 30 – 35 minutes, or until a toothpick inserted into the middle comes out clean.

NO-FAT TZATZIKI SAUCE

Servings: 16(2 tablespoons per serving)

Prep Time: Under 5 mins

(Per Serving)

Calories: 12

Protein: 1 gram

Carbohydrates: 2 grams

Fat: 0 grams

1/2 large cucumber

3/4 cup plain fat-free yogurt

1/4 tablespoon Worcestershire sauce

1/8 cup fresh mint, finely chopped

salt, to taste

> Peel the cucumber and cut in half lengthwise, scoop out the seeds. Finely slice half the cucumber and place into a large mixing bowl. Take the other half and puree in a food processor or blender, add to the mixing bowl.

> Add the remaining ingredients to the mixing bowl and mix well. For guaranteed freshness I recommend using within 3 days.

EGG WHITE BITES

Servings: 6

Prep Time: 5 mins

Cooking Time: 8 – 10 mins

(Per Serving)

Calories: 50

Protein: 7 grams

Carbohydrates: 3 grams

Fat: 1 gram

10 egg whites

1 whole egg

1 tomato, seeded and finely chopped

1 medium onion, finely chopped

1 teaspoon dried basil

salt and ground black pepper, to taste

> Beat the egg and egg whites in a medium bowl.
> Divide mixture among a 6-cup muffin pan. Top each cup with tomatoes, onions and basil. Sprinkle with salt and pepper.
> Bake at 350 °F/180 °C/Gas mark 5 for about 8 minutes.

MEAN GREEN SALSA

Servings: 4 (1 cup per serving)

Prep Time: 5 – 10 mins

(Per Serving)

Calories: 141

Protein: 4 grams

Carbohydrates: 17 grams

Fat: 8 grams

2 poblano chilli peppers, halved and seeded

2 serrano chilli peppers, halved and seeded (if you cannot find these peppers, use 2 hot and 2 medium hot)

1 avocado

1 clove garlic

1 bunch coriander

1/2 green bell pepper, seeded and chopped

1/2 medium sweet onion, chopped

1/4 head iceberg lettuce, chopped

1/2 cup water

2 limes, juiced

1 can (14.5 ounces/410 grams) no-salt diced tomatoes, drained

> Place all of your ingredients excluding the tomatoes in a blender or food processor. Blend until mostly smooth with some chunks. If you can't fit it all at once you can blend in multiple batches.

> Pour into a large bowl and add the tomatoes, mix well.

SIZZLING SALSA

Servings: 8 (1 cup per serving)

Prep Time: 5 – 10 mins

(Per Serving)

Calories: 58

Protein: 1 gram

Carbohydrates: 10 grams

Fat: 2 grams

6 medium vine-ripened tomatoes, chopped

4 sticks of celery, chopped

4 jalapeño peppers, finely diced

4 serrano or other chilli peppers, finely diced (optional)

1 bunch coriander, finely chopped

1/2 yellow bell pepper, seeded and chopped

1 cup mango, chopped (optional)

1/2 cup sweet onion, chopped

1/2 cup key lime juice

1 tablespoon extra-virgin olive oil

pinch of ground black pepper

> Place all of your ingredients in a large bowl, toss, and serve.

CORN TORTILLA CHIPS

Servings: 1

Prep Time: Under 5 mins

Cooking Time: 10 mins

(Per Serving)

Calories: 80

Protein: 2 grams

Carbohydrates: 16 grams

Fat: 2 grams

Cooking spray

2 (6-inch/15 cm) corn tortillas

> Preheat the oven to 350 °F/180 °C/Gas mark 4.
> Cut the tortillas into 6 wedges and place the pieces on a baking sheet. Lightly spray both sides of the chips with cooking spray and bake for 10 minutes, or until crispy and browned on edges.

PERFECT GUACAMOLE

Servings: 2

Prep Time: 5 – 10 mins

(Per Serving)

Calories: 295

Protein: 6 grams

Carbohydrates: 19 grams

Fat: 26 grams

2 ripe avocados

1/2 red onion, finely chopped

2 serrano chillies, seeded and finely chopped

1/4 cup fresh cilantro, chopped

1 tablespoon fresh lime juice

1/2 teaspoon salt

dash of ground black pepper

> Cut the avocados in half, pit them and scoop out the peel and place in a mixing bowl. Add in the chopped onion, coriander, lime, salt, pepper, and half the chilli.

> Mash together, I personally like mine slightly chunky, so I don't mash too much. Taste, add additional lime, salt, and chilli to reach desired flavour and level of spice. I always end up adding a tiny bit more salt and the rest of the chilli, but that's just how I like it!

GARLIC VEGETABLE DIP

Servings: 9 (2 tablespoons per serving)

Prep Time: 2 – 3 mins

(Per Serving)

Calories: 20

Protein: 1 gram

Carbohydrates: 4 grams

Fat: 0 grams

1 cup fat-free sour cream

2 tablespoons fat-free mayonnaise

1 lime, juiced

1/2 teaspoon garlic powder

pinch of ground black pepper

> Place all of your ingredients in a medium-sized mixing bowl, mix well, and serve.

DESSERTS

Don't worry—I haven't forgotten the sweets. Don't think of your hard training as a license to indulge in treats regularly, though. You can kill your fat loss pretty quickly by simply adding a couple hundred calories too many each day.

That being said, there's nothing wrong with having a dessert every week or two. When I'm eating to gain muscle, I usually have one dessert per week (although some weeks I skip it—I'm not really into sugar). When I'm dieting to lose weight, I never have more than one small, (100-calorie) dessert per week, and I usually have one every two weeks.

The recipes I give here are better than your average dessert recipes in that they have no sugar and little fat. They use higher-quality carbs than your average junk at the store, and they are high in protein.

PROTEIN PUDDING

Servings: 2

Prep Time: Under 5 mins

Cooking Time: 20 mins

(Per Serving)

Calories: 266

Protein: 32 grams

Carbohydrates: 31 grams

Fat: 1 gram

1 package sugar-free fat-free Angel Delight

2 cups skimmed milk

2 scoops chocolate or vanilla whey protein powder (use same flavour as pudding)

> Place all of your ingredients in a medium-sized bowl, stir together to combine everything, then mix with an electric hand mixer until it starts to thicken. Place in the refrigerator for at least 20 minutes to set.

PEACH COBBLER

Servings: 6

Prep Time: 10 – 15 mins

Cooking Time: 30 – 35 mins

(Per Serving)

Calories: 154

Protein: 11 grams

Carbohydrates: 25 grams

Fat: 1 gram

3 tablespoons blueberry, raspberry, strawberry, or mixed-fruit preserves

1 can (15 ounces/425 grams) diced peaches in water or 100% juice, drained

1/2 cup low-fat cottage cheese

1/2 cup water

2 scoops vanilla whey protein powder (available at Holland & Barratt)

1/4 cup all-purpose flour

2 packets (2 grams/0.06 oz) stevia or other sugar alternative

1/2 cup quick cooking oats

1 tablespoon honey

> Preheat the oven to 350 °F/180 °C/Gas mark 4.

> Pour the fruit preserves into an 8 x 8 inch/20 cm x 20 cm baking dish and spread evenly. Add the peaches, spread evenly.

> In a mixing bowl, add the cottage cheese, water, protein powder, flour, and stevia. Mix well and pour over the peaches, spreading evenly.

> In a small mixing bowl, mix together the oats and honey. Pour over the cheese mixture.

> Bake for 30 minutes, let sit 20 minutes before serving.

KEY LIME PIE

Servings: 6

Prep Time: 10 – 15 mins

Cooking Time: 55 mins – 1 hr

(Per Serving)

Calories: 317

Protein: 9 grams

Carbohydrates: 61 grams

Fat: 3 grams

4 sheets low-fat digestive biscuits, crushed into crumbs

1/2 cup apple sauce

1 cup quick cooking oats

1 teaspoon ground cinnamon

3 egg yolks

1 can (14 ounces/400 grams) fat-free condensed milk

1/3 cup fresh lime juice

St. Ivel Low Fat Spray Whipping Cream

> Preheat the oven to 350 °F/180 °C/Gas mark 4.
> In a large mixing bowl, add the biscuit crumbs, apple sauce, oats, and cinnamon. Mix well. Remove 1 tablespoon of the mixture and set aside.

> Pour the cracker mixture in a 9 x 1.5 inch/23 x 4 cm pie pan. Spread evenly and lightly pack it into and along the sides of the pan to form the crust. Bake for 15 minutes.

> In a medium-sized bowl, add the egg yolks, condensed milk, and lime juice. Whisk until smooth. Reduce the oven temperature to 250°F/130 °C/Gas Mark 1/2, pour the juice mixture into the crust. Bake for 40 minutes, or until the filling is firm.

> Remove from heat, let sit until completely cool. Transfer to refrigerator for 4 – 6 hours, or until fully chilled. Top with a 2-inch/5 cm layer of the whipping spray, sprinkle with the 1 tablespoon of crumb mixture, and serve immediately.

PROTEIN MILKSHAKE

Servings: 1

Prep Time: Under 5 mins

(Per Serving)

Calories: 259

Protein: 25 grams

Carbohydrates: 33 grams

Fat: 2 grams

1 cup skim milk

1/2 cup low-fat frozen yogurt

1/2 teaspoon vanilla extract

1/2 scoop whey protein powder (your choice of flavour) (Holland & Barratt)

> Place all ingredients in a blender and blend on low for a few minutes, until desired consistency.

HONEY-BALSAMIC STRAWBERRIES

Servings: 4

Prep Time: 5 mins

(Per Serving)

Calories: 117

Protein: 2 grams

Carbohydrates: 29 grams

Fat: 1 gram

2 large punnets of strawberries, washed, tops cut off, and halved

4 lemons, juiced

1 tablespoon balsamic vinegar

1 teaspoon honey

> In a large mixing bowl, add the strawberries and lemon juice, mix well and refrigerate for 2 hours.
> After the strawberries have chilled, in a separate bowl, mix the vinegar and honey. Drizzle the honey vinegar over the strawberries and serve.

BONUS SPREADSHEET

First, I want to say THANK YOU for reading my book, *The Shredded Chef.*

I'm thrilled at how many people have written me to say how much they like the recipes for helping with losing weight, building muscle, and staying healthy.

Chances are you'd like to use the recipes in this book to plan out your daily meals. This handy spreadsheet will help!

In it you'll find a list of every recipe in the book along with their calories, protein, carbs, and fats. When you're planning your meals, all you have to do is skim over the spreadsheet and pick foods that fit your caloric and macronutritional targets. No need to browse through the entire cookbook!

Visit the link below to download this free spreadsheet today!

Visit WWW.BIT.LY/TSC-SPREADSHEET to get this spreadsheet now!

WOULD YOU DO ME A FAVOR?

Thank you for buying my book. I hope that you enjoy the recipes I've included and that they help you in your muscle-building and fat-torching endeavors.

I have a small favor to ask. Would you mind taking a minute to write a blurb on Amazon about this book? I check all my reviews and love to get feedback (that's the real pay for my work—knowing that I'm helping people).

Visit the following URL to leave me a review:

WWW.AMZN.TO/TSC-REVIEW

Also, if you have any friends or family that might enjoy this book, spread the love and lend it to them!

Now, I don't just want to sell you a book—I want to see you use what you've learned to build the body of your dreams.

As you work toward your goals, however, you'll probably have questions or run into some difficulties. I'd like to be able to help you with these, so let's connect up! I don't charge for the help, of course, and I answer questions from readers every day.

Here's how we can connect:

Facebook: facebook.com/muscleforlifefitness

Twitter: @muscleforlife

G+: gplus.to/MuscleForLife

And last but not least, my website is www.muscleforlife.com and if you want to write me, my email address is mike@muscleforlife.com.

Thanks again and I wish you the best!

Mike

ALSO BY MICHAEL MATTHEWS

Thinner Leaner Stronger: The Simple Science of Building the Ultimate Female Body

If you want to be toned, lean, and strong as quickly as possible without crash dieting, "good genetics," or wasting ridiculous amounts of time in the gym and money on supplements...regardless of your age...then you want to read this book.

Visit www.muscleforlife.com to get this book!

Bigger Leaner Stronger: The Simple Science of Building the Ultimate Male Body

If you want to be muscular, lean, and strong as quickly as possible, without steroids, good genetics, or wasting ridiculous amounts of time in the gym, and money on supplements...then you want to read this book.

Visit www.muscleforlife.com to get this book!

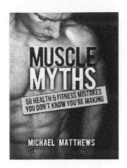

Muscle Myths: 50 Health & Fitness Mistakes You Don't Know You're Making

If you've ever felt lost in the sea of contradictory training and diet advice out there and you just want to know once and for all what works and what doesn't—what's scientifically true and what's false—when it comes to building muscle and getting ripped, then you need to read this book.

Visit www.muscleforlife.com to get this book!

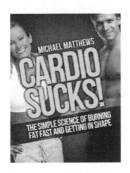

Cardio Sucks! The Simple Science of Burning Fat Fast and Getting In Shape

If you're short on time and sick of the same old boring cardio routine and want to kick your fat loss into high gear by working out less and...heaven forbid...actually have some fun...then you want to read this new book.

Visit www.muscleforlife.com to get this book!

Awakening Your Inner Genius

If you'd like to know what some of history's greatest thinkers and achievers can teach you about awakening your inner genius, and how to find, follow, and fulfill your journey to greatness, then you want to read this book today.

(I'm using a pen name for this book, as well as for a few other projects not related to health and fitness, but I thought you might enjoy it so I'm including it here.)

Visit www.yourinnergenius.com to get this book!

Approaches to curriculum management

OPEN UNIVERSITY PRESS

Management in Education Series

Editor
Tony Bush

Senior Lecturer in Educational Policy and Management
at The Open University

The series comprises five volumes which cover important topics within the field of educational management. The articles present examples of theory and practice in school and college management. The authors discuss many of the major issues of relevance to educational managers in the post-Education Reform Act era.

The five readers are components of The Open University M.A. in Education module *E818 Management in Education*. Further information about this course and the M.A. programme may be obtained by writing to the Higher Degrees Office, Open University, PO Box 49, Walton Hall, Milton Keynes, MK7 6AD.

TITLES IN THE SERIES

Managing Education: Theory and Practice
Tony Bush (ed.)

Approaches to Curriculum Management
Margaret Preedy (ed.)

Financial Management in Education
Rosalind Levačić (ed.)

Human Resource Management in Education
Colin Riches and Colin Morgan (eds)

Educational Institutions and their Environments:
Managing the Boundaries
Ron Glatter (ed.)

Approaches to curriculum management

EDITED BY
Margaret Preedy
at The Open University

OPEN UNIVERSITY PRESS
MILTON KEYNES · PHILADELPHIA
in association with The Open University

Open University Press
Celtic Court
22 Ballmoor
Buckingham
MK18 1XW

and
1900 Frost Road, Suite 101
Bristol, PA 19007, USA

First Published 1989
Reprinted 1992

Selection and editorial material
copyright © The Open University 1989

British Library Cataloguing in Publication Data
Approaches to curriculum management. – (Management in
    education)
    1. Great Britain.   Schools.   Curriculum.   Planning
    I. Preedy, Margaret   II. Series
    375'.001'0941

    ISBN 0-335-09249-7
        0-335-09248-9 (paper)

Library of Congress Cataloging-in-Publication Data
Approaches to curriculum management / edited by Margaret Preedy.
        p.   cm. – (Management in education series)
    Includes indexes.
        ISBN 0-335-09249-7—ISBN 0-335-09248-9 (pbk.)
        1. Curriculum planning – United States.   2. Curriculum evaluation –
    – United States.   3. Educational law and legislation – United States.
    4. School management and organization – United States.   I. Preedy,
    Margaret.   II. Series.
    LB2806.15.A67   1989
    375'.001'0973—dc20   89-34691 CIP

Typeset by Rowland Photosetting Ltd
Bury St Edmunds, Suffolk
Printed and bound in Great Britain by
Biddles Ltd, Guildford and King's Lynn

Contents

Acknowledgements

All possible care has been taken to trace ownership of the material included in this volume, and Open University Press would like to make grateful acknowledgement for permission to reproduce it here.

1   S. Maclure (1988). *Education Reformed*, pp. 1–33, London, Hodder & Stoughton.
2   Task Group on Assessment and Testing (1988). *National Curriculum: Task Group on Assessment and Testing – A Report*, London, DES. Reproduced with the permission of the Controller of Her Majesty's Stationery Office.
3   Further Education Unit (1989). *Towards a Framework for Curriculum Entitlement*, London, FEU.
4   K. Morrison and K. Ridley (1988). *Curriculum Planning and the Primary School*, London, Paul Chapman Publishing.
5   T. Becher (1989). Commissioned for this collection.
6   J. Campbell (1989). Commissioned for this collection.
7   A. McIntyre (1989). Commissioned for this collection.
8   J. Shackleton (1988). 'The professional role of the lecturer', *Planning the FE Curriculum* edited by B. Kedney and D. Parkes, London, FEU.
9   K. Reid, D. Hopkins and P. Holly (1987). *Towards the Effective School*, chapter 9, Oxford, Basil Blackwell.
10   E. Hoyle (1986). *The Politics of School Management*, pp. 51–73, London, Hodder & Stoughton.
11   M. Fullan (1987). 'Managing curriculum change', *Curriculum at the Crossroads* edited by M. O'Connor, London, School Curriculum Development Council. Also R. D. Laing (1970). *Knots*, London, Tavistock Publications.

12   D. Barnes, G. Johnson, S. Jordan, D. Layton, P. Medway and D. Yeomans (1988). 'TVEI and the school as a whole', *A Second Report on the TVEI Curriculum*, London, Training Agency. Reproduced with the permission of the Controller of Her Majesty's Stationery Office.

13   P. Ribbins (1986). 'Qualitative perspectives in research in secondary education: the management of pastoral care', *Research in the Management of Secondary Education* edited by T. Simkins, Sheffield Papers in Educational Management, No. 56, Sheffield City Polytechnic.

14   M. Wallace (1988). 'Towards a collegiate approach to curriculum management in primary and middle schools', *School Organisation*, Vol. 8, No. 1, Carfax Publishing Company.

15   S. Ball (1987). *The Micro-politics of the School*, chapter 9, London, Methuen & Company.

Grateful thanks are due to my secretary, Betty Russell, for her help in typing and other preparation work on this collection with great patience and good humour. Thanks are also due to members of the E818 course team for reading and commenting on drafts.

Introduction

Margaret Preedy

Curriculum management is a central activity for schools and colleges, creating the framework for effective teaching and learning to take place. This collection of papers examines various aspects of the curriculum management process and the context in which it occurs. The intention of this volume is to encourage greater reflection about and understanding of the elements of curriculum management.

The organizing framework and content of this book rest on a number of themes which are outlined below, followed by a brief review of the issues raised by the contributors. For our purposes here, curriculum management is taken to include organizing and co-ordinating curriculum planning; changing the curriculum in response to internal and external needs and demands; dealing with issues that arise in implementing curriculum change and evaluating the work of the school or college; and negotiating the curriculum in practice with the various groups and interests involved.

A major theme of the collection is the importance of the context in which curriculum management takes place. It is a truism now to suggest that external constraints and accountability demands play a large part in shaping curriculum decisions within the school or college. Yet it is not such a very long time ago (1959) since David Eccles (the then Minister of Education) described the curriculum as 'a secret garden', the preserve of professional teachers, into which politicians and the public at large strayed at their peril. The garden gate is now wide open. There has been a very significant increase in central control of the curriculum, accompanied by a growth in influence of other external groups – parents, school/college governors, employers. Much of the reduction in professional autonomy took place as a result of the radical legislation of the Conservative governments of the 1980s – particularly the 1986 (no. 2) Act, and the 1988 Education Reform Act (ERA), which set out the framework for the national curriculum and associated pupil assessment arrangements. The radical nature of these innovations contrasted with developments in education (and, indeed, other areas of public provision) in the 1950s, 1960s and 1970s when change had proceeded in a much more gradual and incremental way.

Lawton's (1983) model identifies five levels (national, regional or LEA, institutional, departmental, and individual) and three areas (aims, pedagogy, and evaluation) of curriculum control. In terms of this typology, the 1988 ERA brought about a significant increase in central control, a reduction in LEA control, and considerably circumscribed the area for curriculum decision-making within schools, especially in the areas of aims and evaluation. However, schools arguably retain a considerable degree of discretion in terms of *implementing* the national curriculum and assessment arrangements and also in the area of teaching/learning styles and approaches – pedagogical issues – which are not prescribed by the 1988 Act.

None the less, it can be argued that the cumulative impact of the assessment arrangements, together with other aspects of the ERA, all act as a strong constraint on the area of pedagogy in Lawton's typology. Thus the requirement to publish assessment results, coupled with the impact of parents acting as 'discriminating consumers' in comparing results between schools, and open enrolment, may provide a strong incentive to adopt forms of curriculum organization and teaching styles which maximize 'good' assessment results (see also Ranson's discussion of the impact of the publication of exam results as required by the 1980 Education Act: Ranson *et al.*, 1986). These and other aspects of curriculum control in the light of the ERA are explored by various chapters in this volume.

The ERA did not deal directly with curricular issues in further and higher education. None the less, in further education (FE) at least, there was by the end of the 1980s evidence of a move towards more overall planning and standardization of provision, and a national framework for vocational qualifications with the National Vocational Qualification (NVQ) due for implementation in the early 1990s. The ERA required each LEA to produce strategic plans for all its further education provision, for approval by the DES. The secretary of state also indicated a wish to move towards a core curriculum for further education.

External curricular control is thus an essential consideration when looking at curriculum decisions within the institution. Another major influence on curriculum management is formed by the *ideologies* or underlying sets of values and beliefs of those involved. Curriculum decisions are guided by these ideologies and by the interplay of the competing values which exist within and between the various decision-making levels identified by Lawton. Indeed, individuals may espouse elements of different ideologies with respect to various issues or at different times. Closely linked with individual and group ideologies are their perspectives of the management process. Until recently, the dominant perspectives in educational management were broadly functionalist or systems approaches which saw institutional decision-making as a generally rational and systematic process (see e.g. Cuthbert, 1984; Bush, 1986).

These approaches have however been increasingly questioned. An influential paper by Greenfield (1975) put forward the case for an alternative approach to the study of educational management. He and other writers argued for the insights offered by a phenomenological or interactionist approach, focusing on individual actors' meanings and interpretations rather than on organizational structures and goals. Similarly it has been argued that political, collegial, and organized anarchy perspectives can offer important insights into curriculum management (see Hoyle, 1986, and Reader 1 in this series).

The debate on alternative perspectives of management was paralleled by an increased concern for curricular *processes* as opposed to *products*. Kelly (1982) and others argued that traditional models of curriculum decision-making gave an undue emphasis to products or outcomes – especially in terms of test and exam results – and neglected processes: teaching and learning activities as perceived and negotiated by teachers and students themselves.

The later 1970s and the 1980s also saw a number of practical curriculum developments which promoted a greater emphasis on processes. These included work by the Further Education Unit (FEU) and further education colleges on pre-vocational courses, which included learner-centred elements such as negotiated curricula, the provision of guidance as an important curricular element, formative and profiled assessment. These, it was argued, developed greater student motivation. Hargreaves (ILEA, 1984) put forward similar points about the management of the school curriculum, arguing the need for a greater emphasis on learning processes and negotiation with the student, and approaches which would enable students to show attainments in broader areas than merely exam passes, and hence enhance their commitment to school. TVEI and CPVE incorporated elements of a student-centred process approach, and in some schools had a significant impact on teaching and learning styles (see e.g. Harland, 1987; DES, 1988). Profiling and records of achievement were also adopted in many secondary schools and their value widely endorsed (see e.g. Broadfoot *et al.*, 1988; TGAT, 1988).

Approaches to curriculum innovation and evaluation also saw a shift from top-down rationalist stances to a more interactionist school-based focus which stressed the importance of the user/classroom teacher in the design, review and evaluation of the curriculum (see e.g. Skilbeck, 1984 on school-based curriculum development; McMahon *et al.*, 1984). Empirical and theoretical studies increasingly recognized the importance of the implementation stage in effective curriculum innovation and the need to change teacher attitudes and values rather than just materials (see Fullan, 1982).

In many respects, recent large-scale top-down curriculum innovations by central government such as the national curriculum and GCSE can be seen as running counter to the school-based, process-focused, learner-centred approaches mentioned above. Many commentators, too, noted that in terms of content the national curriculum and assessment arrangements would tend to inhibit school-based developments, and to marginalize curriculum areas not included in the core and foundation subjects, as well as such developments as cross-curricular approaches and records of achievement (see Haviland, 1988).

None the less, while the framework of subjects and assessments are clearly defined by the Act and by the Orders of the secretary of state stemming from it, there is considerable scope for curriculum decision-making within schools. Indeed, in the light of the major implementation task, affecting all teachers and all schools in the maintained sector, flexible and responsive curriculum management in the schools is all the more important, with the need to phase in the new arrangements over a period of several years while maintaining existing provision, ensuring adequate staff preparation and resources, negotiating between internal school needs and external pressures, and coping with the impact of multiple changes.

The papers in this collection explore the themes outlined above from various angles. Section I (Chapters 1–3) looks at the policy framework for curriculum decision-making. Chapter 1 by Maclure outlines the main provisions of the ERA on the national curriculum and assessment, together with the TGAT proposals, looking at the main implications for local authorities, schools and parents. Maclure emphasizes that the curricular and assessment provisions of the Act create a clear framework for schools within which they are expected to become more open to the operation of market forces and consumer choice under the provisions of the Act dealing with LMS, open enrolment and grant-maintained status.

Chapter 2 comprises the conclusions and recommendations of the TGAT report. The extract shows the fairly 'liberal' approach taken by the task group, which went some way towards reassuring those who had grave doubts about a national system of testing. In particular the report stressed formative aspects, the combination of teacher assessments and standardized assessment tasks, a flexible system of levels of attainment to allow for children's differing rates of development, and the use of a range of methods of assessment, not just written tests.

Turning to further education, Chapter 3 outlines the FEU's general guidance for LEA and institutional staff who are involved in overall curriculum planning in the light of the requirements of the Education Reform Act. The document stresses the importance of considering student access and entitlement, and the essential elements that should be included in all learning programmes.

Section II (Chapters 4–11) looks at contextual factors for curriculum decision-making, particularly the ERA, and at various models of curriculum planning, change and evaluation. Morrison and Ridley (Chapter 4) identify and describe a number of educational ideologies, each suggesting a particular approach to the aims, outcomes, structure and content of the curriculum. A glance at the curricular aims of any school or college is likely to reveal elements of several of these ideologies, reflecting the demands of a pluralist society.

The next four chapters look at the implications of a major contextual factor – the Education Reform Act – for curriculum decision-making in the school or college. Chapter 5 by Becher examines a central issue confronting all schools in the early 1990s: putting in practice the major curriculum changes brought about by the ERA. Becher looks at the national curriculum in terms of the 'implementation gap' between policy objectives and their outcomes in practice, arguing that 'policy-makers cannot operate in isolation: what happens when their plans are put into action depends crucially on those who have to carry them out'. Although the national curriculum has been brought about by what the paper characterizes as a broadly coercive approach to policy change, schools, departments and individual teachers retain considerable scope for the exercise of professional autonomy. Approaches to implementation are likely to reflect the prevailing management styles of the institutions concerned. Becher identifies three broad approaches – coercive, manipulative and rational – and their implications for curricular policies and practice in the schools.

Curriculum diversity, standards and accountability and control are central issues in curriculum policy, at national and LEA levels as well as within the school. Campbell's (Chapter 6) discussion of the implications of the ERA for curriculum decision-making in primary schools assesses how far the Act has effectively addressed these issues. Campbell discusses three fundamental management tasks which the ERA raises for primary schools: curriculum implementation, assessment and public relations. All three, it is suggested, require a collegial approach with a key role for curriculum co-ordinators.

The impact of the ERA is also a central concern in Chapter 7, which looks at the management of curriculum and school evaluation. McInytre reviews various evaluation strategies and argues the need for a collaborative approach, involving groups inside and outside the school in meeting the demands of external accountability and internal school improvement within the framework created by the ERA.

Some of the curriculum management issues confronting the FE sector in the post-ERA period are reviewed in Chapter 8. Shackleton argues that colleges should move beyond a curriculum-led approach to institutional development, adopting instead a student-led perspective. In the context of changes brought about by the National Council for Vocational Qualifications, strategic planning of FE provision, and demographic trends, college managers need to develop a more flexible and responsive approach to client demands, perspectives and needs – to 'empower' the student.

The last three chapters in this section look more generally at curriculum management issues and perspectives. Reid, Hopkins and Holly (Chapter 9) argue that successful teaching needs 'thoughtful and systematic curriculum planning', in which the classroom teacher should occupy a central role. They trace the development of product and more recent process models of curriculum planning, and describe an approach which attempts to incorporate both product/outcome and process considerations.

Hoyle's paper (Chapter 10) raises a number of fundamental problems in the dominant rationalist or systems approach to curriculum decision-making. Focusing on the central rationalist concept of organizational goals, Hoyle discusses the 'organizational pathos' arising, he argues, from the 'chronic discrepancy between proclaimed organizational goals and their achievement'. This has considerable implications for the traditional approaches to curriculum planning which are evident in LEA and institutional planning models as well as in official documents. The ambiguity perspectives discussed by Hoyle may be particularly appropriate to institutions faced with rapid change and uncertainty in their environments – conditions which are confronting schools and colleges in the 1990s.

Finally in this section, the brief paper by Fullan (Chapter 11) looks at some general characteristics of curriculum change and proposes a number of strategies for the management of successful curriculum innovation. Fullan emphasizes the complexity of the change process, the importance of the implementation stage and the need to bring about alterations in teachers' fundamental beliefs and understandings, in order to achieve lasting and effective change.

Section III presents a number of empirically based papers illustrating the application of various approaches to curriculum management. Chapter 12, by Barnes *et al.*, is an extract from a University of Leeds evaluation report on the TVEI curriculum. Basing their analysis on case studies in 26 schools, the authors examine the impact of TVEI on the curriculum and on teachers. The study illustrates the wide diversity in the ways in which schools managed the implementation of TVEI. It explores some of the major issues raised by the innovation, in particular the problems and opportunities of modular curricula, the impact of TVEI on other areas of the curriculum and the perspectives of TVEI and non-TVEI teachers.

Ribbins (Chapter 13) describes the application of an interactionist or 'qualitative' approach to researching the management of pastoral care in secondary schools. Ribbins contrasts qualitative and quantitative approaches to educational research and demonstrates the strengths of an interactionist approach in revealing the differing meanings and interpretations of staff as to what constituted 'pastoral care' and how it was managed in the schools.

Wallace in Chapter 14 argues for a 'collegiate' approach to curriculum management in primary and middle schools. The case which he makes for a collegiate or democratic form of school organization is similar to that put forward by Campbell (1985) – see also Chapter 6 in this volume. Drawing on the experiences of the National Development Centre for School Management Training, Wallace proposes a 'management development' approach which he argues may help to implement collegiate management, despite the constraints and difficulties involved.

Finally, the extract from Ball's book, *The Micro-Politics of the School*, in Chapter 15 illustrates the application of a contrasting perspective, a political approach, in looking at examples of interdepartmental rivalry in schools, particularly over the issues of resource allocation and departmental status. Ball sees the department as a power base for the competing subject interests within the school, a political coalition which acts to promote the status and interests of its members against encroachments by other departments, the head and senior management.

This collection of papers is inevitably selective. It is hoped that it will encourage not only those who read it as part of an OU course, but also a wider readership, to reflect on the management of curriculum planning, evaluation and change within the framework of the ERA and other con-textual factors, and to consider the applicability of various perspectives in understanding curriculum management processes. A flexible approach to curriculum decision-making, informed by an awareness of the 'competing rationalities' (Hoyle) of those involved, is essential in the context of the multiple changes currently confronting schools and colleges.

References

Broadfoot, P., James, M., McMeeking, S., Nuttall, D. and Stierer, B. (1988) *Records of Achievement: Report of the National Evaluation of Pilot Schemes*. A report submitted to the DES and the Welsh Office, London, HMSO.

Bush, T. (1986) *Theories of Educational Management*, London, Harper & Row.

Campbell, R. J. (1985) *Developing the Primary School Curriculum*, London, Holt, Rinehart & Winston.

Cuthbert, R. (1984) Open University Course E324, *Management in Post-Compulsory Education*, Block 3, part 2, 'The management process', Milton Keynes, Open University.

DES (Department of Education and Science) (1988) *Report by HM Inspectors on a Survey of Courses leading to the Certificate of Pre-Vocational Education*, London, DES.

Fullan, M. (1982) *The Meaning of Educational Change*, Columbia University, New York, Teachers College Press.

Greenfield, T. B. (1975) 'Theory about organization: a new perspective and its implications for schools', in V. Houghton *et al.* (eds) *Management in Education: The Management of Organizations and Individuals*, London, Ward Lock.

Harland, J. (1987) 'The TVEI experience', in D. Gleeson (ed.) *TVEI and Secondary Education: A Critical Appraisal*, Milton Keynes, Open University Press.

Haviland, J. (ed.) (1988) *Take Care, Mr. Baker!*, London, Fourth Estate.

Hoyle, E. (1986) *The Politics of School Management*, London, Hodder & Stoughton.

ILEA (Inner London Education Authority) (1984) *Improving Secondary Schools*, The Hargreaves Report, London, ILEA.

Kelly, A. V. (1982) *The Curriculum: Theory and Practice*, 2nd edn, London, Harper & Row.

Lawton, D. (1983) *Curriculum Studies and Educational Planning*, London, Hodder & Stoughton.

McMahon, A., Bolam, R., Abbott, R. and Holly, P. (1984) *Guidelines for Review and Internal Development in Schools: Primary and Secondary School Handbooks*, London, Longman.

Ranson, S., Gray, J., Jesson, D. and Jones, B. (1986) 'Exams in context: values and power in educational accountability', in D. Nuttall (ed.) *Assessing Educational Achievement*, Lewes, Falmer Press.

Skilbeck, M. (1984) *School-Based Curriculum Development*, London, Harper & Row.

TGAT (Task Group on Assessment and Testing), DES (1988) *National Curriculum Task Group on Assessment and Testing: A Report*, London, DES and Welsh Office.

Section I

Policy frameworks

1

The national curriculum and assessment

Stuart Maclure

[This chapter provides a summary and analysis of the 1988 Education Reform Act's main provisions on the national curriculum and assessment, Sections 1–25 of the Act.]

> **1.** (1) It shall be the duty –
>
>   (a) of the Secretary of State as respects every maintained school;
>   (b) of every local education authority as respects every school maintained by them; and
>   (c) of every governing body or head teacher of a maintained school as respects that school;
>
> to exercise their functions (including, in particular, the functions conferred on them by this Chapter with respect to religious education, religious worship and the National Curriculum) with a view to securing that the curriculum for the school satisfies the requirements of this section.
>
>   (2) The curriculum for a maintained school satisfies the requirements of this section if it is a balanced and broadly based curriculum which –
>
>   (a) promotes the spiritual, moral, cultural, mental and physical development of pupils at the school and of society; and
>   (b) prepares such pupils for the opportunities, responsibilities and experiences of adult life.

The Education Reform Act requires all maintained schools to provide for all pupils, within the years of compulsory schooling, a basic curriculum 'to be known as the national curriculum'. Section 1(2) notes that the curriculum for a maintained school 'satisfies the requirements of this section if it is a balanced and broadly based curriculum which:

(a) promotes the spiritual, moral, cultural, mental and physical development of pupils at the school and of society; and
(b) prepares such pupils for the opportunities, responsibilities and experiences of adult life.'

---

2. (1) The curriculum for every maintained school shall comprise a basic curriculum which includes –

(a) provision for religious education for all registered pupils at the school; and
(b) a curriculum for all registered pupils at the school of compulsory school age (to be known as 'the National Curriculum') which meets the requirements of subsection (2) below.

(2) The curriculum referred to in subsection (1)(b) above shall comprise the core and other foundation subjects and specify in relation to each of them –

(a) the knowledge, skills and understanding which pupils of different abilities and maturities are expected to have by the end of each key stage (in this Chapter referred to as 'attainment targets');
(b) the matters, skills and processes which are required to be taught to pupils of different abilities and maturities during each key stage (in this Chapter referred to as 'programmes of study'); and
(c) the arrangements for assessing pupils at or near the end of each key stage for the purpose of ascertaining what they have achieved in relation to the attainment targets for that stage (in this Chapter referred to as 'assessment arrangements') . . .

Section 3 designates three core subjects and seven foundation subjects which must be taught. The core subjects are mathematics, English and science. The foundation subjects are history, geography, technology, music, art, physical education and (at the secondary stage) a modern language. Welsh is a core subject for Welsh-speaking schools and a foundation subject in non-Welsh-speaking schools in Wales.

The curriculum includes religious education for all pupils (Section 2). It must specify in relation to each subject 'the knowledge, skills and understanding which all pupils of different abilities and maturities' are expected to have learned by the end of each 'key stage' – that is, by about the ages of 7, 11, 14 and 16 (the 'attainment targets'). It must also set out how pupils are to be assessed and tested at around the prescribed ages ('the assessment arrangements').

3. (1) Subject to subsection (4) below, the core subjects are –

    (a)   mathematics, English and science; and

    (b)   in relation to schools in Wales which are Welsh-speaking schools, Welsh.

  (2) Subject to subsection (4) below, the other foundation subjects are –

    (a)   history, geography, technology, music, art and physical education:

    (b)   in relation to the third and fourth key stages, a modern foreign language specified in an order of the Secretary of State; and

    (c)   in relation to schools in Wales which are not Welsh-speaking schools, Welsh . . .

---

4. (1) It shall be the duty of the Secretary of State . . .

    (a)   to establish a complete National Curriculum as soon as is reasonably practicable (taking first the core subjects and then the other foundation subjects); and

    (b)   to revise that Curriculum whenever he considers it necessary or expedient to do so.

  (2) The Secretary of State may by order specify in relation to each of the foundation subjects –

    (a)   such attainment targets;

    (b)   such programmes of study; and

    (c)   such assessment arrangements;

as he considers appropriate for that subject . . .

Note that although a list of subjects is specified in the Act, most of the implementation – such as, for example, the setting of attainment targets, the prescription of programmes of study and the outline arrangements for assessment – is by secondary legislation in the form of Orders. The original list of subjects, too, can be amended by Order.

All maintained schools are under a general duty to make sure the national curriculum is implemented (Section 10) – that is to say, a duty is placed on the local authority and school governors in respect of county and voluntary schools (other than aided schools) and on the governors of aided schools and grant maintained schools.

Religious worship and religious education are covered in Sections 6 to 13. Section 6 states the legal requirement for a single act of worship for all pupils, or separate acts of worship for pupils of different age groups or in different school groups. In county schools, responsibility for arranging the form of worship lies with the headteacher after consultation with the governors. In voluntary schools it is the other way round: the governors are meant to make the arrangements after consultation with the head.

Religious education

6. (1) . . . All pupils in attendance at a maintained school shall on each school day take part in an act of collective worship . . .

7. (1) . . . In the case of a county school the collective worship . . . shall be wholly or mainly of a broadly Christian character . . .

The Act adds the rider that in county schools the collective worship 'shall be wholly or mainly of a broadly Christian character' (Section 7(1)). This is qualified by giving schools some discretion to vary the form, provided that 'taking any school term as a whole' most assemblies comply. Among the considerations which may be taken into account (Section 7(5)) are the family background of the pupils. Where heads consider that insistence on a Christian act of daily worship should not apply, they can (Section 12) submit an application to the local Standing Advisory Council on Religious Education (SACRE), which body can decide whether or not the school should have exemption, having regard to the nature of the school community. (SACREs are committees set up by local authorities with representatives of the Churches to oversee the RE curriculum.)

Religious education continues to be non-denominational in character in county and controlled schools, based on Agreed Syllabuses. These, too, are the responsibility of the SACREs, and Section 8 lays down that they 'shall reflect the fact that the religious traditions in Great Britain are in the main Christian, while taking account of the teaching and practices of the other principal religions represented in Great Britain.'

The Act goes on (Section 14) to provide for two Curriculum Councils (one for England, one for Wales) and a School Examinations and Assessment Council to advise the secretary of state on matters relating to the curriculum and its assessment.

Special cases

18. The special educational provision for any pupil specified in a statement under section 7 of the 1981 Act of his special educational needs may include provision –

  (a) excluding the application of the provisions of the National Curriculum; or

  (b) applying those provisions with such modifications as may be specified in the statement.

19. (1) The Secretary of State may make regulations enabling the head teacher of any maintained school, . . .

  (a) to direct as respects a registered pupil . . . the provisions of the National Curriculum –

(i) shall not apply; or

(ii) shall apply with such modifications as may be so specified . . .

(2) The conditions prescribed by the regulations shall . . . limit the period that may be specified . . . to a maximum period specified in the regulations . . .

(3) Where a head teacher gives a direction under regulations made under this section . . . he shall give the information mentioned in subsection (4) below, . . .

(a) to the governing body; and

(b) where the school is a county, voluntary or maintained special school, to the local education authority;

and . . . also to a parent of the pupil.

(4) That information is the following –

(a) the fact that he has taken the action in question, its effect and his reasons for taking it;

(b) the provision that is being or is to be made for the pupil's education during the operative period of the direction; and

(c) either –

(i) a description of the manner in which he proposes to secure the full implementation in relation to the pupil after the end of that period of the provisions of the National Curriculum; or

(ii) an indication of his opinion that the pupil has or probably has special educational needs by virtue of which the local education authority would be required to determine the special educational provision that should be made for him (whether initially or on a review of any statement of his special educational needs the authority are for the time being required under section 7 of the 1981 Act to maintain). . . .

(6) It shall be the duty of a local education authority, on receiving information given to the authority under this section by the head teacher of any maintained school which includes such an indication of opinion with respect to a pupil, to consider whether any action on their part is required in the case of that pupil under section 5 of the 1981 Act (assessment of special educational needs).

All the members are nominated by [the secretary of state]. The Act specifically requires him/her (Section 20(2)) to refer proposed Orders relating to the subject requirements, attainment targets and programmes of study, to the National Curriculum Council, and obliges the Council to consult with local authorities, governors' representatives, teachers' organizations and others (subsection 3). The secretary of state must publish the advice he/she receives from the Council, and if he/she fails to follow it, state his/her reasons (subsection (5)(a)(ii)).

The secretary of state has also a general power to make regulations (Section 17) removing or modifying the provisions of the national curriculum in such circumstances as may be specified.

Certain exceptions to the provisions of the Act on the national curriculum are outlined in Sections 16–19. Section 16 sets out the limited conditions under which the secretary of state may issue a direction exempting a school from the requirements laid down in the national curriculum or modifying them. Such a direction can be given in a county, controlled or maintained special school on the application of the local authority with the agreement of the governing body, or vice versa; or of the Curriculum Council with the agreement of both the local authority and the governing body. In a grant maintained, aided or special agreement school, applications can be made by the governing body, or by the Curriculum Council with the governors' agreement.

Another exemption (Section 18) applies to pupils with special educational needs, for whom the national curriculum can be modified by a Statement under Section 7 of the 1981 Education Act.

An added flexibility is provided in Section 19, under which the secretary of state can make regulations enabling the headteacher of any maintained school to modify the national curriculum in respect of any pupil for a limited period.

In reporting such action to the parent, the governors and the local authority, the head can either press for a statement of special educational need, or signify how he or she intends to secure in due course that the pupil is brought back on to the full national curriculum course. The section provides for the parents to have right of appeal to the governors, in respect of any action by the head under these regulations.

An important aim of the introduction of a national curriculum is to give parents the maximum information about the programmes their children are following, and regular reports on their progress. Section 22 of the Act empowers the secretary of state to make regulations about the supply of public information which local authorities, governors and heads may be required to provide. Among the topics covered would be the details of how the national curriculum is to be interpreted, and the curriculum policy documents which all authorities and governing bodies are required to produce under the 1986 Education Act.

There is also a general power for the secretary of state to require the local education authorities, governors and heads to provide any other information about the education of pupils that he/she thinks fit.

The secretary of state's power to demand information also means that he/she can insist on the publication of results of assessment and testing, and determine the form which this must take.

Section 23 requires local authorities to establish their own procedures (approved by the secretary of state and therefore subject to his/her guidelines) for dealing with complaints about any maintained or county and voluntary or maintained special school, including complaints that the curriculum has not been followed, or that there has been a failure to provide all the information required under Section 22.

A new orthodoxy

The powers which the secretary of state has taken to prescribe the curriculum are similar in effect to powers which existed under the Codes which governed elementary and secondary education under the 1902 Act. These powers continued till the 1944 Act, though from the mid-1920s their application was relaxed. When the 1944 Education Act was passed, legal control of the curriculum in maintained schools was ascribed to the local education authorities and the governors of aided schools. In practice, they never exercised their powers over the curriculum, which to all intents and purposes became the responsibility of heads and their senior staff. The external examinations exerted a strong influence in the upper forms. So too, in some local authorities, did the local advisers and other support staff.

In the decade before the introduction of the Education Reform Bill, the Department of Education and Science and successive secretaries of state showed increasing interest in the curriculum, and began to intervene by issuing a series of policy documents such as the *Organization and Content of the 5–16 Curriculum* (DES, 1984), *Science 5–16: A Statement of Policy* (DES, 1985a) and *Modern Languages in the School Curriculum* (DES, 1988a).

Her Majesty's Inspectors also increased their output of curriculum papers, and local education authorities were encouraged by DES circulars to review their own curriculum arrangements.

By the time Sir Keith Joseph (secretary of state, 1981–6) issued his White Paper on *Better Schools* (DES, 1985b), it had become clear that curriculum policy had to be considered at three levels: the *national* level in the form of statements of policy issued by the secretary of state; the *local authority* level in the form of each authority's policy statement, which would be expected to have regard to national aims and priorities; and the *school* level, where each governing body would be required to produce its own curriculum paper.

The 1986 Act, mainly concerned with reforming the composition of school governing bodies and extending their powers, demonstrated the potential danger of the three-way stretch which might arise if the secretary of state, the local authority and the school pulled in different directions. It seemed to leave the head in the invidious position of arbitrating between his or her governors and the local authority if a disagreement were to arise.

Though *Better Schools* (DES, 1985b: para. 37) stated that the government had no intention to introduce legislation redefining responsibility for the curriculum, shortly after Mr Kenneth Baker had succeeded Sir Keith Joseph in the early summer of 1986 he had begun to move towards a centrally controlled curriculum.

What had still been regarded as a highly controversial idea in the early 1980s had become commonplace by the time it figured in the Conservative election manifesto at the general election of June 1987. It soon became apparent that it enjoyed a wide measure of political support outside the Conservative party, and controversy concentrated not on *whether* there should be a national curriculum but on the mechanics of it and the setting of attainment targets and methods of assessment.

The 1988 Act made it clear exactly where the legal control of the curriculum lay – with the secretary of state. It removed the confusion built into the 1986 Act, while still insisting that both the local authority and the governing body must adopt curriculum policies to give effect to the national curriculum.

The local authority's curriculum role is downgraded. It is the national curriculum which provides the local authority, the governors and the headteacher with their marching orders. A school which is implementing the national curriculum is working within the law.

The distinction which the Act made in Section 3, between the core and foundation subjects, is more important as a guide to administrative action than as a fine legal distinction.

The core subjects, as their name implies, form the central part of the curriculum. It was with these subjects that the setting up of the national curriculum would begin. Working groups on mathematics and science had reported by August 1988 and the secretary of state had published these with his own proposals. [. . .]

The foundation subjects came afterwards. Technology was intended to be a priority but was not in the first batch. Modern languages differed from the other foundation subjects because they concerned only the secondary school stage. The introduction of a modern languages curriculum had to await some solution to the obvious staffing difficulties implicit in a demand for all pupils to be taught one or more languages *throughout* the compulsory period of secondary education.

[. . .]

The Act is at pains to describe the process by which the secretary of state is to arrive at his/her curriculum Orders, the documents which he/she must lay before Parliament for a positive resolution in both Houses. Any proposals have to be referred to the appropriate Curriculum Council. The Council then puts them out for consultation with local authorities, teachers' bodies, representatives of governing bodies and 'any other persons' thought to be worth consulting. The Council then reports back to the secretary of state, summarizing the views of those consulted and making its own recommendations. The Council can also add any other advice it thinks fit.

The secretary of state is then obliged to publish the Curriculum Council's report. He/she does not have to accept the advice, but if he/she fails to do so he/she must state his/her reasons for setting it aside. He/she then issues the draft Order, after which there has to be yet another period of at least a month for further consultation and representations from interested groups.

The reason for laying down such a detailed procedure was to make sure that the strong central powers vested in the secretary of state are constrained by a due process which ensures extensive consultation and requires the secretary of state to act publicly and explain him/herself. The effect may well be to hand the power over, within a relatively short time, to the powerful curriculum bureaucracy which the Act has created.

Assessment and testing

The reliance placed on attainment targets and the testing and assessment of pupils at the key stages of 7, 11, 14 and 16 made this part of the Education Reform Act of great and controversial interest to those inside the education system. Testing and assessment were to be the public and visible way of enforcing the new curriculum.

It was a prime aim of the Act to make schools more accountable and give parents more and better information about their children's progress. Experience in the USA and elsewhere had shown the likelihood that the curriculum could become 'test-driven' if universal external testing were introduced in a simplistic or clumsy way. The English folk memory returned to Matthew Arnold's strictures on 'payment by results' and the three decades which followed the introduction of the New Code in 1862, spent in dismantling the disincentives to good teaching which that powerful administrative device instituted.

Teaching to the tests was a likely enough expectation. The question was: could sufficiently good tests be created to ensure that teachers who taught to them would do a good job?

Assessment is clearly an essential part of the teacher's job, and teachers regularly use standardized tests to help them. What sort of national scheme could be set up which would build on the best practice and make it the norm? How could it be ensured that assessment would avoid an excessive concentration on pencil and paper tests of a traditional kind?

The task of drawing up the outline of an assessment scheme fell to a group headed by Professor Paul Black of King's College, London, a scientist with considerable experience as a curriculum developer. His Task Group on Assessment and Testing (TGAT) produced a report at Christmas 1987 which became the basis of DES policy and a guide for the national curriculum subject working groups set up to consider attainment targets, programmes of study and assessment arrangements.

The scheme put forward by the Black Committee – generally known as the TGAT Report – envisaged a system of 'formative' assessment drawing heavily on teachers' observations as well as on 'standard assessment tasks' and other tests. The 'standard assessment tasks' could take the form of defined activity which was part of the normal teaching programme. In primary schools, the report suggested, children could undertake an assessment task without necessarily knowing it was a test which would be moderated and form part of a graded assessment.

The aim, according to TGAT, had to be to produce 'a full and well-articulated picture of the individual child's current strengths and future needs'. It was essential to build on good classroom practice:

> A system which was not closely linked to normal classroom assign-
> ments and which did not demand the professional skills and commit-
> ment of the teachers might be less expensive and simpler to implement
> but would be indefensible in that it could set in opposition the processes
> of learning, teaching and assessment.

(TGAT, 1988: para. 220)

This last is the key sentence in the report: it is all about trying to construct a *system* of assessment which runs in parallel with teaching and learning, and yet can be 'moderated' and 'standardized' to produce information about individual, class, school and local authority performance which can be usefully presented to parents and other 'consumers', teachers, adminis-trators, and so on.

TGAT assumed that the attainment targets which the Act required to be established for each subject would be divided up into groups, each group representing a different dimension of the subject. These groups of attainment targets would form what the TGAT Report called the 'profile components'. These components ('preferably no more than four and never more than six') would reflect 'the variety of knowledge, skills and understanding to which the subject gives rise'.

The assessments would be based on these profile components and would include the teachers' own estimates, based on classwork, as well as the performance of the pupils on 'standard assessment tasks' and in tests. Development which would have to be undertaken before the system could be introduced would include the creation of an item bank of test questions to be administered by teachers in connection with their teaching. An important assumption, especially at the primary level, was that there would be consider-able overlap of profile components, to reduce the number of separate assessments which individual teachers would be called upon to make, and to take account of cross–curricular themes.

The assessment of the various subject components would then be put together to form the complete assessment of the pupils' progress.

TGAT was anxious to devise a form of assessment which emphasized progression, and therefore constructed a framework of ten levels through which a pupil might be expected to climb.

At age 7 most (80 per cent) of pupils would achieve levels 1, 2 or 3 according to their assessed performance: 'Two years of learning represents one level of progress.' At age 11, 80 per cent would achieve levels 3 to 5. At age 14, the range would cover levels 4 to 7 and at age 16 there would be an overlap with the GCSE: levels 7 to 10 would, as the report put it, 'bear some relationship to upper GCSE grades'.

This ingenious scheme was intended to prevent pupils from moving through the various assessment points with a static or scarcely changing mark or grade. It would provide a sense of progression. It would also enable the wide spread of achievement in each age-group to be accommodated by the use of levels below or above the national average. The form of assessment would be criterion-referenced (that is, expressed as far as possible in terms of specified tasks) and directly linked to the programmes of study laid down in the national curriculum, thereby providing a flexible scheme with testing at more or less fixed ages which would nevertheless do justice to children of all performance standards.

How the results were to be reported outside the school was a matter of widespread concern. TGAT made a number of sensible recommendations.

Assessment results for *individual* pupils should be confidential to pupils, their parents and teachers.

> The *only* form on which results . . . for . . . a given school should be published is as part of a broader report by that school of its work as a whole.
>
> (TGAT, 1988: para. 227)

The group rejected the idea of 'scaling' results up or down to take account of social factors. It recommended that 'national assessment results for a class as a whole and a school should be available to the parents of its pupils'.

Much concern had been expressed about the impact of formal national assessment and testing on the primary schools. TGAT favoured starting the tests at age 7 to identify at an early stage any who were under-performing, but wished to restrict the number of standard assessment tasks at age 7 to three, each task being designed to give 'systematic assessment of competence in the range of profile components appropriate to age 7'. It opposed any requirement for the publication of school results for 7-year-olds.

By the time they reached the age of 11, TGAT assumed that children would need to be assessed on three or four standard tasks which covered a range of profile components, 'possibly supplemented by more narrowly focused tests for particular components'.

The report emphasized (as such reports usually do) that its recommendations had to be considered as a whole – including the far-reaching sections on in-service training, research and development, and resources in time and materials. The timetable attached to the report provided for a five-year run-in period in which the assessment procedures and the curriculum development would go hand-in-hand, with the first full reporting of the results in year 5, in 1993.

The TGAT Report was produced in five months – a feat in itself. It was an extremely skilful document in that it met the secretary of state's requirement for an assessment scheme which would satisfy the provisions of the Education Reform Act, while at the same time it won the confidence of many teachers who had been sceptical or hostile to the idea of universal testing and assessment. This in itself was enough to arouse suspicions in certain government quarters that the Group had subverted the radical intentions of the Act. A leaked letter from the prime minister's private office reported early doubts about the 'enormously elaborate and complex system' and the philosophy behind the scheme for formative and diagnostic rather than summative assessment. The central importance which the report placed on the role and judgements of teachers was also queried, along with the 'major role envisaged for the LEAs'. There were also doubts about the cost and the long lead time to bring the assessment and testing procedures into operation (*TES*, 1988).

These doubts appeared to be more muted as the Bill moved relentlessly forward to become an Act. It looked as if an attempt would be made, at some point, to simplify the working of the scheme and meet practical difficulties which might arise in its application. An assessment and testing scheme introduced in Croydon, independently of the Education Reform Act, appeared to produce a somewhat simpler method which might be expected to be easier for parents and employers to come to grips with. But the TGAT Report's proposals were the only national scheme on offer and, from the DES point of view, there was clearly a great deal to be said for mobilizing the widest possible support behind a scheme which would stand or fall on the cooperation of teachers.

The essential features of the scheme which the TGAT Report combined were

1 close interdependence between curriculum, teaching and assessment
2 full involvement of teachers
3 varied forms of assessment, including assessment via tasks which form a normal part of classroom activity
4 time for the development of assessment measures and for the training of teachers in their use
5 assessment at the primary level which was compatible with good primary practice
6 sensible ground rules for reporting results
7 a realistic timetable for the introduction of the scheme.

The government's formal response to the TGAT Report came in a parliamentary answer (*Hansard*, 7 June 1988) which set out the main principles on which assessment would be based:

(a) attainment targets will be set which establish what children should normally be expected to know, understand and be able to do at the ages of 7, 11, 14 and 16; these will enable the progress of each child to be measured against national standards.

(b) pupils' performance in relation to attainment targets should be assessed and reported on at ages 7, 11, 14 and 16. Attainment targets should be grouped for this purpose to make the assessment and reporting manageable.

(c) different *levels* of attainment and overall pupil progress demonstrated by tests and assessment should be registered on a ten-point scale covering all the years of compulsory schooling.

(d) assessment should be by a combination of national external tests and assessment by teachers. At age 16 the GCSE will be the main form of assessment, especially in the core subjects of English, mathematics and science.

(e) the results of tests and other assessments should be used both *formatively* to help better teaching and to inform decisions about next steps for a pupil, and *summatively* at ages 7, 11, 14 and 16 to inform parents about their child's progress.

(f) detailed results of assessments of individual pupils should be given in full to parents, and the Government attaches great importance to the principle that these reports should be simple and clear. Individuals' results should not be published, but aggregated results at the ages of 11, 14 and 16 should be, so that the wider public can make informed judgements about attainment in a school or LEA. There should be no legal requirement for schools to publish such results for seven-year-olds, though it is strongly recommended that schools should do so.

(g) in order to safeguard standards, assessments made by teachers should be compared with the results of the national tests and the judgement of other teachers.

The principles followed the general lines of the TGAT recommendations, with some significant differences in regard to the publication of results. TGAT wanted to insist that results should be published only within the context of a report on the work of the school as a whole. This proviso was ignored in the ministerial statement. The TGAT Report was opposed to any requirement for the formal publication of results at age 7. The ministerial statement stopped short of making publication at 7 compulsory, but added a strong recommendation that such results should be published, notwithstanding the TGAT's serious doubts about the usefulness of the comparisons to which this might give rise.

It was clear that the TGAT Report and the principles it adumbrated were only a beginning. A great deal would depend on how the scheme was developed, at every stage – from the setting of the attainment targets and the selection of the profile components, to the presentation of the results in detail and in aggregate. The commitment of human and physical resources which Professor Black's group assumed was great: if this commitment were not wholly forthcoming, the initial support for the TGAT approach could melt away.

[. . .]

Applicability

The national curriculum is mandatory on all maintained schools – that is, county and voluntary schools, and the new category of grant-maintained schools. It does not have legal force in independent schools, though most independent schools will make sure they can satisfy parents that they offer it or something better. New independent schools seeking registration will have to bear this in mind. City technology colleges will have to provide 'a broad curriculum with an emphasis on science and technology'. The national curriculum does not apply to them, though the discussion document on the curriculum issued before the Bill was published indicated that the secretary of state would 'make adherence to the substance of the national curriculum' a condition of grant.

Time allocation

The DES Consultative Paper on the national curriculum (DES, 1987), issued in advance of the Bill, gave an illustrative example of how the timetable for the last two years of compulsory education might work out under the constraints imposed by the national curriculum. This showed the ten compulsory subjects occupying some 75–85 per cent of the available time, with no allowance for religious education, or for additional science or mathematics. Subsequently ministers drew back from this draft illustration and in commending the Bill to Parliament in the Second Reading debate, Mr Baker contented himself with saying: 'it is our belief that it will be difficult if not impossible for any school to provide the national curriculum in less than 70 per cent of the time available.' In reality, nobody could say in advance of the publication of 'programmes of study' how much time would be required.

The first draft of the Bill was amended to underline the refusal to specify any particular periods of time. Section 4(3) makes this an explicit denial. In this it is unusual, in that it spells out what the secretary of state must *not* put in an Order, instead of what he/she must or may.

Special educational need

There was considerable anxiety among those directly concerned with children with special educational needs that their interests might be prejudiced by the introduction of a national curriculum. At various points the Act acknowledges these concerns. Statemented children are exempt from the national curriculum, and headteachers have a procedure they can invoke for other pupils for whom the specified curriculum would be unsuitable.

The Act is clearly not designed to make it easy for schools to take the line of least resistance with pupils who are failing to make the grade. The effect of the legal changes may be to put pressure on local authorities to provide 'statements' for more pupils, and for the needs of slow learners to be considered more carefully because the Act will allow such children to be withdrawn from the regular course only in prescribed circumstances.

Enforcement

The national curriculum is to be policed in local authority maintained schools by the governors, by the local authorities through their own inspectors, and by Her Majesty's Inspectors of schools.

Local authority inspectors are expected to play a key role. [. . .] The inspectors are the advisers who are in closest touch with the schools. It will fall to them, in many cases, to clarify, for the schools, points of difficulty arising from the mountain of curriculum material which is being generated by the DES, the National Curriculum Council and the subject working groups.

In addition to their formal in-service training activities, they will have much informal training to do in their regular school contacts. They will have to help the local authorities develop performance indicators by which schools can be judged. After 1989 they are expected to become increasingly involved in the introduction of teacher appraisal.

All this will be in addition to the essential part they play in matters of staff discipline. More intensive monitoring of performance is likely to increase the demand for reports from inspectors as a first step towards sanctions against ineffective staff and other, less extreme, remedial measures.

In addition to the monitoring functions undertaken by the local authority, direct intervention by parents is made possible through the complaints procedure. In terms of a market ideology, this gives the consumers (i.e. the parents, who throughout the Act are seen as surrogate consumers for their sons and daughters) a chance to act if they believe there is a failure to deliver the curriculum to which they are, by law, entitled. In an ideal market system, pressure by consumers would be all-important. Under the Act it seems unlikely to be of paramount significance, but dissatisfied parents who might otherwise feel impotent are given a weapon with which to fight back. It may also open up opportunities for barrack-room lawyers. Its main significance is likely to be to keep heads and their staff, and governing bodies, on permanent guard against the possibility of local challenge. They will watch their flanks with caution.

Action

The national curriculum requires action from the secretary of state, from the local authorities, from governors, from headteachers and their staff, and from parents.

The secretary of state must activate the machinery to produce the programmes of study, attainment targets and procedures for testing and assessment. This means setting up working groups to prepare the programmes of study and attainment targets, subject by subject, for the ten-subject curriculum laid down in Section 3 of the Act. He/she must set up and keep in being a National Curriculum Council and a School Examinations and Assessment Council. The secretary of state's proposals for the Curriculum must be referred to the National Curriculum Council, starting with those for the core subjects. After receiving the advice of the Council (which must consult widely), the secretary of state must then make up his/her own mind. If the secretary of state rejects the advice, he/she must say why. Finally, the secretary of state must incorporate his/her decision in Orders which have to be approved by both Houses of Parliament.

It then becomes the continuing duty of the curriculum and examinations councils to keep the national curriculum under review. The councils must advise on matters referred to them by the secretary of state; they also have the right to give advice without waiting to be asked.

The timetable for the phased introduction of the national curriculum was set out in DES Circular 5/88:

(i) all primary schools will be required to teach all pupils, and secondary schools all 11–14-year-old pupils, core and other foundation subjects for a reasonable time from September 1989;

(ii) from September 1989 all primary schools will be required by Orders . . . to adopt for 5-year-old pupils the new attainment targets, programmes of study and assessment arrangements for mathematics, science and English;

(iii) Orders will similarly be made with effect from September 1989 for 11–12-year-olds in the third key stage for mathematics and science only;

(iv) Orders relating to technology for 5-year-olds, and to English and technology for 11–12-year-olds in the third key stage, will be introduced in 1990. Orders relating to mathematics and science and probably English and technology will be introduced for 7–8 year-olds in the second key stage in 1990;

(v) thereafter implementation arrangements for these subjects will proceed year by year as the first cohorts move through the first three key stages; requirements relating to the fourth key stage are unlikely to be introduced before Autumn 1992;

(vi) assessment arrangements for each key stage will be introduced alongside attainment targets and programmes of study but on a trial basis for the first year of operation. Thus the second cohort of pupils in a key stage will be the first for whom results of assessments are reported. In other words those who are 5 and 11 in Autumn 1989 will be assessed at the end of their key stage but it will be those who start key stages 1 and 3 in Autumn *1990* who will be formally assessed and *reported upon* in 1992 and 1993.

(DES, 1988b)

Local education authorities must implement the national curriculum (Sections 1 and 10) and have regard to it in undertaking their statutory duties. Under the 1986 Act, they must 'make, and keep up to date' a written statement of their curriculum policy.

How much initiative a local authority retains in regard to curriculum policy also depends on the working out of other parts of the Act (in particular those on financial delegation). In practice, it will mainly be through monitoring school performance and through in-service training and local authority support services that the local authority will be able to give expression to its own curriculum policy. There will also be the chance to take up or reject opportunities offered by government initiatives by way of in-service training grants, Education Support Grants and Training Agency programmes.

Governing bodies are (under the 1986 Act) responsible for the oversight of the curriculum at the school level and they must produce (and keep up to date) a curriculum policy document for parents, to show how they intend to meet the requirements of the national curriculum in the light of the local education authority's curriculum policy.

They have a specific responsibility with regard to sex education, which they have discretion to include in the curriculum or exclude; and they have the obligation to ensure that, if it is included, it is 'given in such a manner as to encourage those pupils to have due regard to moral considerations and family life'. They are also bound by the local authority's duty not to present homosexuality as a pretended family relationship.

Headteachers must see that the national curriculum policy is carried out. Schools will have to take the programmes of study which emerge from the Curriculum Councils and turn them into syllabuses and working timetables. The attainment targets will form the framework within which these syllabuses will have to be fitted together.

It will be for the schools to work out how the 'subjects' of the national curriculum are to be taught and to interpret them alongside the other demands made on them for the teaching of themes which stretch across the curriculum. Similarly, it will be for the schools to decide whether their statutory obligations are better met by strict timetabling of compulsory subjects, or by modular programmes which cover the ground in other ways.

In the case of grant-maintained schools, governing bodies and heads will have the same obligation to implement the national curriculum, but they will not have to have regard to the local authority's policy.

Parents are intended under the Act to become more discriminating consumers, watching school results, as published, and interpreting these results as best they can in the light of local circumstances. The assumption is that they will keep schools up to the mark by making their approval or disapproval known in informal contacts with governors and teachers, and through their formal opportunity to raise points (and pass resolutions) at the annual parents' meeting required by the 1986 Act. If complaints remain unanswered, parents can use the complaints procedure to force the school to deliver the national curriculum, or to force the local authority to use its powers to this end. If unable to get satisfaction, they can appeal to the Secretary of State. And, ultimately, parents have the power to remove their children from one school and send them to another. The procedures for doing so have been made marginally easier by the sections of the Act dealing with open enrolment.

References

DES (1984) *Organization and Content of the 5–16 Curriculum*, London, HMSO.

DES (1985a) *Science 5–16: A Statement of Policy*, London, HMSO.

DES (1985b) *Better Schools*, Cmnd 9469, London, HMSO.

DES (1987) *The National Curriculum 5–16: A Consultation Document*, London, HMSO.

DES (1988a) *Modern Languages in the School Curriculum*, London, HMSO.

DES (1988b) Circular 5/88, London, DES.

TES (*Times Educational Supplement*) (1988) 'In dispute over whether to help parent or pupil' 18 March: 6.

TGAT (Task Group on Assessment and Testing) (1988) *National Curriculum Task Group on Assessment and Testing: A Report*, London, DES and Welsh Office.

2

National curriculum: Task Group on Assessment and Testing Report: conclusions and recommendations

Task Group on Assessment and Testing

[. . .]

Any system of assessment should satisfy certain general criteria. For the purpose of national assessment we give priority to the following four criteria:

1 the assessment results should give direct information about pupils' achievement in relation to objectives: they should be criterion-referenced;
2 the results should provide a basis for decisions about pupils' further learning needs: they should be formative;
3 the scales or grades should be capable of comparison across classes and schools, if teachers, pupils and parents are to share a common language and common standards: so the assessments should be calibrated or moderated;
4 the ways in which criteria and scales are set up and used should relate to expected routes of educational development, giving some continuity to a pupil's assessment at different ages: the assessments should relate to progression.

[. . .]

Conclusions

While the system we propose draws on many aspects of good practice that are already established, it is radically new in the articulation and comprehensive deployment of methods based on such experience. We are confident that the system we describe is practicable and can bring benefits to work both within schools and outside them. In particular, we can see how provision of new types of support within a framework of a new set of procedures can replace much of the large volume of testing and assessment at present in use. A co-ordinated system will use resources to better effect and will complement and support the existing assessment work that teachers already carry out. Thus the system should contribute to the raising of educational standards so that the broad educational needs of individuals and the national need to enhance the resources and skills of young people can be met.

Building on good classroom practice

The proposed procedures of assessment and testing bear directly upon the classroom practices of teachers. A system which was not closely linked to normal classroom assessments and which did not demand the professional skills and commitment of teachers might be less expensive and simpler to implement, but would be indefensible in that it could set in opposition the processes of learning, teaching and assessment.

Formative assessment to support learning

Our terms of reference stress that the assessment to be proposed must be 'supportive of learning in schools'. The four criteria set out on p. 21 are essential if this support is to be secured and we believe that they necessarily follow from the aims expressed in the consultative document on the national curriculum. The formative aspect follows almost by definition. For the system to be formative it must produce a full and well-articulated picture of the individual child's current strengths and future needs. No simple label 1–6 will achieve this function, nor is any entirely external testing system capable of producing the necessary richness of information without placing an insuperable load of formal assessment on the child. The formative aspect calls for profile reporting and the exercise of the professional judgement of teachers.

Raising standards

The system is also required to be formative at the national level, to play an active part in raising standards of attainment. Criterion-referencing inevitably follows. Norm-referenced approaches conceal changes in national standards. Whatever the average child accomplishes is the norm and if the average child's performance changes the reported norm remains the same figure. Only by criterion-referencing can standards be monitored; only by criterion-referencing can they be communicated. Formative assessment requires the involvement of the professional judgement of teachers. Criterion-referencing helps to inform these judgements. Group moderation will enable the dissemination of a shared language for discussing attainment at all levels: the central function of assessment. These three features will help to emphasize growth. They result in progression – a key element in ensuring that pupils and parents receive focused and evolving guidance throughout their school careers. Consistent and de-motivating confirmation of everything as it was at the previous reporting age can be avoided only if pupils and parents can have clear evidence of progress by use of the single sequence of levels across all ages in the way that we propose.

The unity of our proposals

We have considered systems of assessment and testing which are very different from the one that we propose. All alternatives impoverish the relationships between assessment and learning, so that the former harms the latter instead of supporting it. Most of them give no clear information or guidance about pupils' achievement or progress, and they all risk interference with, rather than support of, teachers' work with pupils. Thus we cannot recommend any simpler alternative to our proposals. There is of course room for variation in their implementation: for example, using group moderation procedures for a restricted number of profile components, or not using all such procedures on every annual assessment cycle, or phasing in more slowly to spread the load on teachers and on the support systems. None of these marginal changes would destroy essential features of our system, although they might weaken its impact in the short term. However, any major change that we can envisage would destroy the linked unity of our proposals and lose most of the benefits which they are aimed to secure within and for the national curriculum.

Securing teachers' commitment

The underlying unity of the three aspects of education – teaching, learning, and assessment – is fundamental to the strategy which informs our proposals. The strategy will fail if teachers do not come to have confidence in, and commitment to, the new system as a positive part of their teaching. Securing this commitment is the essential pre-condition for the new system to realize the considerable value that it could bring.

Amongst the conditions which will have to be met to secure this professional commitment will be the following:

1 Clear acceptance that the aim is to support and enhance the professional skills that teachers already deploy to promote learning.
2 Clear recognition that the focus of responsibility for operation of a new system lies with teachers within schools.
3 Stress on the formative aims and on giving clear guidance about progress to pupils and to their parents.
4 Widespread consultation and discussion before proposals are put into effect.
5 A realistic time-scale for phasing in a new system.
6 Adequate resources, including in-service provision.
7 Help with moderation procedures so that the system contributes to communication within schools, between schools, parents and governors,

and to the community as a whole about the realization and evaluation of the aims of schools.

8 Sensitive handling of any requirements for outside reporting, recognizing that simplistic procedures could mislead parents, damage schools, and impair relations between teachers and their pupils.

If there is one main motive to explain our support for the system we propose, it is that we believe that it can provide the essential means for promoting the learning development of children: support for teachers in enhancing the resources and professional skills which they deploy.

A list of recommendations

The recommendations we have made in this report are listed below.

Purposes and principles

1 The basis of the national assessment system should be essentially formative, but designed also to indicate where there is need for more detailed diagnostic assessment. At age 16, however, it should incorporate assessment with summative functions.

2 All assessment information about an individual should be treated as confidential and thus confined to those who need to know in order to help that pupil.

3 For summative and evaluative purposes results should be aggregated across classes or schools so that no individual performances can be separated out.

4 Assessment of attitudes should not form a prescribed part of the national assessment system.

5 To realize the formative purpose of the national assessment system, pupil results in a subject should be presented as an attainment profile.

6 An individual subject should report a small number (preferably no more than four and never more than six) of profile components reflecting the variety of knowledge, skills and understanding to which the subject gives rise. Wherever possible, one or more components should have more general application across the curriculum: for these a single common specification should be adopted in each of the subjects concerned.

7 The national system should employ tests for which a wide range of modes of presentation, operation and response should be used so that each may be valid in relation to the attainment targets assessed. These particular tests should be called 'standard assessment tasks' and they should be so designed that flexibility of form and use is allowed wherever this can be consistent with national comparability of results.

8 Assessment tasks should be reviewed regularly for evidence of bias, particularly in respect of gender and race.

9 Attainment targets should be exemplified as far as possible using specimen tasks. Such tasks can then assist in the communication of these targets.

10 A mixture of standardized assessment instruments including tests, practical tasks and observations should be used in the national assessment system in order to minimize curriculum distortion.

11 Teachers' ratings of pupil performance should be used as a fundamental element of the national assessment system. Just as with the national tests or tasks, teachers' own ratings should be derived from a variety of methods of evoking and assessing pupils' responses.

12 When the subject working groups provide guidance on the aggregation of targets into a small number of profile components, they should have regard to the need for each component to lead to a report in which reasonable confidence is possible.

13 Teachers' ratings should be moderated in such a way as to convey and to inform national standards.

14 The national assessment system should be based on a combination of moderated teachers' ratings and standardized assessment tasks.

15 Group moderation should be an integral part of the national assessment system. It should be used to produce the agreed combination of moderated teachers' ratings and the results of the national tests.

16 An item bank of further assessment instruments should be available for teachers to use in cases where they need additional evidence about particular pupils.

17 The final reports on individual pupils to their parents should be the responsibility of the teacher, supported by standardized assessment tasks and group moderation.

18 Wherever schools use national assessment results in reports for evaluative purposes, they should report the distribution of pupil achievements.

The assessment system in practice

19 The ages for national assessment should be 7, 11, 14 and 16, with reporting occurring near the end of the school year in which each cohort reaches the age involved.

20 Each of the subject working groups should define a sequence of levels in each of its profile components, related to broad criteria for progression in that component. For a profile component which applies over the full age-range 7 to 16, there should be ten such levels, with corresponding reduction for profile components which will apply over a smaller span of school years.

21 Levels 1 to 3 should be used for national assessments at age 7.

22 The formal relationship between national assessment and GCSE should be limited, in the first instance, to this one reference point: and

accordingly the boundary between levels 6 and 7 should correspond to the grade F/G boundary for GCSE.

23 As they develop the upper four levels of their profile components, the subject working groups should adopt present practices for determining GCSE grades at A/B, C/D, mid-E, and F/G as a starting-point.

24 GCSE should be retained in its present form until the national assessment system is initiated at earlier ages.

25 Assessment and reporting for the national assessment system should be at the same ages for all pupils, and differentiation should be based on the use of the single sequence of levels set up to cover progression over the full age range.

26 Support items, procedures and training should be provided to help teachers relate their own assessments to the targets and assessment criteria of the national curriculum.

27 A review should be made of the materials available to schools for detailed diagnostic investigation of pupils' learning problems, and that the need for extra help with production or advice about such materials should be considered.

28 A working group should be established, with some shared membership between the subject working groups, to co-ordinate their proposals for assessment, including testing, at the primary stages, in the light of a comprehensive view of the primary curriculum and of the need to limit the assessment burden on teachers.

29 National assessment results for any individual pupil should be confidential, to be discussed between pupil, parents and teachers, and to be otherwise transmitted in confidence. National assessment results for a class as a whole and a school as a whole should be available to the parents of its pupils.

30 The *only* form in which results of national assessment for, and identifying, a given school should be published should be as part of a broader report by that school of its work as a whole.

31 Any report by a school which includes national assessment results should include a general report for the area, prepared by the local authority, to indicate the nature of socio-economic and other influences which are known to affect schools. This report should give a general indication of the known effects of such influences on performance.

32 National assessment results, for pupils at age 11, aggregated at school level, should be published as part of each primary school's report. There should be no requirement to publish results for pupils at age 7.

33 National assessment results for pupils at ages 14 and 16, aggregated at school level, should be published as part of each school's report.

34 At age 7 the standard assessment tasks for the national assessment should comprise a choice of three prescribed tasks for each child; each task should be designed to give opportunities for systematic assessment of competence in the range of profile components appropriate to age 7.

35 At age 11 the tests for national assessment should include three or four standard tasks which cover a range of profile components, possibly supplemented by more narrowly focused tests for particular components.

36 Records of Achievement should be used as a vehicle for recording progress and achievement within the national assessment system.

37 Eventually changes will be necessary to the GCSE and other criteria. Changes derived from the development of the national curriculum should have priority in an orderly process of amendment.

38 Like all children, those with special educational needs require attainable targets to encourage their development and promote their self-esteem. Wherever children with special educational needs are capable of undertaking the national tests, they should be encouraged to do so.

39 A special unit within a chosen test development agency should be dedicated to producing test materials and devising testing and assessment procedures sufficiently wide-ranging and sensitive to respond to the needs of these children.

Implementation

40 Each subject working group should decide on a limited number, usually four, of profile components in relation to which any pupil's performance will be assessed and discussed. A criterion-referenced set of levels should be set out for each component, to span the full range of performance over the ages for which the component is applicable.

41 Subject working groups should specify, in broad terms and for each profile component, the appropriate tests (standardized assessment tasks) which should be prepared, and the advice and help which should be given to teachers about their corresponding internal assessments.

42 Combination of profile component levels to give a subject level should be by a specified procedure. Uniform ways of describing profile components and the level within each should be specified in language that is helpful to pupils, teachers, parents, employers and other users.

43 Subject working groups should give general advice about the degree of novelty of the assessments they envisage, so that the construction of them and the provision of in-service support for teachers can be appraised.

44 The new assessment system should be phased in over a period adequate for the preparation and trial of new assessment methods, for teacher preparation, and for pupils to benefit from extensive experience of the new curriculum. This period needs to be at least five years from the promulgation of the relevant attainment targets.

3

Towards a framework for curriculum entitlement

Further Education Unit

Curriculum development

A useful starting-point for planning is to consider a model of curriculum development used by the Further Education Unit (FEU). A simplified version is shown in Figure 3.1. The model suggests that the adequacy of provision depends on the quality and appropriateness of all four processes shown in the outer circle, and the existence of the necessary systems required to support them. Thus, however well-resourced the implementation phase may be (for example), this cannot make up for inaccurate needs analysis or inappropriate programme design. This model also suggests that versions of all four processes are necessary at whatever level provision is being planned: from the level of the locality, via individual institutions, down to and including those concerned with specific programmes. Also, at each level, the clients as well as the providers need to be involved, whether the former be identifiable sections of the community or individual learners, vocational sectors or specific companies. Clients and providers need to be involved in the analysis of needs and judgements about priorities, the negotiation of learning programmes appropriate to these needs and priorities, and the evaluation of the extent to which the latter have been met. Implementation must also involve the active participation of the learner, and be flexible enough to adapt to different learning styles.

Like all models, this represents an ideal case. Nevertheless, it does illustrate the variety of factors which needs to be taken into account if the planning process is to achieve its purpose – the efficient provision of better learning opportunities. The role of the LEA is thus to design and support the development of the desired curriculum.

[. . .]

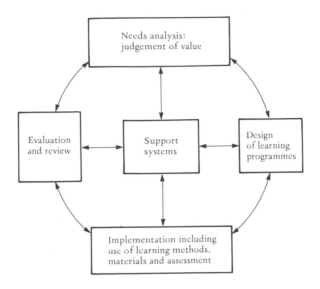

Figure 3.1   Processes of curriculum development

Common curriculum framework

Over a period of many years, FEU has proposed and refined a framework within which the post-16 curriculum should be offered. The curriculum framework, in this sense, refers to the aims, principles and procedures within which all learning programmes should be designed and implemented.

Aims

FEU (1987a) suggests that the education service should aim to provide

1 appropriate learning opportunities, regardless of gender, race, age and ability;

2 o⟨...⟩ners to establish and develop a recognized com-
⟨...⟩dge, skills and experience, sufficient to facilitate
⟨...⟩ment, further education, training, or other roles;
⟨...⟩local and national economic and social environ-
⟨...⟩reciation of the variety of available adult roles in

⟨...⟩ease their self-awareness, to appraise realistically
⟨...⟩cts, and to become progressively responsible for
⟨...⟩sonal development.

This set of generic aims can also be seen as a way of finding commonality across a diverse range of learning programmes.

These aims can be said to form the basis of an agenda of entitlement by providing individuals with equal opportunities to cope with change through progression, role competence and personal development. Alongside these aims, FEU suggests that there should be common learning themes applied to all learning programmes regardless of their content (FEU, 1987a; 1987b). These themes are

1 *relevance:* provided by analysing the needs of the learners and the receiving agencies; integrating education, training, work and other aspects of life; placing a value on experience; developing a negotiated curriculum; and ensuring a balance between competing needs;
2 *flexibility:* provided by timetabling to facilitate learning; allowing for individual differences in pace and style of learning; using formative, profiled assessment; introducing modularity to allow credit accumulation; and developing a curriculum to meet the needs of learners by negotiation and interaction;
3 *competence:* provided by designing programmes that deliver a broad range of skills, knowledge, experience and attitudes; ensuring that the programme is integrated and includes work-based learning; developing a better awareness of standards and the ability to recognize and encourage appropriate performance by learners.

Principles

Value judgements made by providers often manifest themselves directly in the learning experiences which individuals have in schools and colleges. Learners tend to have quite different experiences according to the type of learning programme they are engaged in. This has happened partly because, particularly for 11- to 19-year-olds, we have generally worked to a deficit model of education in which the purpose of the service was to identify deficiency and remedy it, rather than to recognize proficiency and develop it. It is crucial that in developing a common curriculum framework, LEAs should encourage institutions to hold as fundamental principles that

1 learners are of equal value, regardless of their individual strengths and weaknesses;
2 learners have access to appropriate programmes in the locality, within the physical and financial constraints prevailing at the time;
3 learners have the opportunity and positive encouragement to maximize their own potential achievement;
4 all learners are treated equally and benefit from certain common experiences, regardless of the nature of their learning programmes.

Procedures

Over recent years, certain educational procedures have been recognized as effective and have been absorbed into practice. In 1981 FEU proposed (FEU, 1981) a set of connected procedures which can be summarized as: negotiation of the curriculum; provision of guidance; the opportunity to acquire relevant skills; formative and profiled assessment; valuing the experience of learners. This tended to be implemented only with a client group comprising learners with a variety of disadvantages who had previously not been well provided for. The DES supported these procedures but as an alternative to the academic and mainstream vocational curricula, rather than as a common framework for all learners over the age of 16.

The framework described above should be implemented with all learners. No one should be denied access to successful learning strategies and enriching curriculum elements and they should form part of the educational entitlement for everyone over the age of 14. These procedures are:

1 *learner-centredness:* this involves arranging educational provision so that learners are involved in negotiating the content, style, and targets for their programmes – this is often facilitated by valuing their experience and engaging in profiled formative assessment;

2 *maximized accessibility:* this is about ensuring that there are no artificial barriers to programmes, such as unnecessary entry requirements, and that every effort is made to provide for all of the potential learners in a locality;

3 *integrated curriculum:* this involves making connections between the various elements of learning – between the (subject) components of a programme, between activities in an institution and outside it, and between past, present and future experience;

4 *guidance and counselling:* this comprises a wide range of support for learners including educational, vocational and personal guidance provided as a part of both learning programmes and the institutional infrastructure;

5 *personal development:* an important consideration in the design of programmes is to ensure that there is both opportunity and encouragement for the development of personal qualities such as effectiveness and role awareness;

6 *optimized progression:* all learners should have the opportunity to achieve their own personal targets and maximize their progress on a particular programme in order to advance to another programme or employment;

7 *equality of opportunity and experience:* this is a starting-point, and implies that institutions should move from equality of access, through equality of treatment, towards equality of outcomes (having equal regard for different outcomes).

This set of procedures is an essential part of a learner's entitlement, and is about equitable access to learning and the quality of that learning.

[. . .]

Learners' curriculum entitlement

Content

The curriculum framework described on pp. 29–31 is re͟   ͟͟͟
starting-point, but LEAs will wish to require colleges to cc   p͟
lum statement which describes entitlement in more detail.   or
learning programmes have components which may need t
some contexts. FEU suggests that, in doing so, the content ot
should be considered in terms of

1 *skills:* including performance-related (product skills) and activity-related (process skills);
2 *knowledge:* including theoretical and practical understanding;
3 *experience:* gained before and during a particular learning programme;
4 *learning support:* comprising the infrastructure surrounding learning programmes, including guidance.

Breadth and relevance are more likely to be provided by these components than by merely attempting a balance between subjects. The effectiveness of the combination is likely to be judged by its success in developing competence in a variety of vocational and other roles.

The need for a common curriculum within which learning is provided has led some to define a core, and much work has been undertaken by LEAs to design an 'entitlement core' within TVEI. In developing a core, it should be seen as only a part of the entitlement, and not the entitlement itself. A common core of learning content, defined in the national curriculum as single academic subjects, is a requirement up to the age of 16. Post-16, it may not be appropriate to categorize and deliver learning solely within a subject-based core, especially if it is both common and compulsory. It may be even less appropriate for individuals over 19.

HMI have encouraged a shift of emphasis from subjects to areas of experience in the context of the 11–16 curriculum (DES, 1983), and recommended a 'common framework which provides coherence, and, while taking into account individual needs and abilities, still ensures the provision of a broadly based experience'. A core based on learning experiences would seem to be appropriate for all learners, one to which they should all have access and which should form the basis for curriculum planning. It is not, however, something which all learners would necessarily choose to access all of the time.

For some curriculum planners, this core is expressed in the form of a checklist of activities, such as work experience and residential experience, while others use these and/or a list of areas of learning. This was first suggested by FEU in 1979. It describes groups of experiences and outcomes (including skills, knowledge and attitudes) capable of application in a variety of contexts, and has been helpful in providing the basis for consideration of core entitlement.

Outcomes

Learners should be aware of the potential outcomes, as well as the content, of a programme. Some outcomes will be pre-specified according to external criteria, while others may be individually negotiated. An important outcome of all learning programmes will be competence. FEU has defined 'competence' as the possession and development of sufficient skills, knowledge, appropriate attitudes and experience for successful performance in life roles, thus embracing academic, vocational and personal competence.

Learners should also be informed of the range of opportunities following from an agreed programme if it is satisfactorily completed. Some colleges already provide this in the prospectus, but it also needs to be addressed at LEA level. Learners should be allowed to negotiate their own interim targets for achievement within nationally agreed parameters and mechanisms by which this will be checked.

Progression

A comprehensive and impartial description of progression opportunities should form part of the contract between the institution and the learner, and will need to be supported by initial and continuing guidance. For some colleges, this may necessitate a shift of emphasis away from being provision-driven; that is to say, planning should begin with an analysis of clients' needs and not with an analysis of what teachers want to teach. This shift to a needs-driven approach may require colleges to update their staffing expertise. The role for LEAs will be to check that learners' needs are being met.

[. . .]

Experience

Learners will often prefer to attend an institution in which they will feel comfortable rather than one which apparently best meets their extrinsic needs. This part of curriculum entitlement is about the kind of experience which learners have while they attend schools and colleges. Individuals should be able to expect equal and equitable treatment regardless of their individual needs.

An individual learner's entitlement may be described in the form of a learning contract, initially between the LEA and the learner, and then specifically between the learner and the providing institution, or a combination of them. This will, of course, be only a small part of the total provision on offer in a locality, but will be designed within the agreed overall LEA curriculum framework and underpinned by the prescribed principles. This contract may be in the form of a learning plan describing

1 *content:* this will be negotiated within the constraints of prevailing resources;
2 *outcomes:* these will be negotiated within the context of nationally agreed targets, and pre-specified by external bodies;
3 *progression:* this will be individual;
4 *experiences:* these will be common to all learners.

The equity of treatment and quality of experience which learners receive will be determined by the curriculum framework already described.

Curriculum provision in institutions

Following the LEA curriculum statement, the various plans and policies may need to be synthesized into a coherent framework within which all post-14 education and training can be implemented. A development plan should be operationalized and implemented by institutions. This process of working from the LEA statement through a synthesis of plans and description of curriculum entitlement to institutional action plans will be followed by LEAs and colleges which place a value on the quality of provision and intend the curriculum to guide decisions about schemes of delegation. The process will also provide the basis of the framework within which the performance of institutions can be monitored and evaluated.

LEAs must design and monitor the implementation of the plan because they are accountable to constituents in a way that individual colleges are not. Colleges and their learning provision are part of the planned resources for those constituents. Greater institutional autonomy will not ensure coherence or comprehensiveness without LEA guidance. While an LEA will have an obligation to provide a curriculum entitlement in its institutions, a school or college will have an obligation to provide a service which meets local needs. Institutions and LEAs need to give equal attention to individual needs and collective community and employment needs.

Institutional policy

An LEA may start this process by undertaking an audit of community and local employment needs. It will also be appropriate for many colleges to conduct such an audit, together with a thorough analysis of individual learners' needs, before finalizing provision. This will be particularly so if a college is in a large or geographically disparate LEA or intends to provide a comprehensive service. The audit would then become a continuous process. It would result in an institutional policy statement, sometimes called a 'mission statement' (agreed with the LEA), followed by an action plan (agreed with the governing body), and learning contracts (agreed with the individuals).

Colleges may wish to define a local entitlement, in addition to the LEA statement, including a core curriculum of outcomes and experiences for all learners, and may wish to ensure that a system of learner advocacy guarantees its delivery. This may be provided by LEA monitoring, or an external agency acting as an impartial broker, or by the learners taking responsibility for themselves following guidance. This overall process is shown in Figure 3.2.

Equity

The tension between quality and cost-effectiveness will be most acute at college level, and managers will need to consider carefully not only the range of provision on offer but also the range of educational courses and services *not* on offer. The success of a college cannot be judged on high examination pass rates with a selective client group, as the true measure of effectiveness is the amount of progress made by all learners from their level of achievement at entry to their level at the point of exit. Nor is the successful college one which simply provides courses on demand. That student-led model, in which colleges exist to satisfy learners' wants, could lead to a proliferation of unsuitable programmes, reinforcing failure and lacking progression.

The role for the college is in mediating between learner aspiration, available and potential provision, and realistic progression opportunities. In this mediation process, the college entitlement policy will be the yardstick by which the equity of provision is judged. There should be scope for responding positively to an employer's request for short, full-cost recovery, programmes and providing for the individual needs of a disadvantaged student within the common curriculum framework of the college.

[. . .]

Quality

The difference between the minimum and maximum entitlements will often comprise a variety of learning support mechanisms, including guidance, tutoring, individualized negotiated learning, and the package of curriculum

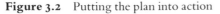

LEA curriculum statement ← public accountability

↓

institutional development plan ← LEA monitoring

↓

individual learning contracts ← learner advocacy

Figure 3.2   Putting the plan into action

enrichment elements described earlier. Enrichment is both expensive and cost-effective; it is not a marginal activity and cannot be provided cheaply. It is, however, investing in efficient learning and, if successfully implemented, it maximizes learning outcomes and optimizes progression. In reducing learning wastage it is a powerful and cost-effective weapon. Once this is realized, there may be a shift of resources from teaching activities to learning support systems.

Curriculum enrichment needs to be carefully marketed both inside and outside the college. Evidence of the intended benefits will need to be shown, and in this connection colleges may wish to work towards defining some performance indicators for curriculum quality. Elements of enrichment will be most effective when integrated into mainstream programmes rather than offered as 'bolt-on' packages or optional modules. In this way, the agreed curriculum principles are embedded in all programmes but specific content remains a non-compulsory (negotiated) element.

Quantity

The preceding paragraphs have discussed curriculum quality as an essential component of entitlement. Another essential aspect is the quantity of provision. LEAs must consider their local staying-on rates and look closely at whether existing provision satisfies the overall needs of the community. The aim should be to ensure that all potential learners are enfranchized and that no one falls through the net. For LEAs, this will require a consideration of fee structures and cost implications. Some may wish to consider the possibility of providing two or three years of free education post-16 for everyone, which could be accessed at 16, or later, or over a period of time.

For a college, the issue of quantity means making some difficult decisions about *what* is offered and what is left out of the college provision. It is also about examining *who* is provided for, and whether that is equitable.

[. . .]

Further education is undergoing a process of modernization. Future developments are likely to encourage further multi-agency provision post-16 in which colleges are essential partners but not sole owners. More institutional autonomy, the growth of private provision, more demand for part-time and modular packages, accelerated technology and ever-changing skill needs could change further education quickly and profoundly. In terms of the curriculum model presented in Figure 3.1 the balance of a college's activities may shift to needs analysis, the tailor-making of learning programmes and evaluation, and away from implementation. Colleges may, therefore, be involved in a shift from being teaching centres to becoming learning resource, testing and accreditation centres. Managing the transition will be difficult and painful for further education staff. The purpose of the service, and changes to it, must be kept in mind at all times – simply, to provide better learning opportunities and experiences for everyone.

References

DES (1983) *Curriculum 11–16: Towards a Statement of Entitlement*, London, HMSO.

FEU (1979) *A Basis for Choice*, London, FEU.

FEU (1981) *Vocational Preparation*, London, FEU.

FEU (1987a) *Relevance, Flexibility and Competence*, London, FEU.

FEU (1987b) *Supporting Vocational Change*, London, FEU.

Section II

Contexts and perspectives

4

Ideological contexts for curriculum planning

Keith Morrison and Ken Ridley

The curriculum is value based. It is founded on the principle of protection and neglect of selected values. Curriculum planners need to expose such values before evaluating how they are brought into the planning debate. A value or ideology can be defined as 'that system of beliefs which gives general direction to the educational policies of those who hold those beliefs' (Scrimshaw, 1983: 4). Different ideologies can coexist with a degree of harmony; different elements of the curriculum being built on different ideological foundations. Alternatively, one can adopt a less consensual line, seeing ideologies not as sets of beliefs of various social groups but – from a Marxian perspective – as that set of values issuing from the dominant powers in society which has imperceptibly permeated the whole class structure; this has the effect of sustaining the dominant class in power (Centre for Contemporary Cultural Studies, 1981).

The significance of this interpretation for curriculum planners is to direct attention to the power of certain groups to make major curriculum decisions, to ask 'whose values are protected in the curriculum?' Educational ideologies will contain values, beliefs and assumptions about children, learning, teaching, knowledge and the curriculum. A curriculum is taken to be all those activities designed or encouraged within the school's organizational framework to promote the intellectual, personal, social and physical development of its pupils. It includes not only the formal programme of lessons, but also the 'informal' programme of so-called extra-curricular activities as well as those features which produce the school's 'ethos'.

More specifically, Meighan (1981) contends that an ideology addresses seven components which concern curriculum planners:

1 A theory of knowledge: its content and structure – what is considered worthwhile or important knowledge, how it is organized (e.g. by subjects or integrated areas) and who shall have access to it.

2 A theory of learning and the learner's role – an active or a passive style, doing or listening, co-operative or competitive learning, producing or reproducing knowledge, problem-solving or receiving facts.
3 A theory of teaching and the teacher's role – formal or informal, authoritarian or democratic, interest in outcomes or processes, narrow or wide.
4 A theory of resources appropriate for learning – first hand or second hand.
5 A theory of organization of learning situations – criteria for grouping pupils.
6 A theory of assessment that learning has taken place – diagnostic or attainment testing, written or observational assessment, defining what is to be assessed.
7 A theory of aims, objectives and outcomes – a view of what is desirable for society, the child, and knowledge.

One can determine how characteristics of different educational ideologies will address these seven main components. Scrimshaw (1983), for example, suggests that ideologies differ in their emphasis on the individual learner, knowledge and society. While these are clearly not discrete, nevertheless the emphasis is useful, and is one way of organizing the potentially disparate number of ideologies which appear in educational literature. Many of these are substantially the same ideology under a different name and are presented in summary form in Table 4.1. The difference between knowledge (a) and knowledge (b) in Table 4.1 lies in the access to high status knowledge. Advocates of knowledge (a) would restrict high status knowledge to an elite minority, whereas advocates of knowledge (b) would make it accessible to all pupils. The difference between society (a) and society (b) lies in the perspec-

Table 4.1 Clusters of educational ideologies

Ideology	Emphasis
Progressivism Child-centredness Romanticism	Individual child
Classical humanism Conservatism Traditionalism Academicism	Knowledge (a)
Liberal humanism	Knowledge (b)
Instrumentalism Revisionism Economic renewal	Society (a)
Democratic socialism Reconstructionism	Society (b)

tives on society. Society (a) tends to regard the existing societal status quo as desirable and worth perpetuating and improving, while society (b) will look to its alteration, its future evolution.

Ideologies emphasizing the individual learner

Ideologies in this sphere represent the 'developmental tradition' in primary education (Blyth, 1965). In them the transmission of knowledge is secondary to discovery and to following the child's impulses, needs and interests. Stress is laid on learning by doing, spontaneity, free expression and developing the child's own nature spontaneously: 'give your scholar no verbal lessons; he should be taught by experience alone' (Worthington, 1884: 56). Knowledge is not imposed from without, but is uncertain, pragmatic, tentative and provisional; it is that which the child discovers rather than reproduces.

Emphasis is placed, then, on originality and authenticity of the child's experience and awareness, on diversity of response and provision, on creativity, enjoyment and the development of the emotional side of the child's personality. The process of learning is as important as the outcomes of learning – the knowledge products. Hence education is seen as intrinsically worthwhile: valuable in itself rather than for what it leads to in later life.

In their challenge to rationalism, objectivity, abstract analysis and universalism, these ideologies celebrate empiricism, subjectivity, personal meanings and particularism. Childhood becomes a state in itself rather than a preparation for adulthood: 'The Child is father of the Man' (Wordsworth, 1807). Adults can learn from children and their childhood innocence (see also Aries, 1973). For curriculum planners such views refute the value of an imposed curriculum: 'put the problems before him and let him solve them himself . . . let him not be taught science, let him discover it' (Rousseau, quoted in Blenkin and Kelly, 1981: 19).

Schools have to protect children from the harmful and unpleasant aspects of the outside world (King, 1978) which might corrupt them. Hence they cocoon the child in a comfortable and secure environment separate from the vagaries of the world outside the classroom. If children fail at school then the school rather than the child is to be censured. One can detect the inspirational and optimistic rather than the analytic tenor of child-centred ideologies; indeed analysis reveals how dangerously loose these ideologies can be. For example, how can one derive and plan a curriculum from needs and interests which may be trivial, ephemeral, irrelevant or morally unacceptable? How will children judge what their needs are until they have a measure of knowledge? How can a curriculum be constructed from aims such as 'development', 'growth', or 'discovery' (Hirst and Peters, 1970)? Will it not lead to Bantock's (1980: 44) fears that 'temporary interest and immediate need are the guiding principle implicit in the attempt to "psychologize" learning; hence the emphasis on motivation and endogenous development too easily fosters a magpie curriculum of bits and pieces'?

Further, in sheltering children from the corruption of the outer world, how adequate an education is being provided for future citizens? How justified is the exclusion or neglect, however partial, of the world beyond the classroom or immediate environment, regardless of the desirability or un-desirability of that world? Similarly, in concentrating on the 'here and now' of the child's existence, how fair or responsible are teachers being to the received wisdoms of prior generations? Children may want, and need, to know about conflict and change as well as consensus and stability.

In approaching child-centred ideologies, then, one has to pare away the romanticism and exhortation, address the criticisms, and then see how they can be usefully employed in curriculum planning, avoiding the curriculum myopia to which such ideologies are prone. The thrust of many of these ideologies towards practical discovery and experiential learning, problem-solving, a process approach to the curriculum, identifying, meeting and developing children's needs, abilities and individual personalities, flexibility rather than uniformity of teaching, and the provision of a stimulating environment, become the elements which curriculum planners can use.

Ideologies emphasizing knowledge

In these ideologies one can detect a strong sympathy with conservative notions of protecting and perpetuating the best of the past as experienced in the present. Their antecedents lie in the 'preparatory' tradition (Blyth, 1965) of primary education and derive too from Plato's 'Republic' through Jesuit education, the mandarins of classical Chinese history (Weber, 1972), Matthew Arnold, T. S. Eliot and Bantock. They are unequivocally divisive and elitist, arguing for a separate and elite education into 'high culture' and a high cultural heritage for a chosen minority, giving them access to power and privilege:

> education should help to preserve the class and to select the elite. It is right that the exceptional individual should have the opportunity to elevate himself in the social scale and attain a position in which he can exercise his talents to the greatest benefit of himself and society. But the ideal of an educational system which would automatically sort out everyone according to his native capacities is unattainable in prac-tice. . . . It would disorganize society, by substituting for classes, elites of brains, or perhaps only of sharp wits.
>
> (Eliot, 1948: 100–1)

Its curriculum is academic and intellectual, non-vocational even though its clients may go on to prestigious positions in employment; it recognizes the permanence of knowledge and of high status knowledge in particular. Children have to be initiated into the received wisdoms of their forebears, the initiation rites of passage often being formal examinations. Subject loyalty is strong, discipline oriented and reliant on instruction rather than experiential learning (Lawton, 1973). Standards are clear, excellence of academic achievement is emphasized, and stress is laid on the development of rationality through a curriculum marked by uniformity rather than diversity (Jenkins 1975). This curriculum runs counter to social justice and equality of opportunity (Lawton, 1983). For the masses who cannot aspire to this, a 'folk' curriculum (Bantock, 1975; 1976) is offered whose result is effectively to debar them from entering the corridors of privilege, providing what is often regarded as low status, practical, vocational and everyday knowledge. Ideologies in this area, then, emphasize a 'dual' curriculum (Scrimshaw, 1976).

Against this perhaps bleak picture an alternative ideology in this area advances a knowledge-based curriculum whose emphasis is less on a stratified than on a unified society, with egalitarian principles at its core. In liberal humanism high culture is to be accessible to all through a common curriculum:

> If, as Tawney said, we think the higher culture fit for solicitors, why should we not think it fit for coalminers? . . . Every child should be initiated into those forms of experience which together constitute this higher culture – the arts, mathematics, the human and physical sciences, philosophy.
>
> (White 1982: 26)

For curriculum planners the significance of debates about knowledge is to clarify which knowledge should be in the curriculum, how it should be organized and who should have access to it.

Ideologies emphasizing society

The ideologies in this group share a common belief that education is valued for what it leads to rather than solely being an end in itself. One can discern two clear directions which society-oriented ideologies take. Instrumental ideologies – instrumentalism, revisionism, and those stressing economic renewal – emphasize the need for education to fit learners to society, particularly in economic terms. Education thus exists to provide a skilled work-force to expand the nation's economic strength; hence resources are developed for vocational (DES, 1985), scientific and technical education. Weight is laid on the relevance and utility aspects of education (Scrimshaw, 1983). The intentions of education are not to alter radically existing society, rather to improve the efficiency of existing organizations, institutions and economic structures (Oliver, 1982).

Table 4.2 Ideologies interpreted by their component issues

Ideology	Progressivism, child-centredness, romanticism	Classical humanism, traditionalism, academicism, conservatism	Liberal humanism	Instrumentalism, revisionism, economic renewal	Reconstructionism, democratic socialism
Emphasis	Individual child	Knowledge – unequal access	Knowledge – equal access	Society – status quo	Society – changed
Theory of knowledge	Empiricist, active, evolutionary, subjective, emphasis on processes, integrated curricula	Disciplines, non-vocational, academic, high culture, emphasis on products, rationalistic	Common culture curriculum	Utilitarian, economically relevant, vocational, scientific, technological	Revolutionary, problem-solving, active, socially relevant, vocational
Theory of learning and of the learner's role	Experiential, spontaneity, emphasis on skills and processes, co-operative, intrinsic motivation	Obedience, passivity, conformity, uniformity	Induction into key areas of experience, active and co-operative learning	Induction into vocationally relevant areas	Apprenticeship, practical, co-operative, problem-solving
Theory of teaching and of the teacher's role	Guide, provider of multiple resources, facilitator, catalyst of child's self-chosen curriculum	Instructor, information transmitter, authoritative, formal tutor	Guide, provider of resources, facilitator	Instructor, trainer, transmitter of vocationally relevant experiences	Guide, catalyst of social changes, disseminator of centralist philosophy, instructor, trainer

Theory of resources	First-hand, diverse, extensive	Second-hand, restricted	First- and second-hand, multiple, extensive	Narrowly relevant to content, practical, vocational	Highly focused to task in hand, vocational
Theory of organization of learning situations	Diverse, flexible, informal, co-operative, group work, discovery methods	Class teaching, formal, uniform, competitive	Open, flexible, diverse	Narrow, practical, relevant to task, class and individual teaching, uniformity	Individual and group work as relevant to task
Theory of assessment	Diagnostic, multiple criteria, informal, profiling	Written, formal, attainment testing, examinations	Diagnostic, norm and written, formal or informal	Formal, written and oral, practical	Flexible, formal or written as appropriate, attainment testing
Theory of aims, objectives and outcomes	Self-expression, individuality, creativity, development of whole personality	Received curricula, elitist, non-vocational, high culture	Equal access to key areas of knowledge, egalitarian	Extrinsic worthwhileness, relevant to economic good, efficient worker	Extrinsic worthwhileness, relevant to social good, citizenship, common good

Contrasted to this are more radical society-oriented educational ideologies. Figuring high at times of social rebuilding or social upheaval, e.g. post-war renewal of society, reconstructionism posits a view of education as a major force for planned change rather than stability in society; what society ought to be rather than what it is (Scrimshaw, 1983). Society in need of reconstruction requires an educated populace whose curriculum has a strong social core with a stress on citizenship, egalitarianism, democracy and participation in decision-making. In this world teachers are catalysts and guardians of social change; creators rather than transmitters of knowledge. There are dangers in this approach. Such a vision is potentially unstable as it is always looking to the future; it is predicated for its success on an educated citizenry – which is perhaps both its greatest strength and its greatest weakness; it relies on a high level of control – running the risk perhaps of centralization or even indoctrination. Finally, one has to question the extent to which education can shoulder the burden of changing society. Do not macro changes require macro and manifold organizations and institutions to change? Reconstructionist ideology, with its positive, perhaps idealistic, tone and central role for education, requires curriculum planners to think from afresh the content, aims and pedagogy of curricula from the perspective of their benefit to society (Hewlett, 1986). From an analysis of key characteristics of different ideologies one can map their expression on to Meighan's (1981) components of ideologies outlined earlier, and they are presented thus in Table 4.2.

Ideological analysis affects primary curriculum planning extensively – at the levels of aims, content, pedagogy and evaluation. The analysis so far reveals the multiplicity of values which underpin the curriculum. There is no exclusive relationship between the ideologies and the everyday activities of primary schools; the same activity in school can support a variety of ideologies, just as one ideology can give rise to several activities. Further, different areas of the curriculum can, and will, serve different educational ideologies. The effect of this analysis is twofold: first, it reveals, importantly, that the curriculum is not a closed system, but that it is open, negotiable, problematic, and has to be constantly reviewed, questioned and discussed. Second, ideological analysis reveals potential conflicts in curriculum decision-making. If one queries why certain ideologies are over-represented or under-represented in the primary curriculum, one is thrust back on to an examination of the power structures operating in curriculum decision-making, to identify whose decisions are holding sway. As mentioned earlier, ideological investigation can reveal the nature of the power of dominant interest groups; ideological analysis is thus political analysis (Mannheim, 1936).

Schools and teachers are caught up in this, like it or not. The study of ideologies, while it separates artificially practices in the interests of conceptual clarity, assists teachers and planners to adopt the reflective and critical stance [which has been] advocated as a requisite of 'good' teaching.

Curriculum planners will need to ascertain the power behind curriculum proposals emanating from diverse sources.

References

Aries, P. (1973) *Centuries of Childhood*, Harmondsworth, Penguin.

Bantock, G. H. (1975) 'Towards a theory of popular education', in M. Golby, J. Greenwald and R. West (eds) *Curriculum Design*, London, Croom Helm and the Open University.

Bantock, G. H. (1976) 'Quality and equality in curricular provisions', Appendix 1, in M. Skilbeck 'Ideologies and values', Unit 3, E203, *Curriculum Design and Development*, Milton Keynes, Open University.

Bantock, G. H. (1980) *Dilemmas of the Curriculum*, Oxford, Martin Robertson.

Blenkin, G. and Kelly, A. V. (1981) *The Primary Curriculum*, London, Harper & Row.

Blyth, W. A. L. (1965) *English Primary Education*, *Vol. 1*, London, Routledge & Kegan Paul.

Centre for Contemporary Cultural Studies (1981) *Unpopular Education*, London, Hutchinson.

DES (1985) *Better Schools*, Cmnd 9469, London, HMSO.

Eliot, T. S. (1948) *Notes towards the Definition of Culture*, London, Faber.

Hewlett, M. (1986) *Curriculum to Serve Society: How Schools can Work for People*, Loughborough, Newstead Publishing.

Hirst, P. H. and Peters, R. S. (1970) *The Logic of Education*, London, Routledge & Kegan Paul.

Jenkins, D. (1975) 'Classic and romantic in the curriculum landscape', in M. Golby, J. Greenwald and R. West (eds) *Curriculum Design*, London, Croom Helm.

King, R. (1978) *All Things Bright and Beautiful? A Sociological Study of Infants' Classrooms*, Chichester, Wiley.

Lawton, D. (1973) *Social Change, Educational Theory and Curriculum Planning*, London, University of London Press.

Lawton, D. (1983) *Curriculum Studies and Educational Planning*, Sevenoaks, Hodder & Stoughton.

Mannheim, K. (1936) *Ideology and Utopia*, London, Routledge & Kegan Paul.

Meighan, R. (1981) *A Sociology of Educating*, Eastbourne, Holt, Rinehart & Winston.

Oliver, D. (1982) 'The primary curriculum: a proper basis for planning', in C. Richards (ed.) *New Directions in Primary Education*, Lewes, Falmer Press.

Scrimshaw, P. (1976) 'Towards the whole curriculum', Units 9 and 10, E203, *Curriculum Design and Development*, Milton Keynes, Open University.

Scrimshaw, P. (1983) 'Educational ideologies', Unit 2, E204, *Purpose and Planning in the Curriculum*, Milton Keynes, Open University.

Weber, M. (1972) 'The Chinese literati', in B. Cosin (ed.) *Education Structure and Society*, Harmondsworth, Penguin.

White, J. (1982) 'The curriculum mongers: education in reverse', in T. Horton and P. Raggatt (eds) *Challenge and Change in the Curriculum*, Sevenoaks, Hodder & Stoughton.

Wordsworth, W. (1807) 'My heart leaps up', line 7.

Worthington, E. (1884) *Rousseau's Emile*, London, D.C. Heath.

5

The national curriculum and the implementation gap

Tony Becher

Introduction

At first sight, the prescription of a uniform national curriculum under the 1988 Act leaves little scope for curriculum decision-making at the classroom level. I want here to suggest that this is an unduly pessimistic view. Many of the most important choices will rest, as they have in the past, within the sphere of responsibility of the professional teachers in each school: curriculum management skills will be no less essential than they have always been.

It may be useful to begin with a reminder that the term curriculum can be interpreted in a number of different ways. At its narrowest, it may be used to stand for no more than a list of the subjects to be taught – the set of entries on the timetable. A slightly broader definition would equate 'curriculum' with 'syllabus', giving it the meaning of a formal list of the topics to be covered over a particular time-span within each subject area. Many people would accord it a wider sense than this, allowing the curriculum to refer to the totality of the planned provision through which any educational organization sets itself to achieve its educative purpose (a notion which would include what are often seen as 'extra-curricular activities'). And there are some who would argue that the concept should cover no less than the institution's total contribution to the student's learning experience (a definition which would embrace the 'hidden curriculum' as well).

Without choosing between these various possible interpretations, it is easy to see that the Education Reform Act itself does not go beyond the first, and most limited, of them. The national curriculum is identified as comprising ten timetable entries: three 'core subjects' (English, mathematics and science) and seven 'other foundation subjects' (history, geography, technology, music, art, physical education and a modern foreign language from age 11). It is only through the subsequently published 'Orders' by the secretary of state that any further specification is given of appropriate attainment targets, programmes of study and assessment arrangements for each of the foundation subjects. These, in effect, comprise the national syllabuses initially proposed by curriculum working groups and further refined through the consultative machinery of the National Curriculum Council (NCC) and the School Examinations and Assessment Council (SEAC).

From one standpoint, the national curriculum can be seen as marking an important educational advance, in that it offers the prospect of a universal entitlement to knowledge, breaking down the increasingly marked differentiation after the early secondary school years between the high-status courses followed by the abler pupils and the low-status offerings commonly provided for the less able. But it is also possible to take a more critical view, arguing that the list of approved items is too narrowly based on the traditional grammar school timetable, and that the curricular model adopted fails to look beyond the mere aggregation of a series of discrete subjects to a more holistic conception of what schools ought to be about.

Be that as it may, any broader view of what the curriculum comprises will remain open to local determination. The Act concedes various subsidiary powers over the individual school's curricular provision to other bodies, and notably the local authority and the governors; but even allowing for this, a large area of discretion remains to the teaching staff.

The continuity behind the revolution

Even if the 1988 Education Reform Act is held to represent a far-reaching reform, the specific provisions it makes for the national curriculum are not especially radical. The seeds of that notion were, after all, sown in the mid-1970s by a Labour prime minister (reviving an older tradition which was enshrined in the Codes which governed elementary and secondary education under the 1902 Act, and which survived for more than twenty years afterwards). To the extent that no major political party voiced its dissent from the views expressed in James Callaghan's 1976 Ruskin speech, the idea of a publicly defined expression of 'the purpose of education and the standards that we need' could be said to be uncontentious.

In any case, there has always been a loose consensus among educationists and lay people about what curricular activities are important. At the upper secondary level, the curriculum in each subject has generally been constrained, if not determined, by national examination requirements; the overall range of subject offerings in schools has been limited by broad, if often unspoken, social expectations. Within the Act, neither the choice of a central core nor that of other foundation subjects is a matter for surprise. Particular interest groups might have wanted to argue for the inclusion of other themes, but there has been little suggestion that any of the existing ones are inappropriate. So the national curriculum may be seen as giving explicit recognition to what many schools would claim they are in large part already doing.

Its symbolic significance should not however be overlooked. It represents the culminating point of a growing sense of dissatisfaction with teachers and with schooling, whose origins lie in the late 1960s and early 1970s, but which was fuelled by more recent events, including the long-drawn-out industrial troubles of the mid-1980s. The imposition by Parliament of a formal set of requirements on the schools may thus be interpreted as a rhetorical device, giving formal expression to a lack of confidence in the education service, though not in practice making a great deal of difference to schools' curricular offerings or policies.

But this line cannot be taken too far, because rhetoric may itself be an important means of enshrining new value assumptions, and hence changing operational practices. It would be as absurd to suggest that the national curriculum would have no noticeable impact on the classroom as it would be to contend that it removes any professionality that the teachers might previously have enjoyed. The truth, as so often, lies between the two extremes.

The government's implementation strategy

It may be helpful to consider what room remains for decision-making within the prescribed curricular framework by standing back and looking at some characteristic ways in which policy initiatives are implemented. There are a number of relevant sources of research literature, each of them somewhat distinct from the others. There are, first, the early accounts of planned change, exemplified in Havelock (1969) and Bennis *et al.* (1969); there are studies of organization and management theory, usefully summarized in Bush (1986); there are the sociological writings on exchange theory, of which Archer (1981) is perhaps the most accessible; and there are the further sets of ideas developed in the context of policy analysis, of which a much-quoted exemplar is Pressman and Wildavsky (1973). None of these exactly catches the distinctions that I now want to make, although between them they give some support to the composite picture which I will try to describe.

There are, I suggest, three broad approaches to the business of putting an innovative idea into practice. The first is some form of coercion: it may be through the direct or indirect exercise of force, or it may rest on an invocation of superior authority. Bennis *et al.*'s (1969) power-coercive strategy approximates to this, in identifying the particular way in which power is applied to limit alternatives for action or to shape its consequences. Archer's 'political' transaction is another variant on the same theme. This 'top-down' approach is perhaps most typically adopted within hierarchical, bureaucratic structures, in which orders are conveyed from central management to those concerned with the day-to-day running of the enterprise.

A second set of tactics encompasses bargaining and manipulation, often operating through emotionally charged appeals, or through a reference to self-interest. Havelock's social interaction model comes somewhere near to this, as does Archer's 'external' form of transaction. Manipulative styles of policy implementation tend to flourish in a setting characterized by rival interest groups.

The third mode of implementation depends on reasoned persuasion, impartial analysis or logical argument – what Bennis terms the empirical-rational approach. Here – though again the correlation is only a rough-and-ready one – one looks for examples most naturally within what Bush (1986) and others have characterized as a collegial or professional form of organization.

This summary of implementation strategies comprises a very simplified account of what is in reality a much more complex situation. It may however serve a useful purpose in bringing out the common structures underlying a number of diverse strands of inquiry into how policy change may be effected. The strategies in question can be illustrated by relatively recent attempts at large-scale curriculum reform.

The last of the three, depending upon the exercise of reason, and operating within a collegial framework, is typified by the Schools Council's approach to curriculum issues. The adoption of the projects it sponsored rested mainly on an appeal to teachers' professionalism, the attempt being to encapsulate existing good practice and to give it wider currency.

In contrast, the then Manpower Services Commission (MSC, now Training Agency) opted for an overtly manipulative technique: its curriculum proposals were supported by the promise of additional resources for schools which adopted them. The MSC's educational arguments were thus less central to the implementation process than the accompanying financial inducements. The context was uncompromisingly one of political bargaining, based on the strongly instrumental view of education characteristic of the MSC's parent agency, the Department of Trade and Industry.

The national curriculum rests for its adoption on the force of statute. Its requirements were promulgated with only a derisory show of consultation. No attempts were made, in the course of framing the Education Act which embodied such requirements, either to enlist professional support along the lines adopted by the Schools Council or to offer the special incentives characteristic of the curriculum schemes promoted by the MSC. It seems reasonable to argue that this particular aspect of the legislation was the product less of party political considerations than of a systematic campaign by the DES and HMI to win back some of the managerial power which had earlier been ceded to the local authorities and professional teacher interests (see Salter and Tapper, 1981). Accordingly it would appear that the national curriculum represents a coercive approach to the problem of adoption, in a context of bureaucratic and hierarchical (rather than collegial or pressure group) relationships between its initiators and those called upon to carry it out.

Coercion would seem a prompt and efficient means of putting any proposal into effect: it is less expensive in terms of money and effort than manipulation, and markedly quicker in its impact than reasoned argument. But its superiority in these regards over other approaches bears a cost. Because those who are required to carry out the resulting policies have no sense of ownership of them, they may – if they have any remaining freedom of action – elect to ignore them or at best to interpret them in ways that serve their own interests. The teaching profession, in so far as its members feel alienated and uninvolved in the process of devising the national curriculum, may well choose to deviate from it to any extent that enables them to avoid its inherent sanctions. Anyone who questions the distinction marked by Pressman and Wildavsky (1973) between policy as formulated and policy as practised has only to look at the provisions of the 1944 Act (reiterated in modified form in 1988) for a daily act of worship and for the teaching of an agreed syllabus of religious education in schools.

This phenomenon – the 'implementation gap' as it is often called – is not of course peculiar to the educational world. Numerous studies of policy analysis testify to its existence across a whole variety of contexts. Thus Lipsky (1971) was able to show how the intentions behind urban renewal policies in the USA could be significantly distorted by the 'street-level bureaucrats' – those relatively low-ranking officials who were charged with making the day-to-day decisions on which the fulfilment of the legislators' plans ultimately rested. More recently, and nearer home, Jordan and Richardson (1987), in their wide-ranging review of governmental policy-making in Britain, noted that 'the most desired goals cannot be secured simply by political will: they require the cooperation of other groups and institutions . . . in fact, the operationalization of policy is often difficult', and added, 'radical objectives [become] compromised in the process of bargaining and implementation'. The following section offers a reminder of the compromises that have already become evident in relation to some recently attempted reforms of national education policy.

Compromise and counter-revolution

It is not, I think, unduly cynical to claim that 'the implementation game' (see Bardach, 1977) was played out with some skill and sophistication by educationists in the 1980s. A state system largely modelled on the liberal-democratic vision which lay behind the 1944 Act was confronted by a radically right-wing government set firmly on course to replace the ideology of the welfare state by a rival dedication to free market principles. At its extreme, that change – which, as we were often reminded, was sanctioned by the mandate of the electorate – resulted in a narrowly instrumental view of schooling. The view which prevailed was that the fundamental rationale for education's call on public funds lay in its contribution to the national economy. Contentions that it should also have intrinsic ends, serving as a source of personal development, and celebrating intellectual knowledge as a worthy goal in itself, were discounted. So, too, were considerations of social benefit, which seek to justify more broadly cultural arguments, along with those which call on humanistic notions of 'the good society'. Yet these reflect underlying values which many people, within the system and outside it, were deeply reluctant to abandon.

The potential here for counter-revolutionary conflict is evident enough: what is interesting is the way in which it gave place to a bargaining process in which the new values have been accommodated without any very drastic sacrifice of the old. By implication, if not explicitly, the proponents of the romantic vision conceded that they were wrong – or at least, that they were at odds with too many of their fellow-citizens – in appearing to scorn the pragmatic aspects of the education process. With the wisdom of hindsight, it was perhaps absurd to pretend, as was once fashionable, that education has nothing to do – and indeed ought to have nothing to do – with the world of work. The message seemed generally to have got home that the public funds on which a public service must depend are themselves the product of a sound economy: that the nation's schools, colleges and universities, if they are to survive in a healthy state, must play their part in contributing to the skilled labour force which such an economy needs. On one reading, the pendulum may – under the influence of the MSC and its successor, the Training Agency – have swung much too far the other way, reducing the concepts of learning and understanding to the narrower notions of job-related competence and entrepreneurial capability. But closer examination may encourage a less gloomy view.

A seemingly endless series of new national initiatives has been promoted in recent years, many of which have at first been greeted with widespread alarm and suspicion. TVEI provides a case in point. The nature of its sponsorship, the rhetoric behind its promotion, and the manner in which it was introduced, led to a quite reasonable expectation that it would have a damaging and restrictive effect on the pattern of teaching provision in the upper secondary years. On the whole, that expectation was not realized: the model it espoused was a fairly open one, and has indeed been compared favourably with the apparently much tighter and more dirigiste structure which underpins the national curriculum.

Teacher appraisal provides another example of an apparent threat which has, in the event, come to look more like a benefaction. Although it was conceived as part of Sir Keith Joseph's campaign to 'cut out the dead wood' in the schools, conjuring up visions of the root-and-branch pruning of classroom staff, the end result has instead been to create far more systematic opportunities than had previously existed for personal and professional development, and to open up (in theory, if not yet in practice) the possibility of a greater measure of career progression for teachers.

Examination reforms, too, have commonly been introduced in the name of 'raising standards', prompting fears that an already excessively competitive and meritocratic system, when judged in an international context, might become even more so. Yet the consequent changes looked very different from those which might reasonably have been predicted. The moves towards profiling and records of achievement represented a broadly enlightened view of the nature of the assessment process; and even the GCSE examination, whose advent at first gave rise to some concern, can now be seen to have provided an impetus for more adventurous methods of teaching and learning. Project work found its way into the secondary schools, filtering down from changes in tertiary education as well as up from long-standing practice in the primary schools; rewards geared solely towards the bookish skills of the academically able were supplemented by a wider recognition of other forms of accomplishment.

These apparent contradictions between what was initially proposed and what has eventually resulted call for some explaining. The transformation in each case is not, I suggest, due to a change in heart on the part of our political leadership, in which proposals intended as punitive measures have been turned miraculously into rewards. Nor can it plausibly be seen as a cunning conspiracy, in which a government in league with the teaching profession has deliberately set out to deceive its hard-line supporters by parading publicly in wolf's clothing, only to reveal itself in private as a wet and woolly sheep in disguise. The truth is likely to be more straightforward. It is that policy-makers cannot operate in isolation: what happens when their plans are put into action depends crucially on those who have to carry them out. However much it might wish to, no regime – whether based on Downing Street, the White House or the People's Palace – can dispense with the agents out there (on the ground, in the front line, at the coal-face) whose job it is to translate policy into practice. And translation is not, one should remember, a purely passive process: a translator has the power to change meanings in a variety of subtle ways.

In each of the examples noted above, one might argue that attempts from the centre to bring schooling into closer line with a 'back to the basics' philosophy were successfully hijacked by the liberal education establishment, who took the opportunity to infuse them with their own, predominantly progressive, ideals. Even where the elitists seem to have won out – as in the rejection of the Higginson Report, which attempted to instil some belated breadth into the sixth-form curriculum and examinations – their victory may have been a pyrrhic one; institutions of higher education, faced with the falling rolls that earlier hit the primary and secondary schools, are finding it expedient to call for a wider range of entry requirements, and hence to extol the virtues of reduced specialization. When one begins to look more closely, the underlying reality is hard to reconcile with the superficial appearance of right-wing radical reform.

Implications for the individual school

If this reasoning is valid, it has obvious implications for the way in which the national curriculum is likely to affect the schools. In turning to consider this question, it must be acknowledged that those who drew up the legislation were in no sense naive enough to suppose that its provisions could be imposed without an accompanying system of checks and sanctions. The guarantee that the relevant provisions of the Act would be properly observed in every classroom, rather than subverted by a silently rebellious teaching force, was seen to lie in the imposition of universal testing at the ages of 7, 11, 14 and 16, whose scores should be published on a school-by-school basis. What was not so clearly foreseen was that the testing process would itself be subverted, in terms of the same liberal pedagogic sentiments that had already dulled the edge of earlier attempts to make education look more like industrial training.

The recommendations of the Task Group on Assessment and Testing must have come as a great disappointment to those who hoped it would give the national curriculum a sharp set of teeth. Although its report was eventually accepted, after some show of prime ministerial reluctance, it represented as forward-looking an approach to the issue as any child-centred educationist could have demanded in the circumstances, allowing a fair amount of scope for teacher involvement and building in a degree of complexity sufficient to defy any too-simplistic interpretation of the results.

To revert to the point with which this analysis began, the national curriculum will certainly impose some greater measure of uniformity on what is supposed to be learnt, and tested, at each given interval in the educational process. But that is about the limit of what can be said. Legislation is silent on how any particular part of the curriculum should be organized and taught; and even with respect to what are now fashionably termed outputs – the required goals at the end of the process – there is likely to be room for a good deal of slippage, since there is no foolproof way known to national legislators of closing tight the implementation gap. The pessimistic, neo-Orwellian vision of a uniform pattern of schooling with centrally controlled teachers, drilled in robot fashion into instilling a set item of the syllabus in exactly the same way at precisely the same moment of time, is a long way from realization.

It may indeed turn out to be almost true, if not intentionally so, that – as the first of the glossy DES bulletins on the Education Reform Act (DES 1988) claimed – 'The framework of the National Curriculum will build on best practice in schools with teachers continuing to have scope to decide what and how they teach, and to develop new approaches.' The 'what' looks pretty questionable, and the 'scope . . . to develop new approaches' may be somewhat more limited than it was before: but for the rest, it seems, *plus ça change* . . .

The room for curriculum decision-making at the level of the individual school may therefore be greater than many of us would initially have foreseen. The next, and final, section will consider some possible approaches to putting the national curriculum into practice, which are likely to reflect the existing management style of each institution concerned.

Some alternative scenarios

Under the Education Reform Act, teachers – at least in principle – cease to have any major responsibility for determining the broad objectives of the curriculum. As an aside, it might reasonably be contended that they have no natural right to do so, nor yet any special expertise that entitles them to act as Platonic 'philosopher-kings' in the matter. Education is a matter for universal concern, and the opportunity to decide where its main emphases should be placed is one which, in a representative democracy, ought to rest with society as a whole.

Professionals, one might concede, should have a legitimate say in determining the most appropriate means to any generally desired end that has close relevance to their particular knowledge and skills: but their sovereignty does not properly extend to the determination of the ends themselves. Doctors cannot be entrusted to decide on behalf of society how the overall resources for medical research and hospital provision should be allocated – between, say, the general improvement of preventive medicine on the one hand and the development of highly esoteric surgical skills on the other; the police cannot be allowed to frame the criminal code or to determine the course of justice. No more should teachers expect to lay down the law on what ought and ought not to be taught in schools. The fact that, for a brief period in history, they were allowed to take this duty upon themselves is no good reason for saying that they ought to have done so. Indeed, one of the factors behind the political backlash of the mid-1970s, as manifested in an upsurge of demands for accountability, may have been the common perception that the teaching profession had begun to get too far above itself.

With this said, there is little sign of widespread public dissent from the view that the insiders should have the major role, if not in deciding what the curriculum comprises, then at least in working out how it can best – to use another revealingly modish term – be delivered. There still remains ample space for variety in this respect: the solutions are likely to remain as diverse as the schools themselves.

We may conveniently explore the implications of the 1988 Act for curriculum management by considering in turn the three structural levels of: the school as a whole, its constituent departments, and its individual staff members. At the school level, the distinction made earlier in relation to national curricular policies between coercive, manipulative and rational approaches to implementation may continue to be a useful one. It is possible to sketch out some likely differences in schools which adopt one such strategy at the expense of the others (though experience should remind us that, in real life, few pure copy-book cases can be found, since most institutions will – perhaps wisely – adopt a mixture of all three, changing the emphasis according to circumstance).

A school with a strongly hierarchical structure, one might predict, will opt to play safe, adopting a coercive managerial approach in which maximizing test scores and examination results becomes the most important consideration. It will be inclined to follow the stipulations of the national curriculum in a generally slavish manner, keeping rigidly to the specified subject boundaries and following the recommended time allocations for each. Little or no attention will be afforded to pastoral issues, the personal and social development of pupils, or any other issue not expressly sanctioned by the NCC and SEAC. Such a school will, in short, behave in much the manner that those who originally drew up the national legislation might have wished.

In contrast, a school in which a traditionally bureaucratic form of organization gives place to a pressure group system of operation is likely to follow a different pattern. Where the process of decision-making depends on constant jockeying for position among powerful departmental baronies and other coalitions of vested interest, the curriculum will in all probability be determined by political manipulation, on the basis of a continuing power struggle for timetable territory. Core subjects will have an in-built advantage; foundation subjects will chip in as best they can; most other activities will be brushed aside, unless a strong voice speaks for them. There will be little attempt at integration or coherence: curricular provision will remain balkanized.

A professionally oriented, collegially based school (a rare phenomenon, it must be said, in its unadulterated form) will incline towards a rational approach based on considerations of the pupils' own best interests. It is here that one might expect to find preserved some of the more valuable features of the previous system – including, for example, mixed ability teaching, cross-curricular integration, topic-based activity, and the fostering of a wide range of talents. In the most professionally confident schools, and perhaps in those alone, the testing process will not be given undue weight, or be allowed to determine the whole emphasis of the curriculum itself. It is such schools that will be least affected by the curricular provisions of the 1988 Act, and will remain distinctly different from the more examination-obsessed grammar and private schools of yesteryear.

If the Education Reform Act now prescribes the main objectives of the education process, one might conclude that it none the less remains to each school to determine the overall pattern of its curricular provision. As has been suggested, both a hierarchically organized institution and one in which pressure-group politics are rife will tend, for different reasons, to maintain a strongly classified, discipline-focused curriculum – the first because that is what the legislation points to and renders most administratively convenient, and the second because subject departments comprise the most obvious configuration of sectional interests. Collegiality, on the other hand, is capable of permitting weak classification – that is a less tightly structured, cross-curricular design in which subject boundaries, and the departments which act as their guardians, are not so strongly emphasized.

Turning next to the departmental level, the most straightforward cases will be those in which the department's ethos reflects that of the school. A hierarchical department in a hierarchical school will be liable to promote a strongly framed curriculum, in which the subject content is clearly laid down and fairly rigidly sequenced; a collegial department in a collegial school may accommodate weaker framing and a greater degree of choice for pupils in terms of curricular content; a department which embodies a diversity of competing factions will tend to allow a relatively unstructured sequence of topics, with little internal coordination.

Complexities are likely to set in when the department's managerial style is at odds with the school's: one may note that it is also possible for a gap to occur between institutional policy and departmental implementation. Thus one might occasionally find an internally contentious or even a collegial department in a hierarchical school; or – perhaps more rarely – a hierarchical or politically fragmented department in a collegial school; and a school organized in terms of baronial interest groups is in any case likely to leave room for a variety of constituent types. In such cases, although the scope for departure from the dominant institutional norms and the prevailing curriculum structure is limited, the department would in all likelihood continue to have a significant measure of sovereignty over the organization and planning of subject content.

Similar considerations apply at the individual level. Teachers who are in tune with their departmental values will present few problems: a traditionally didactic teaching mode will fit comfortably with a strongly subject- and test-oriented curriculum, and a progressive one with a more open, student-centred framework; in a school or department which has not got its own act together, and where the curriculum remains politically contentious, anything goes – though it helps if one can become part of a coterie of like-minded interests.

But perhaps especially here, at the front line of provision, those responsible for shaping the curriculum need to remember that their best-laid plans are vulnerable to the non-conformity of individual practice. The class-teacher may have little control over structure or content, but even in today's constraining climate still enjoys considerable autonomy in the matter of teaching style. At the end of the day, teachers who strongly dissent from existing national or school or departmental policy will retain the professional's scope to do things in their own way. The classroom is a private place, not easily invaded by opposing outside forces. As must always be the case in human affairs, even strongly coercive legislation has its limits.

References

Archer, M. (1981) 'Educational politics: a model for their analysis', in P. Broadfoot *et al.* (eds) *Politics and Educational Change*, London, Croom Helm.

Bardach, E. (1977) *The Implementation Game*, Cambridge, Mass., MIT Press.

Bennis, W. G., Benne, K. D. and Chin, R. (1969) *The Planning of Change*, New York, Holt, Rinehart & Winston.

Bush, T. (1986) *Theories of Educational Management*, London, Harper & Row.

DES (1988) *Bulletin for School Teachers and Governors*, autumn 1988, issue 1, London, Department of Education and Science.

Havelock, R. G. (1969) *Planning for Innovation*, Ann Arbor, Mich., Center for Research on Utilization of Scientific Knowledge, University of Michigan.

Jordan, A. G. and Richardson, J. J. (1987) *British Politics and the Policy Process*, London, Allen & Unwin.

Lipsky, M. (1971) 'Street-level bureaucracy and the analysis of urban reform', *Urban Affairs Quarterly*, 6, 4: 391–409.

Pressman, J. and Wildavsky, A. (1973) *Implementation*, Berkeley, University of California Press.

Salter, B. and Tapper, T. (1981) *Education, Politics and the State: The Theory and Practice of Educational Change*, London, Grant McIntyre.

6

The Education Reform Act 1988: some implications for curriculum decision-making in primary schools

Jim Campbell

The background: 1977–88

The decade that led to the publication of the 1987 Education Reform Bill was characterized by concern over three major issues in the primary school curriculum. These were curricular diversity, raising standards, and accountability and control. Taken together, these three factors provided the evidential and political base for the DES to assert (DES, 1987a), and to some extent to justify, the need for a national curriculum.

The issue of diversity in curriculum practice was in effect an argument about the limits of tolerance of discretion on curriculum matters, exercised either by an individual class-teacher, a school, or a local education authority. What counts as 'undue' diversity is in the end a matter of judgement, but the evidence in the Primary Survey (DES, 1978) had revealed very wide variation (for example, in the provision for science, and in progression and coverage in the humanities). This was used as a basis for arguing that much greater consistency, however defined, in curricular practice was required (Richards, 1983). Other evidence revealed a different kind of diversity, with dramatic variations in the time spent on mathematics and 'language' (even making allowances for definitional problems), by pupils in different schools and classes (Bennett *et al.*, 1980).

Drawing on arguments very similar to those offered for a common curriculum at secondary level (Lawton, 1975; Scottish Education Department, 1977) the Select Committee (House of Commons, 1986) called for an 'entitlement' curriculum for all children, and for the secretary of state to be given new powers to issue broad guidance on the curriculum. Variety, justified by reference to children's interests, local needs, and teacher initiative, lauded in the Plowden Report, had effectively been challenged on the basis of a moral claim that all children should experience a comparable range of curricular experiences. (DES, 1985a; DES, 1985b; Joseph, 1984).

The Primary Survey was also an important source of evidence about unsatisfactory standards in primary schools. It showed reading standards continuing to rise in the post-war period, while simultaneously revealing poor match between work set and pupil capacities, especially in respect of pupils considered able. The poor match was across the curriculum, and was attributed in part to low teacher expectations, with the problem most pervasive in inner-city schools, though there are methodological difficulties with the analysis (Bennett *et al.*, 1983). This general picture was painted more sharply by two school-based studies showing the nature of the mismatch of task to capacities, even in the classrooms of teachers regarded as good practitioners (Bennett and Desforges, 1984; Bennett *et al.*, 1987).

One of the oddest features of the public debate over standards has been its refusal to draw upon the above, rather damaging, evidence and to rely instead upon references to obscure international comparisons, which showed, for example, relatively low attainment in mathematics by low/middle ability children of secondary school age, compared to their German counterparts (Prais and Wagner, 1985).

However, the force of the evidence of the Primary Survey was implicitly acknowledged in the substantial shift in expectations for the role of curriculum co-ordinators as subject advisers to their colleagues (Campbell, 1985; ILEA, 1986; House of Commons, 1986). The extension of this role, while intended 'to support not undermine' class-teachers (Richards, 1986) was in effect addressing the problem of levels of teacher expertise across the curriculum (and, by implication, of standards expected of children). This shift was reinforced by in-service training (INSET) targeted on curriculum post-holders, and the widespread move to appoint advisory teachers through Education Support Grants and other mechanisms, which was also designed to strengthen the subject base of curriculum planning at school level.

The third strand, accountability and curriculum control, is more difficult to analyse, because of the way the admittedly rather broad concept has failed to secure a common meaning. One approach is to restrict its use to the idea of 'giving an account of' the curriculum to parents, governors and other interested parties. At the school level, accountability in this restricted sense has been built up from an ideal goal (Taylor Report, 1977) to a legal requirement in the Education Acts 1980 and 1986 (no. 2) and the Education Reform Act 1988, to enable parents to have a basis, however inadequate in reality, for judging how well a child, a teacher and a school are performing on a publicly known curriculum. The performance indicators to be used for this are assessments on attainment targets differentiated into ten levels for the 5–16 age range (see TGAT Report extract in Chapter 2).

At the local authority level, the casual attitudes to providing curricular statements revealed in Circular 14/77 (DES, 1977) have been transformed by the production of supportive and forward-looking curriculum statements by local authorities, many of them anticipating or following *Curriculum Matters 2* (DES, 1985a). In vivid contrast, accountability at the central authority level has shrunk, with the legal requirement of the 1944 Act that the secretary of state should produce an annual report (a duty still placed on chief education officers of the LEAs) abolished by the 1986 Education Act. This contrast between schools and local authorities moving towards greater account-ability, and central authority reducing accountability, has been powerfully illustrated in the recommendations from an ILEA inquiry into freedom of information about schools (Tomlinson. 1987).

But if we extend the concept to consider aspects of control over the curriculum that may flow from greater accountability, the analysis becomes both more interesting and more problematic. The new right has developed a rhetoric of consumer control as a market force to help to raise standards (CPC, 1986). If the information from accountability rights becomes com-bined with the right to choose schools, it is argued, parents will effectively become controlling consumers, as a counter to the producer-led system operating hitherto. (Producers in this analysis are LEAs, teachers and professional associations generally.) The real problem in a producer-led system is the tendency of corporate interests to dominate consumer interests (Shipman, 1984).

The problem for this analysis, however, is that the Education Reform Act goes against the market forces model in two obvious ways. First, it requires a national curriculum to be implemented in all maintained schools, whereas a market forces model would have allowed the curriculum to be negotiated locally according to parental and community wishes. The curricu-lum in Haringey would be different from the curriculum in Harrogate, if the parents in the two situations wanted different curricula. Second, although the Act effectively breaks much of the power of the corporate interest of the LEAs (the corporate power of the teachers' unions already having been broken under the imposition of the Teachers' Pay and Conditions Act 1987), the power is flowing up to the centre, not down to the localities or to the parents. For the Act gives over 400 new powers to the secretary of state (ACC, 1987). Of those concerned with the curriculum some are very specific (the ability to appoint membership of the National Curriculum Council (NCC) and School Examinations and Assessment Council (SEAC)), but others are catch-all general powers (the ability to redefine the national curriculum and the ages at which children are assessed). This paradox of a government committed to market forces taking greater unitary control over the curriculum has been characterized as a 'fundamental contradiction' in current policies (Campbell *et al.*, 1987).

However, even without the power base provided by a third substantial electoral victory, the Conservative government, by the middle of 1987, had sufficiently strong evidence, and probably wide endorsement amongst pro-fessionals, to enable the case for a national curriculum to be supported. Whether what was proposed in the consultation document on the national curriculum (DES, 1987a) and the Education Reform Act 1988 will deliver what was shown to be needed in terms of reduced diversity, raised teacher expectations and increased accountability and control by consumers is more problematic. The discussion that follows applies these three criteria to the government proposals.

Curricular diversity

At its simplest, the national curriculum model is, for primary schools, a three-part one: religious education; the foundation subjects, including the 'core'; non-foundation subjects. There are three 'core' subjects, English, mathematics and science (plus Welsh for Welsh-speaking schools in Wales) which also form part of the 'foundation' group of subjects.

There are a further six subjects in the foundation, though outside the core. These are art, history, geography, physical education, music and technology (and Welsh for non-Welsh-speaking schools in Wales). (At the secondary stage a seventh subject – a modern foreign language – must be included.) Children's performance is to be assessed by arrangements that include nationally prescribed standard assessment tasks (SATs). A distinction made in the consultation paper was that music, physical education and art would have 'guidelines' rather than attainment targets. This distinction was not explicitly maintained in the Education Reform Act, although Clause 4(2) implies that the secretary of state would have discretion to make such distinctions. A further distinction is that attainment targets and programmes of study in the core subjects are to be specified, in the form of parliamentary orders, and implemented in schools, before those in the other foundations subjects.

Outside the foundation is religious education, which was required under the 1944 Education Act, and was given a distinctive position in the 1988 Act, and other subjects such as home economics, drama, etc., though in practice, aspects of home economics and health have been included in the programmes of study for science, and drama in those proposed for English.

Since the core and foundation and religious education are required by law, the national curriculum as specified appears effectively to address and to solve the problem of curricular diversity; children have a specified entitlement to a curriculum, which is not limited to a narrow basic skills core, and looks set to protect children from the vagaries of provision that has hitherto depended upon the personal inclinations of class-teachers, or particular enthusiasms of heads or governing bodies. Teachers who do not teach art or science or technology, because they do not feel confident or competent to do so, and governing bodies insisting upon a return to narrow basics, will alike find their curricular predilections illicit. Individual schools' practice in this respect is open to scrutiny, since the Act requires that schools' curriculum statements become public documents, available by law to interested parties.

There are two obstacles to the realization of this optimistic analysis. First, the decision to phase attainment targets in the core before the other foundation subjects, will create pressure upon teachers, parents and most importantly pupils, to perceive the core subjects as of greater significance than the others. This is likely to affect the perceived significance of the humanities and the arts adversely, especially as performance arts (Campbell *et al.*, 1987). Second, the Act has tried to clarify the position about which aspects of the curriculum may be subject to 'charges'. The attempt has not been entirely successful, but charges cannot be made for teaching the national curriculum, though voluntary contributions for things like field trips, visits, and swimming are not prohibited. The requirement to delegate financial responsibility to individual primary schools with over 200 pupils, and the possibility of doing so for smaller schools is likely to make parental contributions to school budgets, already a major item (Pring 1987), into a key factor in a school's ability to deliver a high-quality entitlement curriculum. If this happens, the main moral justification for the introduction of the national curriculum identified on p. 62–3 will have been subverted.

Raising standards

The secretary of state, in his statement to the Select Committee in April 1987, gave raising standards as the main generalized justification for the introduction of the national curriculum. He stressed especially the role of attainment targets, which would identify what pupils should 'normally be able to know, understand and be able to do' at or around the ages of 7 and 11. It is difficult to see anyone objecting to the slogan 'raising standards', though logically the published attainment targets will have a chance of raising standards only if they are pitched at a higher level than the implicit targets that teachers previously set for their pupils.

However, we need to think of standards as broader than simply attainment. Educational standards include standards of provision, standards of treatment in school, as well as attainment. It is helpful to think of three related factors:

1 *inputs*: resources for staffing, building and equipment, and learning materials;
2 *within-school factors*: the nature of the curriculum, teaching and learning styles, teacher expectations, school atmosphere and ethos;
3 *outputs*: academic attainment, social and moral development.

At the level of inputs, standards have fallen in respect of building quality (DES, 1982; 1983; 1985c; NCPTA, 1985) to the stage where the neglect of plant and fabric has affected the quality of learning and the safety of staff and children.

In respect of resources for staffing, there has been an improvement in *per capita* spending, though a reduction in real terms in overall expenditure on primary education, between 1975 and 1985 (House of Commons, 1986). The *per capita* improvement is small and has been produced mainly by the impact of falling rolls. There has been an increase in teacher-training intakes for primary schools. This has been interpreted as a government commitment to increase the contact ratio in primary schools, as urged by the White Paper, *Better Schools* (DES, 1985b), and explicitly recommended by the Select Committee (House of Commons 1986). The latter report had obtained confirmation from Sir Keith Joseph that a figure of around 15,000 extra teachers (i.e. above what was necessary to maintain current pupil–teacher ratios) was needed to allow primary teachers to be free from normal class contact time in order to engage in school-based curriculum development, curriculum co-ordination, working with parents, and so on. In December 1987, however, the secretary of state, in a written memorandum, effectively dismissed this recommendation, along with most of the others that were not already built into his Education Reform Bill (DES 1987b). The government had, in effect, refused to endorse the resourcing of the kind of staffing levels which the Select Committee, with full cross-party support, had described as 'essential if any progress is to be made in the classroom' (House of Commons, 1986: para 12.19).

At the level of within-school factors, the specification of attainment targets promises to raise teacher expectations, especially of the more able children. The targets themselves are produced as 'proposals' by subject working groups, and following consultation, amended by the NCC if necessary; they are then sent as advice to the secretary of state who may alter them if he sees fit (and gives reasons). They finally appear as Orders of Parliament. The impact of these orders on teachers' control of the curriculum is discussed further below. A characteristic of the targets is that they are differentiated into ten levels, and thus promise not merely to raise expectations, but to help teachers overcome the problem, identified on p. 63, of classroom 'match' overall.

Two factors that may restrict the potential of such developments are teacher morale and the range of expertise in the overall teacher supply. Teacher morale has not been improved by the imposition of the Teachers' Pay and Conditions Act, or by the legal requirement in the Education Act 1986 and the 1988 Act for teacher appraisal, possibly linked to assessment results. Teacher perceptions of the intentions lying behind the Act are crucial here, and there is little indication that anything practical is planned to restore trust in the relationship between the DES and teachers in primary schools.

At the same time, the academic backgrounds of teachers in primary schools are badly matched to the academic needs created by the specification of the curriculum in subject terms, with severe shortages in mathematics, science and technology, and music, and over-supply in humanities. Even though there is no specification in the 1988 Act that the curriculum should be organized in any particular form, the national curriculum will increase the pressure identified earlier for curriculum-led or 'activity-led' staffing in primary schools, though not necessarily taking the form of curriculum co-ordination in each single subject of the national curriculum. (This point is taken up on p. 75.) The Select Committee anticipated the need for staff time that would follow from curriculum co-ordinators helping to develop whole school policies on aspects of the curriculum, and this need will be enlarged as the implications for developing appropriate assessment strategies in schools come to be realized. It is for this reason that the secretary of state's dismissal of the resource implications of the Select Committee Report is so damaging to the prospects for raising standards in primary schools.

The dismal scenario thus produced is of some schools with disaffected teachers, lacking in confidence to teach some subjects, and without the time for good school-based development, being forced to teach these subjects by premature implementation of parts of the national curriculum. If this comes to pass in only, say, 20 per cent of primary schools, it will undermine much of the potential of the opportunity, provided by the working groups, for raising expectations generally. The pressure for short-term political advantage gained from pressing on with the national curriculum to show results in time for an election, ought to be tempered by considerations of the educational advantages of a longer term development plan, with properly funded and directed in-service training to meet the needs of the schools.

At the level of outputs, the promise that the implementation of the Act will lead to raised attainment, and social and personal development (through the subjects) is unconvincing (if raised standards overall is meant) for three reasons.

First, the attainments of children with special needs have been virtually ignored in both the consultation paper, and the Act. For statemented children the Act seems to envisage the statement becoming a reason for excluding the children from some aspects of the national curriculum. It becomes, so to speak, a ground for withdrawing educational provision, in contrast to the conditions of the 1981 Act, which saw the statement as a claim on resources to meet needs.

Second, open enrolment and financial delegation may lead to raised output standards in popular schools, but may well lead to lower standards in unpopular schools, leading to a three-tier school system: well-resourced independent schools; well-resourced maintained sector schools, financially supported by parents; and unpopular schools, with falling rolls, teachers with low morale, resourced at a minimal level, unable to attract substantial financial support from their parent bodies (Campbell *et al.*, 1987).

Third, there is the logical problem that if targets and national assessment help to raise standards through their impact on teacher and pupil motivation, they will do so only in some subjects, and not in the rest of the curriculum, since art, physical education and music will not have attainment targets.

Thus, although some schools and some pupils may have attainment levels raised, the overall picture looks set to be very patchy. The gap between good and poor schools will widen. This may be intentional, as a market forces exercise to let the poor schools wither on the vine; but schools take a long time to wither, and even longer to close down, and in the mean time, children will still be attending the withering schools.

Accountability and control

I have hinted (p. 63) at the conceptual vagueness involved in notions of accountability and control. At this stage it is helpful to separate out the idea of accountability from that of control, despite their interrelatedness, in order to analyse the Act's impact at school level.

Accountability

The Education Reform Act, by its assessment arrangements and by the requirement to publish curriculum and assessment results, has required schools to give better accounts of the curriculum to parents as 'consumers', to help them to exercise their right to choose schools. For this to be effective, at least three conditions would need to be met.

First, there would need to be a sophisticated and informed constituency of parents able to use curriculum documents and assessment results in a sensitive and aware manner. The relatively low interest shown in the annual meetings for parents held by school governors does not suggest that this constituency is at a highly developed stage, nor that it is uniformly spread.

The second condition is that assessment results should be able to be technically aggregated in a way that does not do damage to the range of characteristics being assessed, and yet is easily comprehended by a lay audience. In addition, the scores would need to have built into them some calculation to take account of social characteristics in a school's intake. The assessment arrangements proposed by TGAT do not meet either of these conditions, since reporting will be based on results unadjusted for social background. Instead there will a broad statement of the work of the school as a whole as a background to the moderated results on assessment tasks.

A third condition concerns the relationship between parents and school that is envisaged in the Act, with its requirement on LEAs to set up complaints procedures. The last decade has been characterized by apparently effective attempts to involve parents in supporting the schools' efforts, and 'deprived' schools especially, in improving their children's progress. These developments, which began by focusing on parental involvement in reading

(Tizard and Hewitson, 1980; Hannon and Jackson, 1987; Widlake and Macleod, 1984), have moved into mathematics (Merttens and Vass, 1987). Although the quality of the evidence in these studies is variable, the fundamental shift in them all is towards co-operation between the parents and the school, with the common aim of raising standards. If parents are put into the role of inquisitorial consumers, such developments may be discouraged, either from teacher mistrust of how parental involvement may be exploited by unscrupulous parents, or because parents may see more benefit in moving school, as open enrolment comes in, than in the arduous and time-consuming work involved in participatory schemes. Thus it is possible to see the exercise of choice by parents becoming a reality as the provisions of the Act come in, but it is difficult to envisage such choice arising from more authentic forms of accountability.

Curriculum control

The likelihood of an actual increase in central control of the curriculum in practice following the 1988 Act, was disputed by the then secretary of state (Baker, 1987) but a massive power base in principle has been established. Amongst other things, the secretary of state has power to appoint all the members of the NCC and SEAC, the bodies intended to give him/her independent advice on the curriculum; he/she has power to change the national curriculum, or to suspend it in order to allow a school to experiment. Above all, he/she has the power to change the recommendations of the NCC for attainment targets and programmes of study before they become incorporated into orders, and thus become the statutory specifications of the school curriculum, provided he/she gives reasons for doing so.

Thus on the face of it, there has been an enormous shift in power to define the curriculum, away from a *de facto* decision-making at school or classroom level to a *de jure* control at central government level. This shift, allied to other increases in power in the Act, has been so great as to raise serious constitutional issues, according to MacAuslan (1988).

From the point of view of control over the curriculum alone, however, Lawton (1983) has produced a simple model, with five system levels (central government, local government, school, department, and classroom) and three dimensions of curriculum (content, pedagogy, and assessment). This model is shown in Figure 6.1. If we use this model, power to define the curriculum appears to have been taken away from the local government level, and shifted to the central government. At the same time there has been some increase in power to regulate curriculum practice, within the centrally defined framework, through the delegation of responsibility to the governing body, and to parents through the complaints procedure referred to above. This applies both to content and assessment, though state control of pedagogy is intended to be excluded.

However, models are constructions invented to help in the analysis of

Aspect / Level	Curriculum content	Pedagogy	Evaluation
1 National			
2 Regional			
3 Institutional			
4 Departmental			
5 Individual			

Figure 6.1   A model of curriculum control

reality, and do not necessarily reflect the real world of decision-making on the curriculum, especially in situations where the system itself is being changed. The key question is how far decision-making over the curriculum at school and classroom level will effectively be controlled by the state, and how much will really remain *de facto* in the hands of the professionals – the teachers and headteachers. It is this issue that the following discussion attempts to analyse.

The national curriculum and school-based decision-making

The crucible in which the range of power given to the central government will be most severely tested lies in the way in which targets of attainment are finally specified. The procedure is a three-step one. First, the subject working groups appointed by the secretary of state make proposals on which the NCC is statutorily obliged to consult. Second, on the basis of the consultation exercise, the NCC gives advice to the secretary of state, including rec-ommendations for draft orders. Third, on the basis of the advice, the secretary of state lays orders, containing programmes of study and attain-ment targets, which become the legally required specifications for the national curriculum. At the time of writing, we have evidence about the first two stages in mathematics and science and the first stage in English (DES, 1988a; 1988b; 1988c; NCC, 1988a; 1988b), as well as the changes made to the recommendations of the TGAT (DES, 1988c: Appendix 4). The evidence is all in the same direction, and suggests that the procedures are being used to try to curtail the scope for school-based decision-making on the curriculum.

The evidence is most substantial in respect of mathematics and science. In the case of mathematics, the working group's final report produced a recommendation that there should be three clusters of attainment targets (profile components: PC):

PC1 Knowledge, skills and understandings in number, algebra and measures;

PC2 Knowledge, skills and understandings in space and shape and handling data;

PC3 Practical applications of mathematics including personal qualities, communication skills and using mathematics.

For assessment purposes the working group recommended 30 per cent, 30 per cent and 40 per cent weightings respectively. The final report was published by the NCC, with a preamble in which the secretary of state's views of its recommendations were made clear. These included a request not to separate the attainment targets concerned with practical applications into a distinctive component, but to merge them into the knowledge-based targets, and an expression of disapproval about the relatively low weighting given to knowledge as against applications.

A similar fate befell the final report of the Science Working Group. It had proposed, for the primary stages, three profile components also, the first concerned with knowledge skills and understanding, and the other two with the exploration/investigation, and communication. Although welcoming the general approach, the secretary of state again expressed disapproval of the relatively low weighting for assessment purposes given to knowledge and understanding; and he proposed reducing the number of profile components in Exploration and Communication, and combining the latter with the knowledge and understanding components where possible. The NCC's response here was to recommend two profile components, one for Exploration in Science (one attainment target) and one for Knowledge and Understanding (sixteen targets), each component weighted for reporting assessment, 50/50 per cent at age 7, and 45/55 per cent respectively at age 11.

The interventions by the secretary of state in the consultation process, contained in a letter to the chairman of the NCC, were extraordinary in one particular sense. In addition to general directions (e.g. 'Are the proposals achievable bearing in mind the time that can be made available?') some requirements dealt with fine detail and, despite the promises in the consultation paper, were concerned with teaching *methods* (e.g. 'Is it justifiable to exclude the pencil and paper methods for long division and long multiplication from the attainment targets for mathematics?').

The impact of the interventions is difficult to assess without insider knowledge of the NCC, but on this particular point the NCC recommended:

that pupils should be able to use mental, paper and pencil methods and calculators as appropriate, and should be able to carry out the operations of multiplication and division using 2- and 3-digit numbers by paper and pencil methods.   (NCC, 1988a: 16)

It is an irony that elsewhere the NCC refused to recommend a science attainment target called Working in Groups because, amongst other things, it prescribed 'too closely the teaching methods to be used by teachers' (NCC, 1988b: 20).

Likewise on the general points, about combining the profile components concerning Applications in Mathematics, and Investigation and Communication in Science, the NCC recommendations appear to give way to the secretary of state, despite its own evidence from the consultation exercise that 80 per cent of those responding wanted the profile components kept separate. The NCC recommendations were accepted by the secretary of state and became incorporated in draft orders (DES, 1988d). Thus, on the face of it, decision-making about the primary curriculum has been effectively removed from schools and teachers in respect of Lawton's content and assessment dimensions, and even to some extent in respect of pedagogy. About pedagogy it should be noted that the central control through specification of attainment targets implying a particular pedagogy is not directed only in favour of formal methods. Both the mathematics and science working groups specified targets that, at least by implication, and frequently explicitly, required 'progressive' approaches, especially those involving investigations and problem-solving methods, often using co-operative group work. It all makes the claim of the 1987 consultation document that there should be 'full scope for the enterprise and initiative of teachers' sound rather hollow.

The need for collegial approaches

However, the above analysis takes too superficial a view of curriculum decision-making. This is because there is a world of difference between national policy and its delivery in schools. The national curriculum as specified in the Act (and to be specified in the orders) has created three fundamental management tasks for its delivery in primary schools. They concern the implementation of the curriculum, specified as subjects; assessment; and public relations. All three point toward the need for an approach to management, advocated and analysed throughout the 1980s, referred to as 'collegiality' (Coulson, 1976; Alexander, 1984; Campbell, 1985; House of Commons, 1986; Southworth, 1988). Although there are differences of interpretation, collegiality implies delegation of curriculum leadership to members of staff with designated curriculum responsibilities – curriculum co-ordinators – and distinctive subject expertise.

The effective implementation of this kind of role by curriculum co-ordinators is crucial in the three aspects mentioned above, and I shall now briefly illustrate the management issues in respect of each of them.

Implementation of the curriculum specified as subjects

First, the attainment targets are fundamentally statements of objectives, and do not in general specify the means by which they should be achieved, which remain the responsibility of the school. For example, Attainment Target 3, concerned with the Processes of Life, in the statutory orders for Science (DES, 1989) is:

> Pupils should develop their knowledge and understanding of the organisation of living things, and of the processes which characterise their survival and reproduction.

> (DES, 1989: 8)

Part of the relevant programme of study for the 7–11-year-old stage is:

> Children should investigate some aspects of feeding, support, move-ment and behaviour in relation to themselves and other animals. They should be introduced . . . to basic ideas about the processes of breathing, circulation, growth and reproduction.

> (DES, 1989: 69)

Even when the general attainment target is specified in ten levels (e.g. Level 4 'be able to name the major organs and organ systems in flowering plants and mammals': p. 8), it remains a framework of objectives, not a strait-jacket of content and/or method. It is still a fundamental task of the school's curriculum management to organize progression in the sequence of learning experiences within the Key Stage 2 (7–11-year-olds) by which children come to such understandings, and to create a through-school policy on curriculum organization, for example, whether learning of science is integrated into cross-curricular topics and themes, or is dealt with in separate subject lessons.

Assessment

Second, the responsibility for creating systematic assessment of children's performance against the attainment targets also remains with the school. The *requirement* to assess is part of the Act and legally enforceable. An element of the assessment arrangements is nationally specified through the externally developed standard assessment tasks (SATs), and administered at the end of each key stage. Even here, the schools are able to choose SATS from an item bank, to take account of local needs. But assessment through teachers' classroom judgements ('teacher ratings' in TGAT-speak), ongoing through-out each year in each key stage, will be an important contribution to the assessment alongside the SATs.

A key management task in this respect is to ensure that such classroom-based judgements are made consistently through the school, and systematically related to the attainment targets. The recording of such judgements, and their match or mismatch with pupil performance on the SATs, also need to be taken into account, probably through the adoption by the school of an LEA-wide information technology system.

Public relations

The third reason relates to the need for school management to be accountable for its curriculum practice, the way it 'delivers' its version of the national curriculum to those with an interest in it. Interested groups include governors and parents, of course, who have a right to information about the curriculum, and also the staff and governors of other schools. For primary schools, this latter set of relations comprise its 'cluster' of primary schools, through which the choice and moderation of SATs are effected, and its receiving secondary school, which will be concerned not only to recruit primary pupils, but also to ensure curricular progression and continuity across Key Stages 2 and 3. In addition, of course, the need to account for the curriculum in practice to annual meetings of parents, and to show the quality of a school's curriculum to a consumer-oriented constituency of parents, with free choice of school, will become even more pressing.

Not all these co-ordination tasks are simple subject responsibilities. They illustrate one change affecting the management of the curriculum in primary schools, from the earlier collegiality models. They represent a shift from the allocation of responsibility for curriculum subjects exclusively (a curriculum-led management model) to responsibility for curriculum-related activities (an activity-led management model). Where the former specified subjects or clusters of subjects, such as topic work, as the key organizational responsibilities, the latter identifies key tasks or activities related to the curriculum, but not necessarily subject specific. For example, responsibility for assessment and public relations as discussed above might be regarded as more important than responsibility for, say, geography. In infant schools, home–school liaison, or learning through play, might take precedence over some subject responsibilities. The actual tasks would have to be agreed by the governors and staff, but activity-led management is likely to be the way that school management responds to the new political context of education, brought about by the 1988 Act. This kind of model, originally devised by the Audit Commission for secondary schools (Audit Commission 1986) and called activity-led staffing, should prove applicable by primary schools, both as a management model and as a basis for calculating a more appropriate staffing formula than the simple pupil–teacher ratio.

Thus the three curriculum management tasks identified earlier, together with others, have been turned, by the passing of the 1988 Act, into imperatives for schools that wish to flourish in the new political situation.

Collegiality was advocated in the early 1980s as a means of responding to the pressure for both democratic decision-making and higher standards across a broader curriculum in primary schools. But in the 1990s schools in which a collegial approach has been adopted, in which staff are accustomed to collective decision-making, and in which curriculum co-ordinators already exercise effective leadership in their subject or 'activity', will be better placed than most others to deliver the curriculum to which children and their parents are now entitled by law.

References

ACC (Association of County Councils) (1987) 'Annex E, agenda item 2, Education Committee', 17 December, London, ACC.

Alexander, R. (1984) *Primary Teaching*, London, Holt, Rinehart & Winston.

Audit Commission (1986) *Towards Better Management of Secondary Education*, London, HMSO.

Baker, K. (1987) speech to the North of England Conference, Nottingham.

Bennett, N. and Desforges, C. (1984) *The Quality of Pupil Learning Experiences*, London, Lawrence Erlbaum Associates.

Bennett, N., Andrae, J., Hegarty, P. and Wade, B. (1980) *Open Plan Schools: Teaching, Curriculum and Design*, Windsor, NFER for the Schools Council.

Bennett, N., O'Hare, E. and Lee, J. (1983) 'Mixed age classes in primary schools', *British Educational Research Journal*, **9**(1), 41–56.

Bennett, N., Roth, E. and Dunne, R. (1987) 'Task processes in mixed and single ages classes', *Education 3–13*, **15**(1), 43–51.

Campbell, R. J. (1985) *Developing the Primary School Curriculum*, London, Holt, Rinehart & Winston.

Campbell, R. J., Little, V. and Tomlinson, J. R. G. (1987) 'Multiplying the divisions?', *Journal of Education Policy*, **2**(4), 369–78.

Coulson, A. A. (1976) 'The role of the primary head', in R. Peters (ed.) *The Role of the Head*, London, Routledge & Kegan Paul.

CPC (Conservative Political Centre) (1986) *Save Our Schools*, London, CPC.

DES (1977) *Circular 14/77*, London, DES.

DES (1978) *Primary Education in England: A Survey by HM Inspectors*, London, HMSO.

DES (1982) *Report by HMI on the Effects on the Education Service of Local Authority Expenditure Policies*, London, HMSO.

DES (1983) *Report by HMI on the Effects on the Education Service of Local Authority Expenditure Policies*, London, HMSO.

DES (1985a) 'The curriculum from 5–16', *Curriculum Matters 2*, London, HMSO.

DES (1985b) *Better Schools*, Cmnd 9469, London, HMSO.

DES (1985c) *Report by HMI on the Effects on the Education Service of Local Authority Expenditure Policies*, London, HMSO.

DES (1987a) *The National Curriculum 5–16: A Consultation Document*, London, HMSO.

DES (1987b) 'Memorandum by the Secretary of State for Education and Science on the Third Report from the Education, Science and Arts Committee,

Session 1985–6 Achievement in Primary Schools', 16 December, London, HMSO.

DES (1988a) *National Curriculum Mathematics for Ages 5–16*, London, HMSO.

DES (1988b) *National Curriculum Science for Ages 5–16*, London, HMSO.

DES (1988c) *National Curriculum English for Ages 5–11*, London, HMSO.

DES (1988d) *National Curriculum: Draft Orders for Mathematics and Science*, London, HMSO.

DES (1989) *Science in the National Curriculum*, London, HMSO.

Hannon, P. and Jackson, A. (1987) *The Bellfield Reading Project: Final Report*, London, National Children's Bureau.

House of Commons (1986) '3rd Report of the Education, Science and Arts Committee, Session 1985–86', *Achievement in Primary Schools*, 1, London, HMSO.

ILEA (1985) *Improving Primary Schools*, London, Inner London Education Authority.

Joseph, Sir K. (1984) speech to the North of England Conference, Sheffield.

Lawton, D. (1975) *Class Culture and the Curriculum*, London, Routledge & Kegan Paul.

Lawton, D. (1983) *Curriculum Studies and Educational Planning*, London, Hodder & Stoughton.

MacAuslan, P. (1988) 'The Bill – Does it offend against the constitution?', in J. Haviland (ed.) *Take Care, Mr Baker!*, London, Fourth Estate.

Merttens, R. and Vass, J. (1987) 'Parents in school: raising money or raising standards?', *Education 3–13*, **15**(2), 23–8.

NCC (National Curriculum Council) (1988) *Consultative Report: Mathematics 5–16*, London, NCC.

NCPTA (National Confederation of Parent-Teacher Associations) (1985) *The State of Schools in England and Wales*, Gravesend, NCPTA.

Prais, S. J. and Wagner, K. (1985) 'Schooling standards in England and Germany: some summary comparisons bearing on economic performance', *National Institute Economic Review*, 112, 53–76.

Pring, R. (1987) 'Privatisation in education', *Journal of Educational Policy*, **2**(4), 289–300.

Richards, C. (1983) 'Curriculum consistency', in C. Richards (ed.) *New Directions in Primary Education*, Lewes, Falmer Press.

Richards, C. (1986) 'The Curriculum from 5–16: implications for primary teachers', *Education 3–13*, **14**(1), 2–8.

Scottish Education Department, Consultative Committee on the Curriculum (1977) *The Structure of the Curriculum in the Third and Fourth Years of the Scottish Secondary School*, Munn Report, Edinburgh, HMSO.

Shipman, M. (1984) *Education as a Public Service*, London, Methuen.

Southworth, G. (1988) 'Collegiality and the role of the head', in G. Southworth (ed.) *Readings in Primary School Management*, Lewes, Falmer Press.

Taylor Report (1977) *A New Partnership for our Schools*, London, HMSO.

Tizard, B. and Hewitson, J. (1980) 'Parental involvement and reading attainment', *British Journal of Educational Psychology*, **50**, 209–15.

Tomlinson, J. R. G. (1987) *Informing Education*, Report of a committee chaired by Tomlinson for ILEA, London, Inner London Education Authority.

Widlake, P. and Macleod, F. (1984) *Raising Standards*, Coventry, Community Education Development Centre.

7

Evaluating schools in the context of the Education Reform Act

Anne McIntyre

Introduction

This chapter is concerned with the problems, possibilities and implications of evaluating schools within the terms set by the 1988 Education Reform Act. School managers are faced with the task of planning and implementing school evaluation policies which satisfy two sets of demands. On the one hand, there are the requirements of outside agencies for judging how far and in what respects schools have met external demands for accountability. On the other hand, school evaluation policies must also serve the needs of school managers and staff for improving their own practices.

First, this chapter describes evaluation strategies which have been developed by professional educators to meet accountability demands. Second, some characteristics of economic accountability are defined. Third, major assumptions which appear to underlie the arrangements for implementation of the national curriculum, standard assessment tasks and publication of results are outlined. The final section formulates some evaluation questions, and suggests strategies by which such questions may be answered.

Requirements that schools be evaluated come from a wide variety of groups with differential powers to assert the importance of their own criteria and to demand the provision of evidence that such criteria are being met. *Performance Indicators For Schools* (SIS, 1988) discusses the nature of possible performance indicators for use by schools in meeting public accountability demands. For the purposes of making a distinction between professional and educationist interests and concerns for evaluation and those of non-professionals, this chapter draws on the SIS notions of 'professional accountability' and 'economic accountability'.

Professional accountability

By professional accountability, I mean a form of accounting where the demands being made upon schools – for example, by local or national government, parents and employers – are interpreted and translated into action and criteria for success within the frames of reference of professional educators. Several different strategies adopted by schools for meeting the demands of accountability are distinguished according to their focus for evaluation, their purposes, their evaluation strategies, the positions adopted by the evaluators, and the audiences for whom reports are made available. The strategies dealt with here are: *school prospectuses*, accounts of *self-evaluation*; *validation* of institutions and programmes; and school *reports* to individual parents.

School prospectuses

The main focus of the school prospectus tends to be on descriptions of aspirations, rationales, policies, curriculum plans, extra-curricular activities, expectations of standards of attainment, dress, behaviour, time-keeping, parental support, and so on. The purposes for circulating such descriptions are to recruit pupils and parents, and to alert them to expectations of the school. Prospectuses highlight what the school does well and can offer to different groups of pupils with different interests or needs. The evaluation strategies are those adopted by parents in comparing statements of school intent with their own experiences, and those of their children, as to what happens in the day-to-day running of the school, and what its achievements are. Parents also compare the concerns and claims of the school with those apparent in other school prospectuses. The evaluators are therefore the clients: parents and their children.

Self-evaluation

In the recent past in this country, professional accountability in schools has been largely conceived within a tradition of 'self-evaluation' with the emphasis on critical examination by schools of their own plans and related processes and outcomes. Adelman and Alexander (1982) give some indication of their expectations in this respect, in a description of 'formal' approaches to institutional self-evaluation. Formal evaluation is

> distinct from 'informal' not so much in terms of judgemental process itself as by virtue of the accessibility of that process, the intentions which lie behind it and the uses to which it is put. By formal educational evaluation we mean the making of judgements of the worth and effectiveness of educational endeavours at a public level, sometimes as a matter of deliberate institutional policy. These judgements . . . may reasonably claim to be valid and fair.
>
> (Adelman and Alexander, 1982: 6)

The implications of making public school decision-making, its processes and outcomes, are explored, for example, by Elliott *et al.* (1981). Significant contributions to the debate had earlier been made by House (1972), who was reacting against his experience of what he calls the 'productivity model' of accountability in the USA based primarily on economic and administrative concerns for efficiency, tidiness and value for money. MacDonald (1978) and, more recently, Simons (1988) have also been actively engaged in promoting the idea of self-evaluation as an appropriate way for educationists to respond to demands for public accountability.

These authors, and many others within this tradition, agree that accountability procedures of the self-reporting kind which render educational practice 'open to view and responsive to critique' can usefully serve both improvement purposes in schools and those of public accountability. Within this same tradition, Elliott and others (Elliott, 1981; Brown and McIntyre, 1981; Carr and Kemmis, 1986) have adopted and developed the idea of 'action research' as one way to fulfil the requirements of an explicit approach to self-evaluation. Action research can be described as:

> research carried out by practitioners with a view to improving their professional practice and understanding it better.
>
> (Cameron-Jones, 1983)

Validation

Professional accountability may also be served by the validation and accreditation of institutions and courses. The aims of the procedures instigated are to provide clear and informative descriptions of the nature of institutions, their planned activities, clear and convincing rationales for these activities and how they will be organized and presented. Validation strategies are derived from attempts to make educational planning more considered and more explicitly justified. They rely on the acceptance of the idea that professional educators with qualifications and experience can be relied on to uphold the standards of attainment required by institutions and those they aim to serve. Importantly, the nature of the information generated is made available to a validating group who are usually drawn from a number of institutions, expert, sympathetic, sensitive to practical realities, and in a position to make comparisons between institutions. Most importantly, their judgements are made from independent positions by professionals who have no personal vested interests either in the plans they are being asked to validate or in their costs, the viability and availability of which are assumed to be negotiated elsewhere.

School reports: profiling and records of achievement

For some time now schools have been working to improve their reports to parents and to prospective employers in ways that avoid 'invidious comparisons' between pupils, and which give credit to the specific things that pupils know and can do over a range of activities and contexts. The thinking which has informed much of the work on profiles and records of achievement has been based on criterion-referencing which is described by Brown as

> assessment that provides information about the specific knowledge and abilities of pupils through their performances on various kinds of tasks that are interpretable in terms of what the pupil knows or can do, without reference to the performance of others.
>
> (Brown, 1980: viii)

Many teachers have responded enthusiastically to profiles and records of achievement and, to varying degrees, have attempted to build criterion-referenced assessment into their reporting schemes. Profiles and records of achievement have been seen as helping teachers to work to sustain the motivation of pupils who may otherwise have been classified as 'below average' on the basis of single aggregated scores on tests or examinations (norm-referencing). One of the early advocates described the principles underlying profiles and records of achievement as follows:

> Student profiles or records of achievement are documents constituted by professional teachers . . . , in conjunction with their students, describing as accurately and succinctly as possible the knowledge, skills and experiences of an individual relative to a particular curriculum. They are meant to be read in their final (summative) form by (amongst others) employers, parents and educational personnel. . . . In the formative stage they are a common focus for concern between teacher and taught, . . . a basis for face to face discussion and reflection, and an opportunity to appraise the suitability . . . of the learning programme.
>
> (Mansell, 1986: 25)

Criterion-referenced assessment can, of course, be used in the same way as norm-referencing. While pupils' responses to individual test items can be criterion-referenced, and at this detailed level, provide useful information for professional purposes, they can also be added together to give an overall score or grade by which pupils are accorded a status relative to other pupils. Not only is important information lost in this process, but also the tendency is once more to compare one pupil with another on the basis of their assessment grades.

While profiles and criterion-referenced reports are not intended primarily for school evaluation purposes, they do provide the evidence from which parents can evaluate the school's contribution to their children's education; when reports from a whole year group of pupils are collated, patterns of strengths and weaknesses can be identified for either summative or formative purposes.

All these strategies of professional accountability in their own ways, directly or indirectly, can serve the interests of the public and also those of teachers wishing to improve the quality of learning for their pupils. The effectiveness of professional accountability approaches for these contrasting purposes depends upon the selection of evidence and the presentation of accounts in such a way as to be responsive to the concerns of different audiences, and so as to enable each audience to make valid interpretations of what is presented. On the one hand, there is the danger, to which professionals are likely to be alert, that a naive public will interpret evidence in over-simplified and unfair ways. On the other hand, a danger of all professional accountability, to which members of the public are likely to be alert, is that the professionals will, unwittingly or deliberately, be self-serving in their selection of criteria or of evidence. It is primarily because of this danger that there are demands for economic accountability.

Economic accountability

The demands for economic accountability are that schools demonstrate value for money in relation to the interests and concerns of those bearing the costs. At one extreme, it is conceivable that economic accountability requirements could be met through the explicit professional evaluation activities of schools outlined above, without any further measures. However, schools have clearly been under pressure to justify the costs entailed. Responses in terms of reports by professionals on the benefits and values of their plans and processes, have not been regarded as sufficient. It has also been argued (SIS, 1988) that schools should respond in strictly economic terms. At the other extreme then, taking as the starting-point the general concerns of accountants and economists, value for money may be conceived in terms of such easily quantified variables as pupil–teacher ratios, costs per pupil, occupancy rates, and standards of pupil performance in examinations.

From this perspective, emphasis is laid on objective evidence, standard-izable variables, ready quantification and simple answers. It is clear that there is a significant tension between such an emphasis and a concern for profess-ional relevance and qualitative approaches to the benefits of schooling. The SIS report on 'performance indicators' reflects this tension. The report attempts to achieve a compromise which gives greater weight to the econ-omic perspective, seeking 'a range of suggested quantified indicators in accordance with certain basic principles'. The indicators should be:

(a) related to the school's own aims and objectives;
(b) reliable so far as possible, and able to be standardized;
(c) as few as are needed to achieve their purposes;
(d) as acceptable as possible to those who need them;
(e) capable of conveying messages and throwing up warning signs.

(SIS, 1988: 4)

Economic accountability may be seen as involving four possible categories of variables:

1 outcome, or benefit, variables
2 cost variables
3 process variables
4 context and uncontrolled input variables.

Benefit and cost variables

If schools were to operate in a competitive open market in accordance with a *laissez-faire* 'market' ideology (Lawton, 1988), evaluation of schools would be unnecessary because it would be implicit in the mechanisms of the market. Successful schools would be able to charge more, would attract more clients, and would therefore have high incomes in comparison to their costs: the measure of their success, their profits, would itself provide the 'natural' reward for their success.

However, so long as the state continues to meet even some of the costs of schooling, such a simple model is inadequate, and it is necessary to specify the outcomes of schooling which are valued. These may be very diverse, including the manifold understandings, skills and attitudes which it may be desirable for pupils to acquire, their enjoyment of school life, the contribution that the school makes to the life of the community, and the professional development of teachers working in the school. These various possible benefits may be difficult to describe, more so to quantify, and may differ subtly from school to school; but within an economic accountability framework they are more likely to be considered if they can be both quantified and standardized – for example, the 'simple' and 'objective' measures provided by publication of external examination results as required by the 1980 Education Act.

Within a state-funded system of schooling, it is the benefits and outcomes potentially provided by schools which are most likely to interest both general public and professional teachers. To politicians and administrators, however, costs are likely to be of equal concern. A school's performance in economic terms is a function of the benefits achieved for given costs and of the costs incurred in achieving given benefits. Again, a sensitive analysis of costs would include the stresses and difficulties experienced by teachers, and indeed by pupils and their parents; but unless these can be quantified, and qualified in financial terms, it is unlikely that an economic accountability analysis will include them.

Process variables

While it is in terms of its outcomes or products that a school is likely to be judged within an economic framework, the school has greater control, over its own internal processes, and these may in some respects be more easily observed and measured. 'Process-product' research studies of teaching, and increasingly in recent years of the operation of whole schools, have sought to establish through correlational analyses across schools the processes which are conducive to the achievement of various desired outcomes (Rutter *et al.*, 1979). In so far as such work has been successful, it would seem possible for schools to be evaluated not only in terms of the outcomes they achieve, but also in terms of whether their internal processes are likely to facilitate such desired outcomes.

Context and uncontrolled input variables

Research studies have tended to show that schools' performances, in terms of the outcomes achieved for given costs, correlate more highly with external factors over which schools seem to have no control than with any significant internal process variables (Coleman, 1969; Jencks, 1972). Prominent amongst such variables are characteristics of schools' catchment areas, and the measured abilities or attainments of pupils on entry to the school. In the light of these findings, it may very reasonably be argued that an adequate model of economic accountability would judge the outcomes achieved by schools, and even the processes in which they engaged, only after statistical account had been taken of such major uncontrollable variables.

These then are some of the major considerations which have informed strategies for evaluating schools during recent years, reflecting the diverse values and interests inside and outside schools. Given this diversity, evaluation strategies have been aimed very often at resolving the major problem of reconciling professional interests with those of the public at large.

To know how best to develop our thinking from here, we now turn to the 1988 Education Reform Act to examine some major assumptions which appear to underlie the arrangements for implementation of the national curriculum, assessment, and publication of results. These are outlined, and their possible implications for professional and economic accountability are discussed.

The 1988 Education Reform Act: national curriculum and standard assessment tasks

The aim of this section is to identify the major shifts in power relations that were brought about by the Act. The discussion focuses on the arrangements which are being made for the implementation of the national curriculum and its associated testing programme. The notion of power is useful in understanding who is accountable for what, and what pressures can be brought to bear on different groups to take account of the needs or demands of other groups, and to provide evidence of meeting such demands. Three aspects of the changes are of special significance for a re-examination of professional and economic accounting procedures.

First, the shift in responsibility for development of curricular aims and objectives. Teachers have been relieved of much of the responsibility for decision-making about which 'subjects' might be important, how much time will be devoted to them and what aspects of these subjects are to be given special emphasis. Instead, various subject groups are developing broad curriculum outlines and guidelines which teachers will use to implement their own strategies.

Second, the shift in responsibilities for determining the standards to be achieved. Arrangements have been made for selected consortia to develop appropriate, valid and reliable ways to assess pupils' performance against predetermined standards (or statements of attainment) at various stages throughout their school career. Aggregated results, which must be published, allow comparisons to be made between groups of pupils and schools. (The exception is results for 7-year-old pupils, though it was 'strongly recommended' that these should also be published: *Hansard*, 7 June 1988.) Despite a growing literature on making fair, adjusted comparisons of school performance (Goldstein and Cuttance, 1988; Nuttall, 1988), the school-level results are not to be adjusted for context and uncontrolled variables, but set within a report of the school as a whole and accompanied by a description of the socio-economic characteristics of the school's community. Through publication, for example, in a school's prospectus, parents will have access to these unadjusted test scores so that they can evaluate schools and choose the one they prefer. Competition between schools was anticipated by the government as one outcome of these arrangements. It was argued that this competition could be expected to lead to a raising of standards, although the precise mechanisms through which testing and publication of results might lead to the benefits envisaged were not made explicit (Gipps, 1988).

Third, the shift of powers in favour of government, school governors and parents. Schools have the choice of opting out of local authority control to be maintained directly by central government. The local school management arrangements also gave much greater autonomy to secondary and larger primary schools that remain under LEA control. However, central control is fairly firmly in the hands of government through its control of the curriculum and the standards to be achieved.

What implications, then, do these radical changes have for school evaluation procedures? The first implication would seem to be that, in future, professional accountability operations will be constrained within an economic accountability framework. The powers and obligations of school governors, combined with opportunities for parental choice, mean that teachers and managers have to account for their activities increasingly in terms set by other people.

More specifically, in terms of the categories of variables suggested above in relation to economic accountability, the Education Reform Act would seem to have the following implications:

1 *Outcome variables*: The external prescription of the curriculum, imposition of standardized assessments, and the obligation on schools to publish the results of these assessments, will surely mean that schools will, from now on, be primarily held accountable in terms of their pupils' performance on these assessment tasks.

2 *Cost variables*: Whether or not schools opt out, their funding will be determined by standard and 'fair' formulae. The relative costs which may be appropriately incurred by schools as a result of their differing circumstances (e.g. disadvantaged catchment areas) will not be, one may guess, a major factor in the economic accountability demands made upon them.

3 *Process variables*: Because of local school management, schools will be able to use their resources in meeting the demands of the national curriculum and the standards set as they consider best, with substantially more freedom than before. It must be expected that *how* they use this freedom will be a primary focus of accountability concern.

4 *Context and uncontrolled input variables*: Despite considerable controversy over this aspect of the initial report of the Task Group for Assessment and Testing (TGAT, 1988), it is clear that no formal procedure has been initiated to take account of schools' contexts or recruitment in publishing or evaluating their pupils' performances. Schools will, of course, be able, for example, to explain away poor results at the 14-year-old stage by pointing to the poor results of 11-year-olds entering the school. Such excuses are not, however, likely to be very persuasive to parents. Parents rightly tend to believe that their children's chances of academic success are likely to be poorer in schools where the attainments of entrants are generally low (see e.g. Rutter *et al.*, 1979). The more that the school emphasizes such low attainments, the less the school is likely to be valued. Schools need to find other ways of coping with this central problem.

The 1988 Education Reform Act therefore puts schools within a narrow framework within which they are held accountable. Furthermore it would seem that the relative success of different schools will be largely determined, unfairly, by factors over which they have no control. That is a depressing scenario. It is therefore necessary to ask whether there is any more optimistic and fruitful way of construing the situation.

The narrowing of the accountability framework for schools is primarily in terms of the national curriculum with its imposed attainment targets. Within the core subjects for which these targets have been specified, however, it would be difficult to argue that the attainment targets are inherently inappropriate. Criticisms have been largely about relative emphasis or lack of flexibility. It can be argued that the main problem which schools faced in recent years was an over-extension of commitments that teachers were asked to undertake. The national curriculum with its imposed attainment targets may be seen positively as offering a welcome restriction of the increasingly unmanageable range of tasks for which teachers were previously held accountable.

The plausibility of such an argument depends, of course, on whether or not schools have a genuine opportunity to engage in solving the problems which have been defined by given curricula and attainment targets. In a number of respects they clearly do. As noted, local management of schools enhances the substantial freedom schools already have to use their resources in whatever ways they think most effective. Also, the framework provided by the national curriculum and related assessment tasks does at least provide opportunities for meaningful accounting to parents in terms of what specific aspects of the curriculum have or have not been attained by a pupil and to what standards. None of this is much use, however, unless schools have that most crucial prerequisite for effectiveness: a sense of efficacy on the part of their teachers. Teachers, as much as pupils, have to believe that the problems with which they are faced are problems which they have the power to solve.

The fundamental question then relates to the possibility of a school being able to give valid and positive accounts of its efforts when, as has been suggested, its achievements are likely to be very heavily dependent on input variables beyond its control. Any alternative to the pessimistic scenario painted previously has to be dependent on construing the reality with which schools are faced in some way other than in terms of uncontrollable variables.

One such alternative can be found in the writings of Benjamin Bloom. He is interested especially in interpreting the available process-product research evidence on effective teaching in order to maximize pupils' attainments. The current situation as described would justify a brief reconsideration of some of the points which inform his work. In his book, *Human Characteristics and School Learning* (1976), Bloom establishes a way of analysing causal influences on pupils' attainments. Three sets of variables are at the heart of his thesis:

1 cognitive entry characteristics (knowledge, skills and understanding);
2 affective entry characteristics (attitudes to subject and school, and academic self-concept); and
3 quality of teaching.

Two major assumptions inform his thinking about these variables:

> Each learner begins a particular course . . . with a history which has prepared him [her] differently from other learners . . . [and] that the characteristics of the learners as well as the characteristics of the instruction can be modified.
>
> (Bloom, 1976: 13–14)

Bloom argues that cognitive entry characteristics are the most important explanatory variable in accounting for differences in attainment. In doing so, he rejects more traditional views which assume that the most useful way of explaining differences of attainment is by attributing them to relatively stable ability characteristics of the pupil.

He explains cognitive entry characteristics as various kinds of knowledge, skills and understandings which pupils will need to benefit from a course, and which they may or may not have acquired. This implies that criterion-referenced assessments should have been recorded on previous occasions and that there will be a clear continuity between those assessed prior attainments and the objectives of each new section of the curriculum. Given that most schools have been working towards profiling and records of achievement of the kind required by Bloom's analysis, and that national subject curricula have been articulated to demonstrate required continuities, the above demands are consistent with established policy. The usefulness of standard assessment tasks (SATs), for example, is dependent on internal profiling arrangements of a criterion-referenced kind so that continuity between the various stages of the national curriculum and its related assessment procedures is assured.

Bloom argues on the basis of a review of research evidence, that most differences in pupil attainments can be explained in terms of these three sets of variables: cognitive and affective entry characteristics and quality of teaching. Most crucially he demonstrates that, in explaining differences in attainment, one does not need to refer to such global and unalterable variables as general intelligence or verbal reasoning ability. He argues that the 'cognitive entry characteristics' which are the major determinants of pupils' success in learning *are* alterable and therefore potentially within the control of the school.

If this is so, then schools need not despair about being held accountable for outcomes which depend very largely on input variables beyond their control. Instead they are faced with evaluating their work on the admittedly very demanding criterion, among others, that their pupils should start each new learning task with the skills and understandings necessary to attain the learning objectives for that task.

In the final section, I draw on Bloom's ideas in looking at the evaluation questions which it might be necessary or appropriate for schools to ask in responding to accountability demands in the light of the Education Reform Act.

Evaluation questions and strategies

It is well established that the abilities of pupils entering school are closely related to their home backgrounds, most notably in terms of social class and ethnic group. Furthermore, differences in attainment amongst children from these groups tend to grow steadily wider throughout the years of compulsory schooling. At every stage of schooling, the extent to which children bring with them the abilities they need to benefit from school tasks are powerfully dependent on relationships between cultural experiences and these tasks. This being so, there can be little doubt that school effectiveness in taking account of cognitive and affective entry characteristics is largely dependent on the quality of collaboration which can be established between home, community and school in relation to these tasks. Evaluation questions about the quality and effectiveness of this collaboration would therefore have to be at the top of every school's evaluation agenda.

A second issue relates to the way differences among pupils are dealt with. If it is supposed that pupils differ widely in their inherent abilities and their potential for learning, then the increasingly wide variations in attainment predicted by TGAT (1988) in their report must be seen as inevitable; the focus for accountability will be on the adequacy with which schools *manage* the problems raised by these inevitable variations. If, on the other hand, all pupils are seen as having a similar potential for success on the national curriculum, the important evaluation questions are about how far the school has ensured that temporary differences do not become permanent, and has mobilized its resources to ensure success in tests and examinations for all pupils. To accept such a demanding responsibility may on the face of it seem rash. However, to accept anything else is to resign oneself to being held accountable for what one believes to be outside the school's control.

It is proposed therefore that schools think about their in-school development and evaluation initiatives within a *collaborative* framework:

1 teamwork incorporating groups outside the school.
2 teamwork incorporating groups within the school.

Teamwork: outside groups

Parents
Strategies of accounting such as school prospectuses and reports to parents can be used entirely as school accounting devices, whereby the school sets up a one way form of written communication with parents. While parents may learn a great deal from prospectuses about the requirements of the school, and about how well their children are meeting these requirements from school reports, schools learn very little about the home, and parental attitudes towards their children's school work.

If the schools are to establish effective ways of working with parents, much more information of this kind is required. Parent–school links have been established in some schools over such matters as reading and homework, especially with groups of parents whose children are seen to be 'at risk'. Very often, however, such innovative attempts to engage parents in the work of the school have been developed without much regard for understanding parents' perspectives or for the costs and benefits experienced by teachers, parents and pupils. If such measures were to be institutionalized as a part of school life, and in such a way as to attempt to maximize all pupils' attainments, then it would be necessary for the school to evaluate more carefully parental understandings, to evaluate existing provision and, on the basis of evaluation, to develop frequent and regular opportunities for exchange of views.

Because school prospectuses and reports are important ways of representing the work of the school to parents, and provide sources of evidence from which parents can make decisions about school effectiveness in and between schools, they are an important focus for school evaluation. If schools set out to recruit parents and to persuade parents of their collaborative intentions both prospectuses and reports can be used to communicate these aims. Thus, for example, prospectuses would include descriptions of the procedures through which the school proposes to maximize pupils' attainments and of the ways parents and teachers can collaborate (e.g. through homework) to make sure this happens. Neither prospectuses nor reports would refer to explanations which are beyond the powers of teachers or parents to change. They would concentrate instead on making explicit the standards to be met and the positive measures that can be taken by teachers in collaboration with parents to ensure that these standards are met. Evaluation of prospectuses and reports would set out to establish to what degree and in what respects they reflect such aspirations.

Other professional groups

The idea of teamwork can be extended to include other professional groups. Many schools, for example, have links with local industry and with community groups including local health and social services. While all these sources of help and support can be used to maximize pupil attainments, the schools' concerns have not always been focused on collaboration with a view to establishing prerequisites which pupils may need to meet future curriculum requirements. One useful kind of collaboration would be between primary and nursery schools, or between secondary and primary schools, where prerequisites are identified and negotiated, and the curriculum strategies in each school planned accordingly.

Schools can also make good use of professional educators from higher education, or teachers from other schools, to validate their plans for national curriculum implementation and for related assessment initiatives. The major aims of validation would be to raise consciousness amongst the planners in the school by identifying problems or gaps in the planned provision. The exercise would enable the identification of a focus for evaluation, the clarification of evaluation questions and the reconceptualization of the plans in the light of new information.

Teamwork: within the school

Drawing on Bloom's ideas, the priorities for evaluation in the school would be those questions about how far and in what respects the school has managed to ensure that temporary differences between pupils do not become permanent, and has mobilized its resources to ensure success in tests and examinations for all pupils. It is towards these ends that the principles and procedures developed within the self-evaluation tradition can be most useful.

The literature on evaluation and research techniques is extensive and can be referred to in order to explore the possibilities. Once the school has established the specific nature of the questions to be asked, then the task of finding appropriate techniques for answering the questions is not so daunting. Action research, for example, lends itself well to whole-school developments with staff in various posts studying their own practices in relation to one aspect of school policy. If evaluations are intended to serve the purposes of economic accountability, then they must also fulfil the criteria for explicit and systematic self-evaluation. What is meant by 'explicit and systematic' in this context, is that the procedures adopted should explore the validity of underlying assumptions, interpretations, implementation of plans, achievement of goals, and also possible explanations of potential failure to achieve these goals. (However, if the evidence is for internal use only then some degree of shared understandings can be assumed, although the more closely evaluations meet the criteria outlined above, the more useful they can be for sensitizing school decision-making.)

It is in the classroom, however, that pupils' attainments can be most directly influenced. It is there that learning problems are most likely to be encountered on a day-to-day basis. Following Bloom's proposals, the teachers' task would not be a simple or an easy one. In general, heads and senior staff rely on teachers to identify and solve their own classroom problems. What school managers can do to facilitate evaluation at the classroom level is to initiate, sustain and support questioning attitudes and practices among staff throughout the school. They can most usefully take measures to find out what kinds of internal or external support would be most welcomed by classroom teachers or departments; and how extra time might be found for teachers engaging in problem-solving or action research activities where time for reflection is crucial. They can also attempt to minimize administrative demands on teachers by taking on many of these tasks themselves.

With an emphasis on teamwork, senior staff in their policy-making would have to be sensitive to teachers' varying needs. There will be, for example, differences in subject philosophies and so there are likely to be aspects of a department's work which would benefit by non-standard approaches. There may also be differences in the stages of development which various departments or individuals may have reached in their understandings of what is required. In view of the considerable demands on teachers of undertaking evaluations within the self-evaluation tradition, balancing the costs and rewards for teachers would be an important factor to take into account. For example, there are increasing opportunities for teachers to undertake school-based evaluations as a way of meeting the requirements of part-time, award-bearing courses in higher education. Evaluation projects can be negotiated to suit the purposes of the school, and the scope and quality of such evaluations would benefit from the help and support of higher education personnel and local education authorities.

References

Adelman, C. and Alexander, R. (1982) *The Self-Evaluating Institution*, London, Methuen.

Bloom, B. (1976) *Human Characteristics and School Learning*, New York, McGraw-Hill.

Brown, S. (1980) *What Do They Know?*, a review of Criterion-Referenced Assessment, Edinburgh, HMSO.

Brown, S. and McIntyre, D. (1981) 'An action research approach to innovation in centralised educational systems', *European Journal of the Sociology of Education*, 3(3), 243–58.

Cameron-Jones, M. (1983) 'A researching profession? The growth of classroom research', paper given at a day seminar, University of Glasgow.

Carr, W. and Kemmis, S. (1986) *Becoming Critical*, Lewes, Falmer Press.

Coleman, J. S. (1969) 'Summary of the Coleman Report', Equal Educational Opportunity, Cambridge, Mass., Harvard University Press.

Elliott, J. (1981) 'Action research: a framework for self evaluation in schools', Working Paper, Cambridge, Cambridge Institute of Education.

Elliott, J., Bridges, D., Ebbutt, D., Gibson, R. and Nias, J. (1981) *School Accountability*, SSRC Cambridge Accountability Project, London, Grant McIntyre.

Gipps, C. (1988) 'The debate over standards and the uses of testing', *British Journal of Educational Studies*, 36(1), 21–36.

Goldstein, H. and Cuttance, P. (1988) 'A note on national assessment and school comparisons', *Journal of Educational Policy*, 3(2), 197–201.

House, E. (1972) 'The dominion of economic accountability', *Educational Forum*, 37(1).

Jencks, C. (1972) *Inequality*, New York, Harper & Row.

Lawton, D. (1988) 'Ideologies of Education' in D. Lawton and C. Chitty (eds) *The National Curriculum*, Bedford Way Papers/33, pp. 10–20, University of London, Institute of Education.

MacDonald, B. (1978) 'Accountability, standards and the process of schooling', in T. Becher and S. Maclure (eds) *Accountability in Education*, London, Holt, Rinehart & Winston.

Mansell, J. (1986) 'Records of achievement and profiles in further education', in P. Broadfoot (ed.) *Profiles and Records of Achievement*, London, Holt, Rinehart & Winston.

Nuttall, D. (1988) 'National assessment: complacency or misinterpretation?', lecture given at University of London, Institute of Education, March.

Rutter, M., Maughan, B., Mortimore, P. and Ouston, J. (1979) *Fifteen Thousand Hours*, London, Open Books.

Simons, H. (1988) *Getting to Know Schools in a Democracy*, Lewes, Falmer Press.

SIS (Statistical Information Services) (1988) *Performance Indicators for Schools*, London, Chartered Institute of Public Finance and Accountancy.

TES (*Times Educational Supplement*) (1989) 'A lump sum of low standards', reported by W. Norris, p. A17.

TGAT (Task Group on Assessment and Testing) (1988) *National Curriculum Task Group on Assessment and Testing: A Report*, London, DES and Welsh Office.

Acknowledgement

I must thank my colleague, Caroline Gipps, for her helpful comments and suggestions throughout the drafting of this paper.

8

Planning for the future in further education: beyond a curriculum-led approach

Jenny Shackleton

Introduction

The 1988 Education Reform Act is a large piece in a jigsaw of change, but not the only piece. [. . .] In 1987 it was still possible, and even easy, for many college lecturers not to know about, or to feel, the impact of curriculum trends, demographic trends, the needs of adults, the National Council for Vocational Qualifications (NCVQ), [. . .] performance indicators, the role of the Manpower Services Commission (MSC: later the Training Agency) in further education (FE), and the impending removal of barriers within the European Economic Community (EEC). [The year 1988 also saw the settlement of a new pay and conditions agreement for lecturers in further education.] The post-settlement world [. . .] includes all the above developments in more concrete form and pointed up by the Education Reform Act (ERA). If public sector FE is to have a positive role in education and training in the future, both college managers and lecturers now have a shared responsibility and an urgent need to engage in joint action which recognizes and responds to these new circumstances.

The 1980s: a decade of change

Students

The 1980s brought changes for colleges in respect of their students, curriculum, delivery methods and resources. The scale, range, timing and complexity of these changes impinged upon college lecturers in very varied and uneven ways, and added to the differences which inevitably arise from the breadth and diversity of FE's role, and the range of expertise required. Since the 1970s the patterns of movement among 16- to 19-year-olds [. . .] have been subject to major changes. Certain options such as employment dramatically declined; others expanded. The nature of each option also changed. More young people than hitherto moved into full-time education and training post-16, and the Youth Training Scheme (YTS) established the credentials of work-based learning. Among the nations which have ensured substantial participation in education and training beyond the compulsory stage, much of that education and training is explicitly work based or work related. In the United Kingdom the movement towards greater participation in post-compulsory education and training, and the involvement in this of large numbers of employers and work-places, have been a relatively recent one which is still associated by many college lecturers with youth unemployment, exploitation, and short-term crisis measures.

The piecemeal fashion in which provision for 16- to 19-year-olds, and more recently for adults, has arisen, has created confusion and ineffectiveness which has largely not been of lecturers' or colleges' making. The regulations restricting and controlling young people's and adults' entitlements have often undermined that essential sense of partnership between and among clients and providers to which the curriculum has subscribed.

Curriculum

The overwhelming majority of students and lecturers still expect their course or programme content and processes to be determined by the examining and validating bodies. The trend towards the validation of institutions by awarding bodies, and the greater involvement of staff in course design and in learning and assessment strategies is, however, having an important developmental effect upon college lecturers. In sponsoring the Technical and Vocational Education Initiative (TVEI) and YTS, the MSC (and later the Training Agency) has itself acted as validating body, but since it has had rather broader aims, and has normally not held for lecturers the esteem of an examining and validating body, it has needed to use resources, incentives and penalties to ensure compliance. The major changes which we are now witnessing in qualifying procedures have been inevitable since the MSC became involved in education and training and, in doing so, highlighted the damaging effect upon learning and achievement of a fragmented array of awards.

A number of curriculum principles have managed to survive the years of experimentation and short-term remedies, and have now achieved respectability. These include a core of learning for all students to address, together with understanding and skills for new technology.

The process of

1 induction and initial assessment
2 activity-based, individual and open learning opportunities
3 negotiation of learning programmes and targets

4 planned work or community experience
5 formative assessment and reviews
6 continuing guidance and personal support

are no longer rejected outright. However, they are subscribed to more readily than they are fulfilled. There is also broad agreement that vocational qualifications should comprise statements of attainment in competence form.

Achievement and progression

College lecturers have considerable expertise in assessment but may have applied this outside their own colleges on behalf of the examining and validating bodies, rather than internally, because of the nature of the assessment procedure laid down. However, the 1980s saw a shift away from external assessment and examinations towards internal processes. Continuing assessment, leading to profiles of achievement, encouraged less reliance on traditional examination structures and a greater sharing of aims between students and lecturers. However, the scope of these practices varies widely, as do the techniques and procedures involved.

Since college lecturers are by and large still preoccupied with developing their expertise in formative and summative assessment, they have not addressed in an incisive way the major boundary issues which are highlighted once student achievement is put to use: the currency of vocational qualifications relative to general education ones, and the interfaces between pre-16 and post-16 education, and between FE and HE and training.

In the 1980s much was spoken and written about student access and progression, but with limited effect. Provision for non-traditional students is still managed and delivered as a marginal remedial activity. Most colleges have not yet been able to provide these students with equal attention, an equal curriculum, or qualifications with high currency. Most colleges have not yet found ways of redeploying their resources to provide adequate learner support. By and large, therefore, access has come to mean exceptional entry to elements of the normal curriculum for specified disadvantaged groups. Progression through FE colleges and onwards has not been tackled in a systematic way.

A spectrum of perceptions and practices

As a result of a decade or more of frenetic change stimulated for many different reasons by a variety of agents, individual college lecturers vary dramatically in their attitudes, capability and performance. Some still live in a world which assumes student confidence and motivation, common starting-points for students, regards teaching as equating to learning, thinks only of vertical progression routes, uses set time-scales for learning and courses, uses traditional delivery methods, monitors course inputs and puts the institution first.

In the same colleges, though, increasing numbers of lecturers are acquiring the ability to

1 set achievement targets relative to assessed needs
2 accredit prior attainments
3 support individual pathways
4 apply learning and course time-scales provisionally and flexibly
5 use varied and flexible teaching and learning methods
6 provide personal support
7 monitor and review student outcomes.

To survive and be fully effective in the new circumstances, college lecturers need, consciously and collectively, to espouse and use these latter approaches.

Curriculum-led institutional development

Enormous amounts of time have been spent during the 1980s in encouraging, coaxing, persuading and sometimes bribing colleges to change. During this time, the principles and techniques of curriculum-led institutional development have been invaluable since they take account of, and build upon, the culture of FE. To quote from early working papers:

> FE colleges are concerned with structured student learning. That is what they are there to provide. It is the justification for their existence. Structured student learning is that which is planned and intended, and it is expressed through the provision of a curriculum for the student. Students learn in many other random and unstructured ways, but the responsibility of the college for their learning is bounded by the provision of the curriculum.
>
> If the prime purpose of the college is to facilitate student learning, then it can be argued that all activities of the college should directly or indirectly be supporting that learning, or at the very least should not be making it more difficult. The fundamental proposition is that the organisation, operational activities, and development of the college should be determined by the needs of the student learning programmes. This is our definition of curriculum-led institutional organisation and development.
>
> It follows that the curriculum is as much about support systems as about learning content and pedagogy, and those support systems include not only counselling and guidance for the student, but also a comprehensive management support system. It is true to say that the whole college and all its operations are part of the curriculum. It all impacts upon the students' experiences and their learning. The belief is that the management and organisational structures of colleges are

frequently not perceived in this relationship to student learning and are not defined as part of the total curriculum. Consequently they are as likely as not to work against student learning, or at least do nothing to help it. A curriculum–led approach constantly and consciously tries to keep students and their learning at the heart of things.

The adoption of a curriculum-led approach

Equally, the expression of a curriculum–led approach through seven areas of attention has enabled colleges to adjust their collective behaviour in order to become more sensitive providers of courses and more acute listeners to students' explicit or implicit messages. The headings used for applying a curriculum–led approach to

1 policy-making
2 selective resource allocation
3 managing boundary transactions
4 harnessing staff skills
5 innovative capacity
6 management systems and organizational structure

can be used to include college lecturers in audits of their collective behaviour and operations, and to achieve well-supported strategies for developing a college mission, righting historical imbalances in resourcing, structuring to encourage professional behaviour, training and support to enhance staff capability, introducing response mechanisms for change, using information for quality assurance and management, as well as for administration.

Beyond a curriculum-led approach

Curriculum–led development has a virtuous and moderate air, and wins ready support among lecturers who, as the most direct representatives of students given this approach, are also put at the 'heart of things'. However, for the circumstances we now find ourselves in, we must move forward and beyond a curriculum–led approach. We must question the implicit assumption of a curriculum–led approach that the college lecturer and the student are one and the same, and give the student a separate identity and a greater degree of autonomy. An outright learner–led approach is essential in order to redefine the role and function of colleges, and of college lecturers.

The market-place in which we offer our services is increasingly competitive. Public sector colleges will be no less partisan and competitive than the private sector wherever local authorities do not or cannot exercise their powers of strategic management within the terms of the Education Reform Act, and this may well put some colleges' survival at risk. By and large the quality assurance measures of the MSC and Training Agency eliminated most of the worst private training organizations. Within the remainder there may be people of considerable talent whom we would, in different times, be pleased to employ in our colleges. Many of those who have found a career route within the private sector, or in non-college public sector education and training, did so because at an earlier point they themselves were prevented from advancement in FE colleges. The mystique with which we at times justified our fee levels, our grip on certain qualifications, and particular student attendance patterns, has been seen through, and we have to be more honest and careful about the reasons we advance for a favourable place in the market. Further than that, we have to start providing new services and benefits which are based upon our primary purposes – to educate and train – but which go well beyond the current offering.

The lecturer-student relationship

Competitiveness in FE is being sharpened by both the fall in numbers among the younger students who are available for our traditional provision, and the impact of selective economic growth. Despite the normally very positive relationship between lecturers and students, the basic relationship is not an equal one. Younger students are not consistently viewed as clients requiring a service, and they in turn generally do not assert their rights to personal choice and respect. Our colleges may still be essentially custodial, and the physical accommodation, with its classrooms, canteens and peremptory notices, may reinforce this. The battle for access for students of all needs and abilities is being won, if to some extent because of demographic trends. However, the campaign to give students equality of esteem with lecturers is only just beginning.

The reasons for such equality are to do with the rights of an educated population, the good health of corporations and communities, and the necessary conditions for positive and recurrent learning. The pressure for a more balanced relationship is strong and irresistible, and stems from several sources. Changes in the school curriculum are, it is hoped, leading to more aware young learners who recognize that they have choices in terms of learning methods and environments, and clear rights to a wider range of services.

Alternatives to college are attractive, and have to be competed with on stronger grounds than future career prospects or HE. This is not to say that the relative powers of lecturers and students should be reversed, but that students should have assigned to them a responsibility for managing their own learning, and be equipped and expected to do so in both schools and colleges. Fortunately, in attempting to compensate for the loss of school-leavers, FE colleges are turning to the adult learner, and the services, environments and relationships which develop for older age-groups should attract and benefit the younger students also.

As the average age of our students increases, more is having to change besides the prevailing lecturer–student relationship and the setting within which they meet. Much FE provision lacks clarity of purpose either generally or in its elements. It can easily come to be seen as a good thing without further definition and evaluation. However, for adults, and increasingly for young people, education and training needs to be more overtly supportive and purposeful (though not necessarily serious) if it is to increase its attractiveness. To achieve this, purposes need to be expressed at a series of levels: the institution; the course team; the individual lecturer; the course or programme; and the learning encounter. To bring this about we must dispel the notion that by making purposes explicit we are embracing training and behaviourism. Greater clarity of purpose should include the recognition that we have a national deficiency of educational attainment, as well as of training, and the resolve to address that problem in an open manner.

The impact of NCVQ

It is evident that examining and awarding bodies have exerted, and still exert, a very powerful influence upon college lecturers' perceptions and behaviour. As a result, the number and disparateness of examining and validating bodies and qualifications has been reflected in the variety and lack of co-ordination of qualification schemes in colleges. Hierarchized and other distinctions have developed in colleges, based on external qualification factors, and types of qualifications are often still used to define boundaries between various post-16 institutions. For this reason NCVQ seems set to have at least as large an effect upon lecturers' roles and activities as the Education Reform Act or demographic trends. NCVQ has the remit to

1 secure standards of occupational competence and ensure that vocational qualifications are based on these
2 design and implement a new national framework for vocational qualifications
3 approve bodies making accredited awards
4 obtain comprehensive coverage of all occupational sectors
5 secure arrangements for quality assurance
6 set up effective liaison with bodies awarding vocational qualifications
7 establish a national data base for vocational qualifications
8 undertake or arrange for others to undertake research and development to discharge these functions
9 promote vocational education, training and qualifications.

Its framework, comprising outcomes in competence form, units, aggregate qualifications and levels, is introducing some welcome order into the proliferation of awards. However, by not setting minima and maxima to the number of units which make up a qualification, or to each unit's specificity, NCVQ may exacerbate the problems for colleges attempting to introduce a large number of the new or revised qualifications quickly. Greater consistency in both units and qualifications would assist lecturers with the design, preparation and sharing of learning materials and environments, with assessment, and with the acceptance of units and qualifications for purposes of progression. Credit transfer is an unknown and unpractised concept for many lecturers who have generally been encouraged to emphasize the distinctions between awards.

Faced with the general need to raise the nation's educational base, and the specific requirement by both TVEI and the national curriculum 5–16 to provide a core of learning, it is essential to specify a series of achievement levels in core areas such as language, mathematics, science and technology, which can support progressive and flexible vocational education and training post-16. These levels or grades would contribute another element of consistency to the vocational qualifications, could support the guidance and counselling needed to underpin a credit transfer system, and also provide a foundation for higher levels of vocational attainment. However, to help lecturers to adjust their perceptions and activity in a really radical way, NCVQ also needs to help break down the major barriers mentioned above: the distinctions between vocational and general education qualifications, and between vocational and professional qualifications and university degrees.

Whatever it has not yet managed to address, NCVQ is none the less having an impact upon colleges, setting direct challenges for lecturers at the centre of their professional identity. The National Record of Vocational Achievement has been launched, bringing with it a new type of student expectation. A significant wave of competence-based qualification schemes is now with us in the colleges.

The future?

FE tends to have been under-managed and fragmented locally, and there is a danger of its becoming more so. Concurrently, though, the service is being shaped in new ways at a national level. Alongside the less protected operating conditions for individual colleges, a stronger national framework for strategic planning for the post-16 age range emerged through NCVQ, WRNAFE and TVEI, and the provisions of ERA such as unit-based resourcing. Taken together, these devices touch all aspects of a college: its curriculum, delivery, organization, resourcing and relationships. It is essential that they are seen as a whole, and do not, in effect, cut across each other either locally or nationally. Given the pace and scale of the anticipated changes, college lecturers will be vulnerable to the effects of poor college or local management, and they need urgently to develop their means of influencing decision-making.

If we assume that the changes, trends and requirements which are evident remain and take effect, then FE colleges may in the future have the following characteristics:

1 The students' average age will be higher owing to the reduction in the number of 16- to 19-year-olds, the increase in the number of young adults, and a greater participation rate among adults of all ages. Their fees and other costs will come from a wider variety of sources, some of which the students will have needed to tap on their own behalf, with extensive assistance from colleges. Other funding sources will liaise directly with the colleges.

2 The students will regard colleges as learning centres in a broader sense, offering a variety of direct and indirect learning and qualification services. These will include information and advice, initial assessment, accreditation of prior learning, group and individual learning opportunities, assessments of achievement on demand, work learning placements, final assessments, and assistance with transfer and progression.

3 College environments will be trying to look more like other centres offering community or commercial services, with information and advice points, meeting and relaxation areas. Classrooms and workshops for group learning will take up rather less of the total available space than they do now, but supported study areas will be much in evidence for overall learning purposes, and particularly for the core curriculum.

4 More of the college's resources will be going towards its activity and image in its locality. Industry and commerce and the open community will have access to such college facilities as assessment centres, consultancies, exhibition space and publishing units as part of this. A wider range of staff will be employed, therefore, and the college will be open for the equivalent hours of a leisure or community centre.

5 A much-expanded admissions service will exploit every opportunity to recruit, offering a continuous information, assessment and advice service, and monitoring students until well into their programmes. Family classes, Saturday and Sunday opening, and summer schools will be regarded as normal and essential features of a life-long learning facility.

6 Back-up services for students and the community will include careers education and work placement facilities, information about job vacancies, and support for employment and self-employment projects.

Where will the college lecturers be in this? Perhaps they will maintain existing practices and conditions, be distinct and valued for the job done, but also less dominant within FE colleges. In this event the more autonomous student will spend more time with non-teaching staff trained in learner support techniques. Alternatively, lecturers may find ways of broadening their roles and modifying their conditions of service to take on, at a reasonable cost, a number of those support roles for which so many are ideally equipped through their insight, training and experience. Any such broadening and modification need not imply any deterioration in conditions, remuneration, effectiveness or respect. However, it does require acceptance of wholly new approaches, and also of the open, honest feedback from students, colleagues and others which is the hallmark of healthy, purposeful organizations.

To move from curriculum-led approaches to learner-led or student-led ones requires an enormous shift in the thinking and behaviour of many college lecturers, and of most colleges as a whole, including their managers. There are many good reasons as well as irrational ones to be cautious about separating learning and students from teaching and lecturers. None the less, it is time that we move on from affording students access to learning to the stage where we help to empower students and the public as a whole as responsible achievers. Such a mission could harness the considerable talents and potential of college lecturers, who are otherwise in danger of losing their confidence and creative energy in the face of accelerating change and discontinuity.

Responsible student empowerment is still some way ahead, and needs careful evolution. For the present, while most college lecturers realize and accept that changes are occurring, few have yet had the chance to grasp their significance in terms of freeing learning and personal achievement from lecturers and the act of teaching. Yet this is central to the future activities of colleges and their lecturers, and urgently calls for a shift in professional thinking and identity.

Reference

Curriculum-led Institutional Development (1984) A working paper by the FE Staff College and NICEC for FEU, January.

9

Beyond the sabre-toothed curriculum?

Ken Reid, David Hopkins and Peter Holly

One of the most entertaining and perceptive accounts of curriculum development is the parable of *New-Fist-Hammer-Maker*, New Fist, as he is more commonly known, lived in Chellean (early palæolithic) times and, according to Harold Benjamin (1939), was the first great curriculum theorist and practitioner. He is remembered best for the development of the sabre-tooth curriculum. The sabre-tooth curriculum had its origins in New Fist's aspirations for a better life for his children and, by the same token, for the tribe as a whole. Motivated by this vision he developed a curriculum that included activities such as sabre-tooth-tiger-scaring-with-fire which he taught in a practical way to his children. The benefits of such an induction into these forms of knowledge soon became evident. Despite initial objections by the more conservative and theologically minded members of the tribe (objections that New Fist, being a statesman as well as a curriculum theorist, deftly overcame), tiger-scaring and the other activities soon became accepted as the heart of true education.

All continued well for some generations until the approach of a new ice age drastically changed the environment. The skills acquired through the sabre-tooth curriculum were no longer appropriate to the new conditions in the cave realm and the prosperity and equanimity of the tribe suffered. The spirit of New Fist, however, lived on in the new generation, some of whom proposed a new curriculum more suited to the current situation. These radical proposals were ridiculed by the tribal elders as being mere training; the suggestion that the new activities required as much intelligence and skill as the traditional curriculum was regarded as facetious. Unlike New Fist the tribal elders were neither thinkers nor doers, theorists nor statesmen, as evidenced by statements like:

We don't teach tiger-scaring to scare tigers; we teach it for the purposes of giving noble courage which carries over into all the affairs of life . . . true education is timelessness. It is something that endures through changing conditions like a solid rock standing squarely and firmly in the middle of a raging torrent. You must know that there are some eternal verities and the sabre tooth curriculum is one of them.

The parable [. . .] raises so many issues that we would require another chapter at least to elucidate them. Issues such as education versus training; vocational relevance; transfer of learning; the implementation of innovation; and the calumny of vested interests . . . are all as important now as they were in 1939, let alone Chellean times. Space obviously precludes such discussions but there are three points that we want particularly to highlight. The first is that the term curriculum is an ambiguous one; it is open to many differing interpretations and can be put to many different purposes. The second is that successful teaching is related to thoughtful and systematic curriculum planning. The third is that the responsibility for curriculum development needs to be located close to the classroom. We begin with the sabre-tooth parable because it is entertaining and illuminating, the lessons one can derive from it provide a context for what follows – the attempt to see how far we have progressed in curriculum development since Chellean times.

[. . .]

Perceptions and models

[. . .]

We must be aware of the distinction between the 'formal' and the 'hidden' curriculum. The formal curriculum comprises the academic intentions of the course of study; what is supposed to be taught and learned in school. The hidden curriculum, on the other hand, is concerned more with the social side of education; the values and expectations that pupils acquire as a result of going through the schooling process. Although not part of the formal intentions of schooling, the hidden curriculum has the most powerful and lasting impact on most children. We are inevitably concerned with the formal rather than the hidden curriculum but this does not reflect their respective importance, either in our eyes or in reality. As Cusick (1973) among others, has argued, high schools tend to spend over two-thirds of their time involved in maintenance (or hidden curriculum) activities rather than instructional (or formal curriculum) activities; and, of course, the two are inevitably connected. The derivation of content for the curriculum – what is taught or not taught (see Eisner's *Null Curriculum* (1979)), what subjects are accorded high and low status and who is taught what, are all arguably aspects of the hidden curriculum. So, too, is how we teach the content – because differing teaching styles imply differing classroom climates and levels of pupil participation. The 'nurturant conditions', to use Joyce and Weil's (1980) phrase, are associated with different models of teaching that have a wide and differential impact on pupils. [. . .]

Eisner (1979) points to five basic orientations to the curriculum that underlie the purposes of schooling. Others have described similar influences: Lawton (1983), for example, discusses three or four basic educational ideologies; and Carr and Kemmis (1983) identify eight traditions in the study of education.

The differences between these ideas are less important than the general point. Behind any educational enterprise there is an ideological or philosophical force or forces pushing it forward, which provide a context or set of parameters in which to consider that form of schooling. Schooling and education are always embedded in a set of wider values and although they are often vague, implicit and even contradictory, it is important for us to realize their existence, because to some extent they control and inhibit our freedom of action and inevitably our purpose.

The first of Eisner's orientations is the 'development of cognitive processes'. Here the emphasis is on developing pupils' intellectual capacity and helping them learn how to learn more effectively. The second, 'academic rationalism', refers to the induction of pupils into worthwhile activities and forms of knowledge. The goal is the developing of an educated person, one who is competent in and familiar with the products of humanity's highest achievements. By engaging with these ideas and achievements the individual will inevitably develop rationality and acquire wisdom. The third orientation is 'personal relevance', and its most common expression is the child–centred curriculum. This approach requires that the curriculum and the teacher are aware of each pupil's abilities, experience and predisposition, and that a course of study is developed which builds on those unique qualities. The fourth orientation is 'social adaptation and social reconstruction'. In this approach it is the society's needs that are paramount and the school's purpose is seen explicitly as serving these needs. The billion dollar investment in the USA in science and math curricula in the decade following the Soviet success with Sputnik in 1957 is an example of this. So, too, is the recent emphasis on vocational education in the UK and the instrumental nature of many national curricula in the Third World. Finally, Eisner points to the idea of 'curriculum as technology'. Here the emphasis is not so much on the aims or context of curricula but on the means of achieving them. It is an approach that values efficiency, the measurement of observable achievement, and making schools, teachers and curricula accountable. Mastery teaching, standardized tests, systematic instruction and school accountability are all examples of this tendency. The behavioural objectives model for curriculum planning that we will soon be discussing is perhaps the most common example of this orientation.

In this brief description of the five orientations [. . .] we have not claimed that one orientation is necessarily better than another. Each has been discussed because it enables us more clearly to analyse the purpose of schooling. They provide us with a context within which to consider our own practice and aspirations. Also, it is unlikely that any school or educational system will exhibit characteristics of just one orientation. They are more likely to be found in combination. A useful exercise is to create a matrix using the five orientations and contemporary examples of schooling in England and Wales. Such a matrix would look a little like Figure 9.1.

There are virtually as many models of how to go about developing the curriculum, as there are definitions of the term. Model development is a game that academics play and on the whole it is of little help to teachers, because many models tend to be descriptive rather than prescriptive or specific. They describe their originators' somewhat idiosyncratic views of the educational world, which may or may not be very interesting, and give little information to the practitioner on how to proceed. Naturally there are exceptions, and in the following section we describe a curriculum model that we believe possesses some practical utility. There are also a number of models that deserve mention on the grounds of tradition, usage or appositeness. To two of these we now briefly turn.

The Tyler model

The best known of the curriculum models is that associated with Ralph Tyler, derived from his seminal book *Basic Principles of Curriculum and Instruction* (1949). So ubiquitous is Tyler's model that many claim that it is the *only* way to develop curricula. Somewhat dismayed by the capricious and whimsical, if not downright sloppy, approach to curriculum development

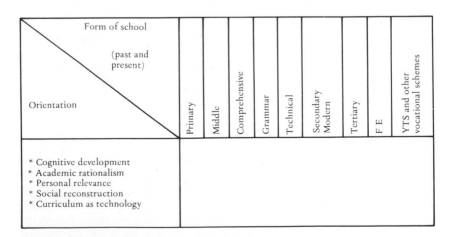

Figure 9.1 The five orientations of schooling

that he witnessed in the USA in the 1940s, Tyler proposed as an antidote a systematic and beguilingly simple approach to curriculum planning based around four questions:

1 What educational purposes should the school seek to attain?
2 What educational experiences can be provided that are likely to attain these purposes?
3 How can these educational experiences be effectively organized?
4 How can we determine whether these purposes are being attained?

The so-called 'Tyler rationale' is often expressed in an even more simplified form:

Objectives
↓
Content
↓
Organization
↓
Evaluation

The Tyler model has been enormously influential, so much so that most curriculum or lesson plans appear to be based on this approach to some extent. Two points should be made about the model at the outset. The first is that by beginning with objectives one begs the question: where do they come from? Some of Tyler's students, who became important curriculum figures in their own right, provided some answers. Benjamin Bloom and his colleagues (1956) produced a taxonomy of educational objectives that provide a ready-made solution for the problem. Hilda Taba (1962) proposed a needs assessment stage that precedes the derivation of objectives. These solutions have served to satisfy most practitioners, but in many ways the problem still remains a real one. The second point relates to the evaluative aspect of the model. The only way to evaluate this type of curriculum scheme is through observing some change in behaviour on the part of the pupil that signifies achievement of the objective. In turn, that objective has to be expressed in behavioural terms so that the achievement can be observed and evaluated. In its pure form the model looks something like the diagram shown in Figure 9.2.

In the diagram, behavioural objectives result from some interaction between the general aim of the curriculum, the content to be taught, and the perceived pupil characteristics. The resulting list of objectives is then tested on the class and as a consequence possibly changed. This provides a base line measure of the pupils' achievement. The teaching/learning process then ensues and the curriculum episode ends with another test that serves to assess the overall pupil achievement on the curriculum. Rarely is the process like this. Testing, particularly the original test, is often omitted. So too is the revision of objectives. Also, the objectives are usually not established with

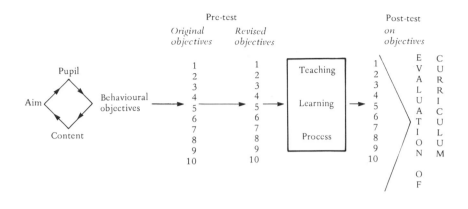

Figure 9.2   The flow of the Tyler model

any degree of precision. But the objectives approach is seen in one form or another in most curriculum designs.

Unfortunately, the objectives model is no panacea. Although it is suitable for certain teaching/learning situations its almost universal application is deleterious. There are a number of well-established critiques of the behavioural objectives model (e.g. Eisner, 1979; Stenhouse, 1975; Rudduck and Hopkins, 1985), but we will briefly rehearse some of the objections here. First, the objectives model trivializes the nature of knowledge. By fitting a subject into an objectives format there is the danger that the essence of, say, history will be reduced to a recitation of the Kings and Queens of England. It is very difficult to represent the deep structure of a subject – in this case, the historical method of inquiry, in an objectives format. How does one prepare an objective or series of objectives for appreciating *Hamlet*? So although the objectives approach may be very effective in transmitting information or skills it is unsuited to more complex forms of knowledge. Second, the objectives model tends to make for predictable pupil outcomes. This is to be welcomed when one is concerned with mathematical or scientific formulae, but to be regretted when one is concerned with poetry or art appreciation. Third, the model does not accord with reality. The teaching/learning process in general does not work like that. We teach in a more idiosyncratic and capricious way; often long periods of effort are followed by a sudden burst of understanding. It is only infrequently that we learn in carefully packaged, uniform and relatively short periods of time. Fourth, the approach, although it often increases the clarity of educational programmes, does little, for reasons already outlined, to increase the quality of educational performance. Finally, the model ignores the ethical, moral and political imperatives surrounding schooling. Questions such as 'Is this the appropriate content to teach?' are of no importance in this approach.

In discussing the objectives model we have tried to point both to its advantages and its drawbacks. It is the most common form of curriculum design. It has had enormous influence, but is appropriate only in certain, often instrumental, subject areas. Later we will propose a process model as a more appropriate means of dealing with more complex subject areas.

Lawton's model

The other approach to curriculum design that we will briefly describe, although not as well known or as useful as Tyler's (being descriptive rather than prescriptive), is that associated with Denis Lawton (1973; 1983). His basic idea is of the curriculum as being a selection from the culture and he argues for a cultural analysis approach to curriculum. A slightly adapted version of his model appears in Figure 9.3.

Lawton has an eminently common-sense approach to curriculum in his writing. We find his 'selection from culture' notion very helpful, especially the tension or dialectic that exists between philosophical approaches, for example Hirst's forms of knowledge, and the sociological or relativist attitude of writers like Young.

Lawton originally envisaged psychology as operating on the selection from the culture, but given current constraints practical issues may be more appropriate. Certainly psychological considerations play (or should play) an

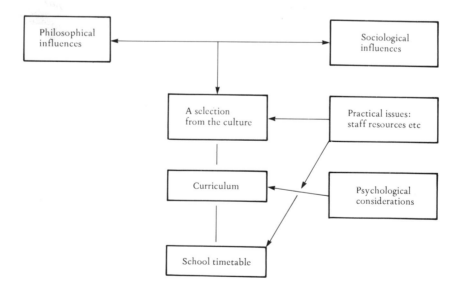

Figure 9.3 Lawton's model

important part in shaping the curriculum and in its presentation to pupils. To us Lawton's model has two main virtues: first, its central organizing concept of curriculum as a selection from the culture; second, the prominence it gives to philosophical, sociological and psychological factors in determining the curriculum. But as we said previously, it is a descriptive model and its utility is limited because it gives teachers no indication of how to proceed. It is to a curriculum development model that offers such practical advice that we now turn.

A model for curriculum development

Figure 9.4 (see p. 113) represents our model for curriculum development (based on Gibbons, 1977: his work on self-directed learning has had a major impact on education in North America). There are seven major stages in the model; each stage has its own kind of task, its own kind of process and its own product (see Table 9.1).

Table 9.1 The seven stages in the curriculum development model

Task	Process	Product
1 *Identify* what job the curriculum has to do	*Analyse* the situation	A clear *purpose* for curriculum development
2 *Formulate* a means of achieving the purpose	*Design* a curriculum concept	A promising *theoretical model* of the curriculum
3 *Select* an appropriate *teaching strategy* for the curriculum	*Establish* principles of procedure for students and teachers when using the curriculum	A specific *teaching/ learning* strategy
4 *Produce* the curriculum delivery system	*Develop* the means required to present and maintain the curriculum	An *operational curriculum*
5 *Experiment* with the curriculum on student learning and the school	*Refine* the model through classroom research and regular improvements	A *refined curriculum*
6 *Implement* the curriculum throughout the school in other settings	*Change* general practice to the new curriculum	A *widely used curriculum*
7 *Evaluate* the effects of the curriculum on student learning	*Evaluate* how effective the curriculum is	A *proven* curriculum

At any point in curriculum development, difficulties may emerge which require returning to an earlier cycle and redoing the work. Alternatively, an opportunity for a major improvement may emerge which makes reconsideration of the earlier work desirable. When the whole cycle is successfully completed, so much will have been learned in the process that the curriculum developer will be well equipped to begin again.

Although the cycle has seven major stages it is, of course, not necessary to complete each stage in order to produce an effective product. An individual teacher might only engage in the Formulation, Teaching Strategy and Production stages if he or she simply wanted to design a new unit. Another teacher may start with classroom research, then find out that the teaching strategy needs altering and, having done that, go back to classroom research again. Alternatively, a fairly major curriculum innovation would most probably require work in each cycle. In a similar sense, the model is generic in so far as it applies to teachers wanting to develop a unit or a course as well as to curriculum developers on major national projects. The model is prescriptive because, as compared with the descriptive models discussed earlier, it provides a guide to action; it helps teachers and others become more systematic and reflective about the curriculum development task.

The model is also relatively value free, in so far as it represents no overt world view (except one that encourages systematic and self-conscious planning and reflection on the part of teachers). This enables the range of ideological perspectives on the curriculum to be accommodated.

An illustration of this last point is given in Table 9.2 (see p. 114), which summarizes a great deal of information about curriculum development. The first column contains the elements of the curriculum development cycle. The second column lists the activities that traditionally occur in each of the seven stages. These are activities that tend to underplay the teacher's role and occur mainly as the result of some external initiative by, for example, the Department of Education and Science. Most teachers will recognize these activities. The third column represents teacher-based activities that can also occur within each of these stages as an alternative to the traditional approach. The table clearly illustrates that teacher- or school-based approaches to curriculum development are both available and viable. The table is not supposed to be taken too literally (or seriously). It certainly does not imply a dichotomy between the two approaches. Its main purpose is to illustrate how a range of experiences, aspirations and activities can be contained within the model. In the following discussion of the stages, however, illustrations of different approaches will be discussed.

Identification

The *identification* stage establishes a clear purpose for the curriculum. It is the rationale; if there is no purpose or rationale then there is no point in

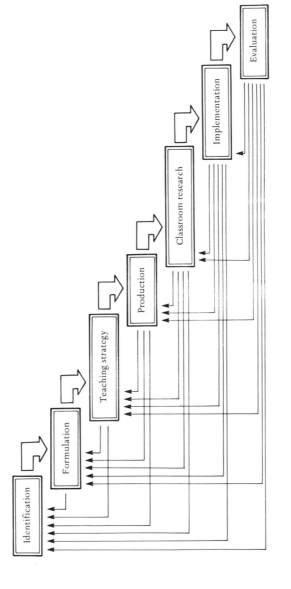

Figure 9.4 A curriculum development cycle

Table 9.2 Alternative approaches to curriculum development

Stage	Traditional	Teacher-based
Identification	Prescribed curriculum/ forms of knowledge	Community based or pupil needs
Formulation	Behavioural objectives	Process model and principles of procedure
Teaching strategy	Teacher centred, didactic	Enquiry/discovery approaches, active learning etc.
Production	Centrally produced curricula	Locally developed programmes
Classroom research	Quantitative analysis	Doing research in your classroom
Implementation	Fidelity	Mutual adaptation
Evaluation	Quantitative, empirical and objective	Qualitative, illuminative and subjective

proceeding. Curricula are, of course, open to varying purposes, a number of which we have already discussed. A well-known polarity within this stage is the distinction between classical and romantic approaches to the curriculum. Lawton's (1973) view of the debate is as follows:

Classical	*Romantic*
Subject-centred	Child-centred
Skills	Creativity
Instruction	Experience
Information	Discovery
Obedience	Awareness
Conformity	Originality
Discipline	Freedom

He continues:

> When it comes to questions of knowledge and curriculum the two views might be polarised as follows (but to subdivide in this way may be unfair to the Romantic view as the following list is set out in the Classical framework):

Classical	*Romantic*
Objectives: Acquiring knowledge	*Processes:* 'Living' attitudes and values
Content: Subjects	*Experience:* Real-life topics and projects

Methods:

Didactic instruction	Involvement
Competition	Co-operation

Evaluation:

By tests (teacher set) and examinations (public and competitive)	Self-assessment (in terms of self-improvement)

Inevitably these views are stereotypical but they do give an indication of the types of activities that can flow from such an orientation. The classical view has probably been best stated by Hirst in his concept of 'forms of knowledge'. Hirst (Hirst and Peters, 1970) argues that we can distinguish seven forms of knowledge:

1 Formal logic and mathematics
2 The physical sciences
3 'Our awareness and understanding of our own and other people's minds'
4 Moral judgement and awareness
5 Aesthetic experience
6 Religious
7 Philosophical

Lawton (1973) summarizes Hirst's position by saying that he justifies the categorization of knowledge into these seven forms on the grounds that all concepts belong to distinct categories, which are marked out by 'certain fundamental, ultimate or categorical concepts of a most general kind which other concepts in the category presuppose'. A good example of the influence of this is found in many DES/HMI publications on the curriculum.

The alternative notion, as represented by the 'romantic' argument, is that the curriculum should be based on the pupils' needs: that we must diagnose them and then build a curriculum around them. [. . .]

From even this brief discussion it can be seen that the identification stage is not only very important but also fraught with opposing views. Two other sources of curriculum purpose, relevant to the contemporary UK scene, need to be discussed. First is the function of curriculum in the eyes of central government. Curriculum innovations like TVEI began with the government (in this case the MSC) identifying the purpose of the curriculum and then allowing LEAs to complete the curriculum development cycle. The other very powerful source of curriculum initiative is the examination boards. Although times are changing a little, past examination papers still play an important part in the identification stage of curriculum development.

Formulation

The formulation stage involves developing new ideas or improving old ones already developed which promise to fulfil the purpose already identified for the curriculum. In other words it offers strategies for answering the question: what is the best design which can be treated to fulfil the rationale for the curriculum?

As we have discussed already, behavioural objectives are the most commonly used method for formulating the curriculum; but teachers also realize that they are not the only way. Behavioural objectives are an excellent means for teaching skills or evaluating rote learning. However, they can be counter-productive in more complex and sophisticated content areas. For example, it is difficult to formulate behavioural objectives for a lesson on *Hamlet* or poetry appreciation and still remain faithful to the subject matter. The over-use of behavioural objectives has sometimes tended to reduce, say, the study of history to a series of dates or geography to a recitation of capes and bays. Stenhouse (1975) has said that 'Education as induction into knowledge is successful to the extent that it makes the behavioural outcomes of the students unpredictable.' In situations such as these it is better to put pre-specified behavioural objectives aside, and utilize some other organizing principle.

The process model is an alternative. This name was coined by Stenhouse to describe his alternative approach to curriculum development as exemplified in the *Humanities Curriculum Project* (Stenhouse, 1975; Rudduck and Hopkins, 1985). The process model does not specify the behaviour the student is to acquire after having engaged in a learning activity, rather it describes an educational encounter. It identifies a situation in which children are to work, a problem with which they are to cope, or a task in which they are to engage. By the use of the process model teachers can formulate educational encounters that respect both the child and the integrity of the knowledge with which they interact.

There are three basic approaches to developing a curriculum on a process model. The first is the approach identified with the work of Eisner (1979). Like many others Eisner was dissatisfied with the behavioural objectives approach, for reasons similar to the ones previously discussed. He advocated the use of expressive objectives in the areas where behavioural (or in his terms instructional) objectives were inappropriate. The expressive objective defines an educational encounter without specifying what the pupil is to learn from that encounter. Eisner (quoted in Stenhouse, 1975) says that 'an expressive objective provides both the teacher and the student with an invitation to explore, defer, or focus on issues that are of peculiar interest or import to the inquirer. An expressive objective is evocative rather than prescriptive.'

He continues by giving examples:

Statements of expressive objectives might read:

1 To interpret the meaning of *Paradise Lost*.
2 To examine and appraise the significance of *The Old Man and the Sea*.

3 To develop a three-dimensional form through the use of wire and wood.
4 To visit the zoo and discuss what was of interest there.

What should be noted about such objectives is that they do not specify what the student is to be able to do after he engages in an educational activity; rather they identify the type of encounter he is to have.

While entirely in sympathy with Eisner's argument we find his examples very loose: they provide no structure within which pupils or teachers can effectively explore their new-found freedom. The lack of structure, guidance or parameters is a serious drawback and will inevitably lead to aimless teaching and spasmodic learning.

A more satisfactory avenue for the process model is provided by Jerome Bruner and his concept of structure (Bruner, 1963; 1966). Following the logic of philosophers like Hirst, Bruner argues that each discipline has a structure which determines the way knowledge evolves or is produced within it. In history, for example, knowledge is produced through locating, analysing and making judgements based upon evidence. This historical method determines the way in which historical knowledge is developed. Similarly in science, knowledge advances through controlled experimentation commonly known as the scientific method. Bruner argues that this structure provides an effective model for teaching and learning. Curricula can be formulated by following the method of 'real' historians or scientists, using the historical or scientific method to structure the curriculum. Instead of teaching historical or scientific knowledge we teach how to do history or science and accumulate our knowledge in this way. Bruner would argue that we should introduce pupils to the process of knowledge. In his own words, 'Knowledge is a process not a product'. He further argues that 'any body of knowledge can be presented in a form simple enough so that any particular learner can understand it in a recognisable form'. The implication of this is that the historical or scientific approach to learning can and should be introduced in the primary school. These ideas and processes are then refined and become more sophisticated as one goes through the school: hence his notion of the spiral curriculum. [. . .] Many of the Schools Council curriculum projects were built on this model. The *History 13–16*, *Science 5–13* and, of course, Bruner's influential *Man, a Course of Study* (MACOS) were all examples of these. However, not all curriculum subjects are dignified by the label 'discipline' – so how does one proceed here?

'Principles of procedure' was the approach that Stenhouse and his colleagues adopted in the *Humanities Curriculum Project*. Faced with producing a curriculum on controversial issues for pupils of school leaving age in an area with no established tradition, they began by specifying the principles upon which the curriculum should be based. The following two extracts illustrate their approach.

The Humanities Curriculum Project, sponsored by the Schools Council and the Nuffield Foundation, was set up in September 1967 to extend the range of choice open to teachers working in the humanities with adolescent pupils.

The work of the Project has been based upon five major premises:

1 that controversial issues should be handled in the classroom with adolescents;
2 that teachers should not use their authority as teachers as a platform for promoting their own views;
3 that the mode of enquiry in controversial areas should have discussion rather than instruction as its core;
4 that the discussion should protect divergence of view among participants;
5 that the teacher as chairperson of the discussion should have responsibility for quality and standards in learning.

If teachers have reserves about any of these premises, the easiest procedure is to adopt them with due scepticism as an exploratory tactic. This will allow them to use the experimental findings of the project for support as they evaluate the likely effects of changing the premises.

The aim of the Project is to develop an understanding of social situations and human acts and of the value issues which they raise.

(Rudduck, 1983: 8)

In this project, discussion was the main mode of inquiry and the teacher acted as a neutral chairperson. Discussion was informed and disciplined by evidence: that is, items of material from history, journalism, literature, philosophy, art, photography, statistics might be introduced. . . . Here are summarised the kinds of demand which this curriculum project made on teachers, pupils and schools:

New skills for most teachers
1 Discussion rather than instruction.
2 Teacher as neutral chairperson – that is, not communicating his or her point of view.
3 Teacher talk reduced to about 15%.
4 Teacher handling material from different disciplines.
5 New modes of assessment.

New skills for most pupils
1 Discussion, not argument or debate.
2 Listening to, and talking to, each other, not just to the teacher.
3 Taking initiatives in contributing – not being cued in by teacher.

New content for many classrooms
1 Explorations of controversial social issues, often in the sensitive areas (e.g. race relations, poverty, family, relations between the sexes).

2 Evidence reproduced in an original form – no simplifications of language.

Organisational demands on schools
1 Small discussion groups, each with teacher chairperson.
2 Mixed ability groups found by many schools to be desirable.
3 Non-row formation of chairs – circle or rectangle appearing to be desirable.

(Rudduck 1984: 57–8)

From these considerations a set of highly specific principles was developed that provided a structure for both pupils and teachers despite the open-ended nature of the curriculum and the radical teaching/learning process it adopted.

In contrasting the behavioural objectives and process models we are not arguing that one is necessarily better than the other. They are complementary approaches; each has the potential of working well but in different areas.

Teaching strategy

Implicit in the formulation stage is a teaching strategy that transmits the content of the curriculum. In our view the teaching strategy is equally as important as the content that the curriculum delivers. There was a time when many teachers felt that there was only one way to teach – the didactic or 'mug and jug' approach – but fortunately times change. We became increasingly aware that pupils learn in different ways and all are not amenable to a uniform approach. The Schools Council in their advocacy of enquiry/discovery learning, and the curriculum innovations like TVEI that promoted 'active learning', were all moves away from the traditional approach.

It is also important to consider at this stage of curriculum development the various assessment procedures associated with the curriculum. The adoption of profiling, for example, had a powerful impact upon teaching style.

Bruce Joyce *et al.* (1981) espoused 'flexibility' as a guiding principle for *professional* development. This represents

a view of humankind that envisions people-in-teaching and people-in-learning as the creators of themselves through their interaction. Flexibility from that stance, becomes an essential characteristic of the teacher as s/he creates her/himself, offers possibilities to his/her students, and creates the schools of the future.

A central component of flexibility is the teacher's ability intelligently to use a variety of teaching approaches, to match them to different goals, and adapt them to different student styles and characteristics. To quote Joyce again:

'Competence in teaching stems from the capacity to reach out to differing children and to create a rich and multi-dimensional environment for them.' In their *Models of Teaching* (1980), Joyce and Weil describe four families of teaching approaches: the information-processing, the personal, the social interaction, and the behavioural models. They argue that 'since no single teaching strategy can accomplish every purpose, the wise teacher will master a sufficient repertoire of strategies to deal with the specific kinds of learning problems he or she faces'. They suggest that teachers begin by mastering one model from each family, and then add others as they are found useful to each individual's particular teaching speciality. It is easier to learn models in collaboration with others (e.g. a colleague or student teacher), because the other person can help coach you (and vice versa) on the finer points of teaching style. [. . .]

Production

Production is the stage where the ideas and aspirations are operationalized. At the end of this stage the curriculum is ready to go, ready to be used and shared. The scale of production will vary according to the size of the product, whether it be a teacher producing a new unit or a team working on a national curriculum project. Nevertheless, resources have to be collected and organized, staff trained in the new teaching methods and the timetable possibly altered.

The following extract from the original model – although somewhat 'North American' in style – gives a good indication of what is required at this stage (see Figure 9.5).

(*a*) production needs
- materials
- methods training
- role changes
- environments
- organisation

(*b*) organise for production:
- cover arranged to free teachers regularly for preparation
- time line for completion of materials and arrangements set
- working teams appointed

(*c*) produce materials and arrangements:
- planning committee receives materials and monitors arrangements
- critical examination of all materials and other elements of setting: they are revised

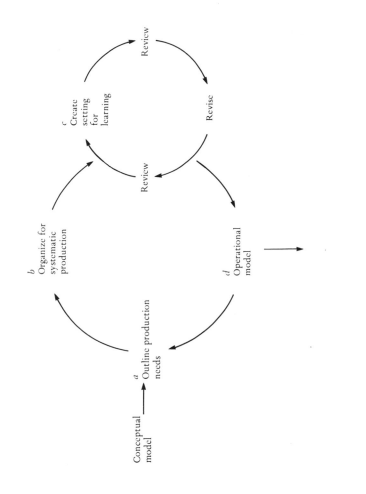

Figure 9.5 The production model

> - materials pilot-tested and modified from feedback; the gaps are filled and further revisions made

(*d*) operational model: - 'central planning' declares the curriculum operational

Gibbons (1977) describes the strategies required for the production stage like this:

> *Production:* Strategies for making the curriculum operational; producing guides, texts and other materials; creating settings, training personnel, and organising the necessary support systems. Strategies for answering the questions, what must be prepared to make this curriculum design usable? How can this be done efficiently and effectively?

He then gives an example:

> The school's curriculum development committee outlined the tasks, divided the work among sub-committees and drew up a production schedule. A new space was found and set up like an editorial room. A teaching handbook of skills and content was written and reproduced. Teaching materials were prepared, reference libraries assembled, and training sessions on the teaching method were provided.

Classroom research

The purpose of this stage is to field-test the curriculum in the classroom, and to refine it through regular improvement. It is important that teachers retain an enquiring and experimental attitude towards a curriculum, irrespective of whether they have produced it themselves or adapted it from elsewhere. A curriculum proposal should never be taken as given but rather regarded as a working hypothetical proposal. Stenhouse (1975) remarks that 'the proposal is not to be regarded as an unqualified recommendation but rather as a provisional specification claiming no more than to be worth putting to the test of practice. Such proposals claim to be intelligent rather than correct.' The ways in which teachers engage in systematic self-study *and* test theory in practice are essentially the same: through the use of classroom research methods.

Classroom research is normally associated with outside researchers measuring the effect and outcomes of classroom activity. In a teacher-based context the phrase has a very different meaning. It implies that the teacher is actively engaged in critically reflecting on his or her teaching by utilizing classroom-based research methods. This is a fundamental role for a teacher who takes professional development seriously, for it is only by understand-

ing our present behaviours, that we can expect to extend or change them.
[. . .]

The purpose of this stage is to revise the curriculum in the light of experience and consequently to produce a better curriculum and so improve the teaching/learning process. When we are dealing with larger curriculum projects then we need to consider the implementation and evaluation stages.

Implementation

Implementation is an aspect of curriculum development that has recently received a great deal of attention. The predominant modality in the traditional approach is 'fidelity': the expectation that a new curriculum will be faithfully implemented and exactly reproduced in the receiving environment. The situation usually occurs when curriculum development begins centrally and then diffuses outwards. Often this expectation is not realized because the context of the local environment is not considered. Under the teacher-based paradigm there is the expectation that the curriculum will be adapted to the local situation. The norm of mutual adaptation implies that both the curriculum and the school or classroom will change as the process of implementation occurs. Thus, the teacher exercises control over the adoption of curriculum in his or her teaching situation.

The implementation process is multidimensional, involving change at a number of different levels. Five components of implementation can be identified. These involve changes in organization, materials, role and behaviour, knowledge, and beliefs.

Changes in organization (e.g. restructuring the timetable to accommodate new options) and materials (e.g. the introduction of a new published reading scheme) are achieved relatively easily. Indeed, it is these two components of implementation that are most often tackled; to the detriment of the others. Yet it is on the necessary changes in teaching style, understanding and commitment, that the success or failure of implementation depends. These are, of course, the most difficult to effect as they also require heavy involvement in time and inservice provision. Successful implementation depends on the meanings and attitudes that teachers give and have towards the curriculum. To recall Stenhouse's evocative phrase 'there is no curriculum development without teacher development'.

Evaluation

A distinction is often made between formative and summative evaluation. The former is concerned with providing ongoing information to improve the quality of the curriculum. Summative evaluation is concerned to provide a judgement on the success of the curriculum. The formative aspects of evaluation occur in our model at the classroom research stage. This final stage is more concerned with summative judgement, on how good the curriculum is after it has been implemented for a period of time. [. . .]

After the conclusion of this cycle, the process of development begins again with the search for new opportunities for growth and new purpose in development.

'No curriculum development without teacher development'

The hidden curriculum behind the curriculum model is that it is a method that teachers can employ to make their curriculum planning more effective. It is a process not only for curriculum development but also for making teachers more skilful and more effective; of putting them more in control of the curriculum and the teaching/learning process. Only teachers can create good teaching, and thus it is imperative that they occupy a central role in developing the curriculum and that *they* develop with the curriculum.

Stenhouse adopted this principle as a central point of his work. As a conclusion to the discussion of the curriculum model, consider this quotation from the work of Lawrence Stenhouse:

> 'No curriculum development without teacher development', reads one of the poker-work mottoes we hung on our wall during the Humanities Project and haven't taken down. But that does not mean, as it often seems to be interpreted to mean, that we must train teachers in order to produce a world fit for curricula to live in. It means that by virtue of their meaningfulness, curricula are not simply instructional means to improve teaching but are expressions of ideas to improve teachers. Of course, they have a day-to-day instructional utility: cathedrals must keep the rain out. But the students benefit from curricula not so much because they change day-to-day instruction as because they improve teachers.
>
> A curriculum, if it is worthwhile, expresses in the form of teaching materials and criteria for teaching a view of knowledge and a conception of the processes of education. It provides a framework in which the teacher can develop new skills and relate them as he/she does so to conceptions of knowledge and of learning.
>
> Only in curricular form can ideas be tested by teachers. Curricula are hypothetical procedures testable only in classrooms. All educational ideas must find expression in curricula before we can tell whether they are day-dreams or contributions to practice. Many educational ideas are not found wanting because they cannot be found at all.
>
> We must be dedicated to the improvement of schooling. The improvement of schooling is bound to be experimental: it cannot be dogmatic. The experiment depends on the exercise of the art of

teaching and improves that art. The substantive content of the arts of teaching and learning is curriculum.

(Rudduck and Hopkins, 1985: 68–9)

References

Benjamin, H. (J. A. Peddiwell 1939) *The Saber Tooth Curriculum*, New York McGraw-Hill.

Bloom, B. (ed.) (1956) *The Taxonomy of Educational Objectives: 1 The Cognitive Domain*, London, Longman.

Bruner, J. (1963) *The Process of Education*, New York, Random House.

Bruner, J. (1966) *Towards a Theory of Instruction*, Boston, Mass., Harvard University Press.

Carr, W. and Kemmis, S. (1983) *Becoming Critical: Knowing through Action Research*, Victoria, Australia, Deakin University Press.

Cusick, P. (1973) *Inside High School*, New York, Holt, Rinehart & Winston.

Eisner, E. (1979) *The Educational Imagination*, New York, Macmillan.

Gibbons, M. (1977) 'A model of curriculum development', British Columbia, Simon Fraser University, mimeograph.

Hirst, P. and Peters, R. (1970) *The Logic of Education*, London, Routledge & Kegan Paul.

Joyce, B. and Weil, M. (1980) *Models of Teaching*, 2nd edn, New York, Prentice-Hall.

Joyce, B. *et al.* (1981) *Flexibility in Teaching*, London and New York, Longman.

Lawton, D. (1973) *Social Change, Educational Theory and Curriculum Planning*, London, Hodder & Stoughton.

Lawton, D. (1983) *Curriculum Studies and Educational Planning*, London, Hodder & Stoughton.

Rudduck, J. (1983) *The Humanities Curriculum Project: An Introduction*, revised edn, Norwich, University of East Anglia/Schools Council.

Rudduck, J. (1984) 'Introducing innovation to pupils', in D. Hopkins and M. Wideen (eds) *Alternative Perspectives on School Improvement*, Lewes, Falmer Press.

Rudduck, J. and Hopkins, D. (1985) *Research as a Basis for Teaching*, London, Heinemann.

Stenhouse, L. (1975). *An Introduction to Curriculum Research and Development*, London, Heinemann.

Taba, H. (1962) *Curriculum Development: Theory and Practice*, New York, Harcourt Brace Jovanovich.

Tyler, R. (1949) *Basic Principles of Curriculum and Instruction*, Chicago, Ill., Chicago University Press.

10

Organizational pathos and the school

Eric Hoyle

The trouble with school [teachers] is that they think all problems are soluble. They aren't.

(Stanley Middleton *The Daysman*)

There is a pathos inherent in all organizations which arises from the chronic discrepancy between proclaimed organizational goals and their achievement. The incumbent of any leadership role in any organization is a modern Sisyphus, constantly pushing uphill a backward-rolling boulder in an effort to mobilize people and resources and move them towards an ever-receding peak. To be sure, limited objectives are constantly being achieved by the organization as a whole or by particular groups within it. Without such achievements organizations would decay and members would remain acutely dissatisfied. But when one considers the goals which society attributes to organizations, and especially to the school, and the goals which organizations establish for themselves, the pathos is obvious.

There are a number of different reasons why this pathos is generated. One is that we tend to view organizations from a rationalistic perspective, the perspective which dominates management theory perhaps even more strongly than it dominates organization theory. This rationalistic ideal of organizational process assumes the establishment of a clear set of achievable goals, the total commitment of organizational members to these goals, the availability of all the necessary resources, the capacity of organizational members to co-ordinate their activities, and the unequivocal achievement of successful outcomes. In this direction lies neuroticism, if one takes neurotics to be people who are preoccupied with the discrepancy between an ideal world which they carry around in their heads and the imperfect world of everyday experience. Of course, the great majority of organizational members do not become neurotic. For many, the organizational world of work is not a central life interest, and problems other than malfunctioning organizations engage most of their attention. And even amongst the professional and administrative classes who invest more of themselves in their work organizations, most come to terms with the shortfall between goals and their achievement. Yet there will be none for whom the organizational pathos does not lead to daily irritations.

The sources of pathos are numerous. One is the fundamental notion of organizational *goal*. It is a term much in play when professionals and administrators discuss their organizations, yet it is a term which is at best problematic and at worst valueless as a guide to organizational processes. Another is that there are inherent limits to the effective co-ordination of organizational activities, partly because there are too many variables entailed to achieve fully a rational co-ordination and partly also because there are logical limits to rationality. Thus organizational members are invariably functioning in a world of imperfect rationality. A third reason, which relates to the empirical limits to rationality, is that contemporary, industrialized and modernized societies are becoming increasingly turbulent as the result of interrelated social, political, economic and technological changes so that the best-laid rational plans for an organization are constantly buffeted and knocked off course by the squalls created by uncontrollable external circumstances.

These themes will be explored in this chapter. To focus on the limits to organizational rationality is to adopt a perspective quite different from the conventional approach which posits an ideal form of rational organization. This focus might be dysfunctional with regard to the management of organizations since it is perhaps desirable that those studying management should not have their motivations impaired by considering the limits to what they can achieve. But here we are concerned with *understanding* organizations and hence with the limitations on what can be achieved.

The problem of goals

The concept of *organizational goal* holds a powerful attraction for both administrators and theorists. One of the distinguishing characteristics of organizations as social units is that they are established for specific purposes. There can be no possible doubt that schools are established for the purpose of educating the young and school goals incorporate this purpose. The achievement of these goals is the administrator's *raison d'être*. They are the touchstone whereby the administrator can check the effectiveness of the various activities undertaken within the organization. The headteacher proclaims the goals of the school in the school brochure, in the staff handbook and to the assembled guests on speech night. Goals give meaning to what the school *does*. Organizational theorists, or those of a functionalist persuasion, find the concept of goal a useful aid to the understanding of organizational processes. Goals provide a focus for their enquiries and enable them to judge the contribution of a particular activity to the whole and, if goals can be operationalized, they provide the yardstick whereby the effectiveness of an organization can be judged both on its own terms (Is the organization achieving the goals which it set out to achieve?) or, taking a comparative view: Of organizations A, B and C, sharing the same goals, which has been the most successful in achieving them?

Goals may appear to offer a means of overcoming organizational pathos but in fact they actually contribute to that pathos, for the truth is that organizations need goals to give them meaning. However, when the goals *of the organization as a whole* are subjected to close scrutiny, their value as a guide to organizational practice becomes questionable. We can examine some of the problems relating to the concept itself, the content of goals and their operationalization.

The concept itself is extremely slippery. As Perrow (1968) puts it,

> The concept of organisational goal, like concepts of power, authority, or leadership, has been unusually resistant to precise, unambiguous definition. Yet a definition of goals is necessary and unavoidable in organisational analysis. Organisations are established to do something; they perform work directed toward some end. We must examine the end or goal if we are to analyse organisational behaviour.

This honest statement by a leading organizational analyst reveals the pathos discussed above: organizations have to have goals, we cannot quite say what they are, but we must endow them with some definition if we are to make any headway. One such definition is the following: 'By organisational goal we understand a state of the organisation as a whole toward which the organisation is moving, as evidenced by statements persons make (intentions), and activities in which they engage' (Gross 1969). This is an adequate definition but reveals some of the difficulties inherent in the concept. One key problem is highlighted in the phrase *the organization as a whole*. A phenomenologically inclined theorist would question whether organizations as such can be said to have goals. It would be argued that this is an unwanted reification, the attribution of a reality to an organization which it does not have. The point would be that only *individuals* can have goals. The phenomenologist would concede that groups of individuals have common interests, and in confronting common problems can, through their interaction, come to recognize these mutual concerns and construct a set of shared goals. It is conceivable that all members of an organization, such as a school, could thus construct a common set of shared goals, but the point would be that these would be the constructed goals of a group of people and not goals which could be objectively ascribed to the organization as an abstract entity. In practice, it is unlikely that organizational goals would be shared to that extent. Although in the case of schools it is possible to conceive of all staff sharing the same goals, it is perhaps stretching credulity to believe that all pupils would share them as well. Thus a goals-model which assumes consensus is criticized by both phenomenologists and conflict theorists. Both argue that what are alleged to be the 'goals' of an organization are, in fact, the goals of those who hold most power in organizations and that these are continuously contested by groups which generate alternative sets of goals. Thus, from these perspectives, organizations are areas in which sets of goals are in conflict. Another problem inherent in Gross's definition is the potential gap between the ideal and reality which is concealed by linking 'statements persons make (intentions) *and* activities' (italics added). Intentions and activities will coincide only where there is either total consensus or total power to realize stated goals, a situation unlikely to occur in the real world. In the case of each of these problems we have the choice between treating a set of goals as an ideal remaining as such however far the activities of an organization fall short of their achievement, or defining goals operationally as the commitments which different sets of participants accept.

The phenomenological and conflict critique of goals has considerable theoretical validity. However, the main significance of this critique is to alert those who run organizations, and those who study them, that a rationalistic, consensual goal-oriented model of organizations can only be an ideal. It can thus sensitize them to limitations of the idea of a shared set of goals and alert them to the validity of the goals of different individuals and groups. The critique cannot, however, dispose of the goal as a symbolic concept for the organizational leader nor as an heuristic concept guiding one approach to the study of organizations. Organizations cannot be wholly devoid of an overall purpose if they are to fulfil the expectations which they are to meet.

If one accepts the paradox that in any strict sense organizations as such cannot have goals but that they cannot function effectively without them, then one is committed to exploring the problems involved in continuing to utilize the term. The major problems are that the goals which might be hypothesized for organizations are of different kinds, are frequently expressed in abstract and non-operational terms, and they often prove to be incompatible with each other. These problems can be explored in turn.

There is a tendency for goals to be initially conceptualized in terms of organizational *output*, not necessarily a physical output as in a factory but, in education, for example, in the skills, knowledge attitudes, etc. acquired by pupils. Yet organizations can have goals other than product goals of this sort. Gross (1969) identifies five kinds of organizational goal for a university, namely:

1 *Output goals*: the inculcation of knowledge, skills and values in students.
2 *Adaptation goals*: the attraction of staff and students, the procurement of resources and the validation of the activities of the university.
3 *Management goals*: the administration of the university, the assignment of priorities, the handling of conflict.
4 *Motivation goals*: the creation of satisfaction and commitment in both staff and students.

5 *Positional goals*: the maintenance of the university's standing in relation to other universities, the improvement on this, and its defence in the face of pressures likely to reduce this standing.

This list is illustrative and is not presented as an agreed list of organizational goals. Other lists could have been suggested, e.g. Perrow (1968) which, although different in some ways, would have made the same point: that there are organizational goals *other than* the obvious output goals. It might be suggested that all the listed goals other than output goals could be reformulated as 'means'. There is some merit in this. When one considers why organizations are established in the first place – in the case of schools for the education of children – only output goals can be the 'true' goals. This broad distinction is useful in pointing to what might be an organizational pathology – a preoccupation with goals other than output goals, particularly management goals – but substantively the distinction is difficult to sustain. Just two reasons can be noted. One is that output goals by no means exhaust the purposes which organizations serve. This is particularly true of schools. It is widely considered that the *process* of schooling is as important as its product. This is held to be so because of the significance for good or ill of the 'hidden curriculum', although this raises the nice point of whether what a child acquires through the hidden curriculum should be construed as an 'output goal' or as an unanticipated consequence. But this aside, it is also held that since children spend much of their time in schools the ethos or climate of a school has an importance independent of its outputs, although one can hardly think that the two would not be related if output is interpreted broadly to cover all changes brought about in the pupil. The other point is that the balance between the various kinds of goal will shift. Although one might expect output goals to be salient, there are situations in which they may be less crucial than other goals. For example, if a school is threatened with closure due to falling rolls, the school organization might be left to 'idle' in relation to the achievement of the output goals of pupil learning, as the goal of survival becomes salient and staff devote more of their energies toward mobilizing support, attracting additional pupils to the school and furthering the school's reputation.

When school goals are articulated they tend to be simultaneously both diverse and diffuse. They are diverse because education tends to be charged with a wide range of tasks to which schools seek to respond, and diffuse because schools seek to bring about changes in pupils which are more than a particular set of knowledge, skills and attitudes. In order to illustrate this point we can consider not the goals adumbrated by a particular school but those set out in the 1977 Green Paper *Education in Schools: A Consultative Document* (DES, 1977).

1 to help children develop lively, enquiring minds, giving them the ability to question and to argue rationally, and to apply themselves to tasks;

2 to instil respect for moral values, for other people and for oneself, and tolerance of other races, religions, and ways of life;

3 to help children understand the world in which we live, and the inter-dependence of nations;

4 to help children to use language effectively and imaginatively in reading, writing and speaking;

5 to help children to appreciate how the nation earns and maintains its standard of living and properly to esteem the essential role of industry and commerce in this process;

6 to provide a basis of mathematical, scientific and technical knowledge, enabling boys and girls to learn the essential skills needed in a fast changing world of work;

7 to teach children about human achievement and aspirations in the arts and sciences, in religion, and in the search for a more just social order;

8 to encourage and foster the development of the children whose social or environmental disadvantages cripple their capacity to learn, if necessary by making additional resources available to them.

We are not here concerned with whether these particular goals are appropriate to schools, but simply with taking them as examples of proclaimed goals in order to explore further the problems inherent in the concept. The first point to note is that they are both diverse and diffuse. As such they are completely open-ended. It would be impossible for schools to achieve these goals completely since they are infinite. This is made even more problematic since these goals, like the goals of most schools, are expressed in terms of the actions which the school will take and do not deal with the outcomes of the process, the notoriously difficult-to-measure changes which have occurred in pupils as a result of their schooling. Goals can be stated in terms of ex-pected outcomes, but this is generally resisted in education because what can be readily assessed, namely the cognitive outcomes of schooling, is regarded as representing only a limited set of school goals which would distort the purpose of the school if confined to this domain. It can be readily seen that many of the goals listed above are not measurable in this way, or achievable in any total sense. Schools must always fall short of achieving these goals and here again we see the pathos of an inevitable gap between goals and achievement. A second point is that they stand in need of far greater specification if they are to become in any sense operational. As stated, they constitute only a general set of guides to action. However, it can be argued that in an organization such as a school which is staffed by professionals, it is sufficient for only the broadest goals to be established, thus leaving the professional with sufficient autonomy to interpret these goals in the interests of clients. A third point is that the goals may be inherently in conflict and that these conflicts will become manifest when the goals are given a specific form in terms of pedagogy and curriculum. From the list given above it could well be, for example, that inducing children to 'esteem the essential role of industry and commerce' when expressed in a curricular form, could be in conflict with the goal of 'the search for a more just social order'. These goals are not necessarily in conflict as they stand, but they could be if each is operationalized in certain ways.

The concept of *organizational goal* is invariably problematic but is particularly so in the case of schools for the reasons stated above: that proclaimed school goals tend to be diffuse, diverse, abstract and non-operational as they stand. If one accepts that proclaimed goals perform the function of guiding the organization, it becomes an interesting empirical problem to relate the avowed goals of a school to the activities undertaken by staff. Because of the diffuse nature of educational goals and the relative autonomy of the teacher, there is considerable opportunity for slippage between avowed goals and their implementation. A number of sources of such slippage can be noted. One is what might be called 'the strain to the instrumental'. There is a broadly accepted distinction within the social sciences between *instrumental* goals which are utilitarian and intermediate to the attainment of other goals, and *expressive* goals which are goals worthwhile in themselves. The avowed goals of many schools contain a strong expressive component, the worthwhileness in themselves of various components of the curriculum. However, because in a complex indus-trialized society schools perform a selecting and differentiating role in relation to the occupational structure, and since occupation is a central concern of pupils and their parents who expect schools to give some priority to this, there is a tendency for schools to give greater prominence to instrumental goals, as embodied in tests and examinations, than to expressive goals. There are few schools which give priority to expressive goals. A. S. Neill's Summerhill would be one.

Another problem is the substitution of control goals for educational goals. Control over pupils is a central organizational problem for schools. However, in so far as the control goal is stated at all, it is stated as an intermediate goal on the grounds that the end-goal of education cannot be achieved without pupil control. However, it is possible for control to become a major goal in its own right. The manner in which the substitution of goals can occur in educational organizations is neatly illustrated in *The Open Door College* by Burton Clark (1960). A junior college was established at San Jose in California with the major goal of providing a technical education for the majority of students who would enter the work-force at the end of their course, and with the minor goal of providing an academic education for a small number of students who would then transfer to a university. But because of the 'open-door' policy which prevailed, students were permitted to choose their own courses, and, in fact, the majority opted for the academic (transfer) courses and only a minority opted for the technical (terminal) courses. The official goals of the school thus changed to a major commitment to an academic education and a minor commitment to a technical education. But since, in the view of the teachers, many of the students enrolling for the academic course did not have the necessary aptitudes, the goal of 'cooling out' the students perceived as academically incompetent was substituted for the goal of teaching these students. A variety of techniques was evolved for persuading such students to drop academic courses in favour of technical courses. For example, counsellors used various kinds of data about students to convince them to withdraw from the transfer courses. 'Need for Improvement' notices were used (as Burton Clark put it: 'If the student did not seek advice, advice sought him'). A course entitled Psychology 5: Orientation to College, compulsory for all transfer students, was designed to encourage the students to make a careful appreciation of their capacity to achieve college entrance by inviting them to compare their own grade point averages and scores on various aptitude tests with those required by colleges.

It is clear from the above discussion of organizational goals in general and school goals in particular that the concept generates considerable theoretical and practical problems. Organizational pathos is inherent in schools since proclaimed goals are frequently unattainable, and thus all schools are thereby 'under-achieving'. There is a proclivity for proclaimed goals to be substituted by others through the everyday practices of teachers. In so far as there is a consciousness of this, it yields further scope for pathos. Moreover, as Musgrove (1971) has pointed out, schools are underpowered for the goals they are expected to achieve.

There is clearly much to be said for the phenomenological critique of the concept of organizational goals. Goals are declaimed by organizational élites who make efforts to have them accepted as operational guides to organizational activities. But since individual members of one organization may have their own contrary goals, and since there is great opportunity for slippage between proclaimed goals and operating norms, it is better to focus on the organization as an area of conflicting perspectives on what *ought* to be done, and to note only that certain 'goals' of certain individuals and groups emerge as dominant. Thus the problem of goals is transformed into a problem of power. And yet it is not wholly possible to dispose of goals in this way. Where the outcome of internal competition results in an organization pursuing 'goals' which are strongly at odds with the mandate bestowed by society, then sanctions might well be imposed. High-level abstract goals at least give some indication of a general expectation of what a school ought to be doing, and as such they at least give some broad direction to the organization.

The limits to rationality

Organizational pathos is endemic because organizations are chronically incapable of achieving the goals which stakeholders and their own members set for them and because, except in relation to limited objectives or through the subjective sense of achievement of members, they are incapable of demonstrating their success in achieving these goals. An associated source of organizational pathos arises from the fact that there is a chronic discrepancy between the 'rational' model of organization, which holds considerable appeal for those who manage, and the less-than-rational reality of life in organizations. Three limitations of rationality can be considered: the *phenomenological* critique of rationality as a universal concept, the critique of those who note the *cognitive* limits to rationality, i.e. the limitations imposed by the limits to human capacities for ordering and relating data – advances in computing notwithstanding – and the *logical* limits to rationality wherein a 'rational' organization is inherently unattainable.

It is impossible in a relatively short section to mount a full discussion of the concept of rationality in its full philosophical splendour. It is perhaps sufficient to note here that the scientific means-ends rationality which underpins much organization theory, and particularly management theory, is widely contested. It is argued that this is not the only form which rationality can take. It is also argued that a distinction can be made between the form of rationality which may be appropriate for certain purposes, particularly scientific research and a different everyday or common-sense rationality which enables people to cope quite adequately with their lives. It is further argued that rationality is not universal and independent of interests but in fact flows from those interests. There are some enormously complicated issues here which have been much debated by philosophers and social scientists. One might dispute, for example, the rationality of the rain dance of the Hopi Indians and the witchcraft of the Azande tribe. These are not 'rational' activities according to the western scientific notion of rationality because there can be no scientific cause and effect relationship between witchcraft and the cure of disease, or between a tribal dance and the appearance of rain, but they may well be 'rational' when perceived from within the culture of the tribe since these activities have functions other than their manifest functions. From the perspective of management, the action of workers in taking strike action may well be irrational since the result could involve a loss of income by the workers. However, leaving aside the question of whether such a loss actually ensued, the strike might well have been 'rational' in terms of the workers' perceptions of their longer-term interests or in terms of their need to demonstrate solidarity. Likewise pupils behave highly 'irrationally' when their behaviour is viewed from the teachers' perspective in which rationality might be seen as the maximization of individual academic attainment. Pupils have other interests – the pleasures of 'messing about', prestige in the peer group, outside jobs, etc. – and their school behaviour may well be 'rational' in terms of these interests. Thus, leaving aside whether or not there is a single form of rationality founded on the principles of the natural sciences, there will be in all organizations competing 'rationalities' arising from differences of real interests or perceived interests which will lead to a gap between the goals of management and their achievement.

Even if one accepts the possibility of a rational model of organization, there are cognitive limits to rationality. This has been the main theme of the influential writings on organization by Simon (1964) and March and Simon (1958). Simon recognized that the model of 'economic man' [sic] who could be expected to optimize his interests by making rational choices was an inadequate account of organizational behaviour. He therefore substituted the concept of 'administrative man' [sic] whose rationality is bounded or limited and who, since he cannot know all the choice alternatives when making a decision 'satisfices' rather than maximizes. March and Simon write:

> Most human decision-making, whether individual, or organisational, is concerned with the discovery or selection of satisfactory alternatives, only in exceptional cases is it concerned with the selection of optimal alternatives.

March and Simon compare the two processes of *optimizing* and *satisficing* with looking for the sharpest needle in the haystack and looking for a needle which is sharp enough to sew with. The assumptions of the classical model are that all choice alternatives are known, that all the consequences of choosing each alternative are known, and that individuals can order these consequences in terms of utility. It is clear that all this is a well-nigh unattainable set of criteria and hence the actor is forced to 'satisfice'. This occurs according to the actor's necessarily limited definition of the situation which is only an approximate model of the 'real' situation. However, March and Simon do not deny rationality in organizational choice; they believe that the actor can achieve a *bounded rationality*. They hold that members work with simplified models which involve, for example, attending to a restricted range of situations and the pursuit of semi-independent or loosely-coupled actions. At the policy level, 'political' challenges to over-rationalistic 'economic' approaches were mounted in the 1950s and subsequently by Lindblom, in his notion of 'the science of muddling through', and others (cf. Dahl and Lindblom, 1953; Braybrooke and Lindblom, 1963; Lindblom, 1959; 1966; 1968). The empirical problem of rationality in organizations is exacerbated by the increasing turbulence of organizational environments. Organizations have long been recognized as being *open-systems* which entails their internal activities being open to influence to a greater or lesser degree by external circumstance. It is difficult to demonstrate that organizations are now, to a greater degree than in the past, subjected to more internal pressures from outside sources, but it would seem to be the case. Schon (1971) for example, argues that we have gone 'beyond the stable state'. He writes: 'Throughout our society we are experiencing the actual or theoretical dissolution of stable organisations and institutions, actions for personal identity and systems of values.' It does appear as though the rate of change, perhaps stemming mainly from technological development and the growing interdependence of social institutions, is accelerating and thus generating an increasingly turbulent environment in which organizations must function. This trend can be seen in relation to the schools. Once considered a 'domesticated' organization which could continue placidly to pursue its goals without need to compete in the market-place like the 'wild' organizations of the business world (Carlson, 1974), the declining birth-rate with consequently falling enrolments has put the continued existence of many schools in doubt. Moreover, schools have become more interdependent with other forms of organization and social institution – commercial, industrial, welfare, legal, community, political, etc. – and the once-strong boundary around the school has become more permeable. The school has become a more open system and has to take into account more, and frequently competing, factors in its decision-making. Thus the cognitive limits to rationality become more acute as the school seeks to take into account the expectations of various sets of stakeholders who are increasingly taking to forms of pressure group activity.

Finally, there is the question of the logical as well as cognitive limits to rationality. There is actually little work on the limits to rationality in schools, or indeed in organizations generally. The writers who have made the greatest contributions to this issue have been more concerned with the limits as they operate in the area of public policy (e.g. Olson, 1965; Hirschman, 1978; 1981). The most wide-ranging and fruitful discussion occurs in a series of books by Elster (1978; 1979). It is not possible to explore these ideas in detail, but essentially they are concerned with the ways in which the rational pursuit of ends by any single individual has an unanticipated outcome of preventing the achievement of those ends when all individuals in the relevant set pursue the same end in a rational manner. For example, in the context of high youth unemployment it is rational for the individuals to seek to improve their employability by enhancing their educational qualifications. However, if all school-leavers maximized their qualifications and no additional jobs were available, employers would increase their demand for qualifications and thus school leavers would be no better off. The individual can succeed only by increasing qualifications while others fail to do so.

A similar problem is that of promotion in a context of declining opportunities. Given the present salary structure and status differences, the teacher is in the same position as the school-leaver described above. Promotion will go to those who acquire the qualifications, using this term broadly to include not only academic qualifications but in-service training and experience of various kinds. But if all teachers pursue the 'rational' courses of obtaining qualifications, none will be better off.

Another fruitful area of analysis would be participation in decision-making. Without entering into a long discussion on the various connotations of *democracy*, it can be seen that in so far as individuals increase control over their own actions, the ultimate outcome may be a reduction of the capacity of all members to attain their individual ends. This can be seen to be the case in those schools which have been able to adapt thoroughgoing patterns of internal democracy. There has been a tendency for those schools to fall short of fulfilling the aspirations of members. It may be that this has been due to an inability to establish appropriate patterns of decision-making, or to respond to the pressures of a hostile environment, but the discrepancy between aspiration and achievement is logically inherent in the attempt to maximize organizational democracy. Elster (1978) quotes Simmel (1968) as stating: 'The all-and-out democrat will not be governed, even if this means that he cannot be served either.' Although Simmel made this statement in relation to the American political system, it can equally well apply to some attempts to democratise school. In Swidler's study (1979) of two highly democratized high schools in California, the power of the students was such that it negated the efforts of school leaders to meet the aspirations of the very same students.

On garbage cans and organized anarchies

Because of the diversity and diffuseness of educational goals and the inevitable limits to rationality in all organizations, the conversion of goals into issues for discussion and decision-making becomes a highly problematic affair. The day-to-day problem of teaching provides the school with a basic stability and predictability, although this is not to say that teaching is an essentially routine process. But at the level of policy, issues emerge and disappear again in ways which are far from predictable. The source of an issue, how it becomes an agenda item, the range of people engaged in the issue, the intensity of the involvement, the direction of that intensity, and the fate of the issue – whether it leads to a decision, to the implementation of the decision, or to the demise of the issue without discernible effect upon the school – are matters which have been considered only rarely in the application of organizational theory to schools, and even less frequently have they been the subject for research. The prevailing model is still underpinned by rationalistic assumptions of goal-setting, decision-making and implementation. However, one theorist who has been attentive to the idiosyncratic nature of organizational decision-making is James March, whose work we can briefly consider as providing an appropriate backdrop to the discussion in the remainder of this chapter.

The collection of papers edited by March and Olsen (1976) questions the fit between the organizational theory and the real world of organizations. In particular, March and his colleagues question the received wisdom about how decisions are made and implemented. They note that this process hardly conforms to the rationalistic paradigm of management theory. The history of the decision-making process in organizations is extremely haphazard, with decisions keenly contested at some times but not at others, with disputes over participating rights sometimes more significant than the issues themselves, with decisions sometimes taken after lengthy and serious discussion, but at other times decisions taken matter-of-factly by a limited number of people. They note that the process of making an organizational choice is often an opportunity for much else, for fulfilling duties, for defining virtue, for distributing praise and blame, for discovering and expressing self-interests, and for the sheer pleasure of being involved in the occasion of making a choice as a decision.

This complexity is increased by the high degree of ambiguity which prevails in organizations, and it can be noted that the diverse goals of schools make them particularly prone to ambiguity. March and his colleagues identify four particular types of opaqueness or ambiguity in organizations: *intention* (i.e. existence of ill-defined and inconsistent objectives), *understanding* (i.e. the difficulty involved in interpreting the organizational world, its technology and environmental pressures), *history* (i.e. the difficulty in interpreting the organization's history and its present consequences) and *organization* (i.e. the variations in the time and attention which individuals give to decisions from one choice occasion to another). The problematic nature of organizational goals and individual preferences, the lack of clarity about how the organization 'works' and the fluidity of participation lead them to put forward the now-famous *garbage-can model of organizational choice*. Rather than decision-making following the apparently rational process of weighing alternatives between organizational goals and then between the different means of achieving these goals, a decision comes out of the 'garbage can' into which have gone four 'streams'. These are as follows:

1 *Problems*: Problems are the concern of people inside and outside the organization. They arise over issues of life-style: family; frustrations of work; careers; group relations within the organization; distribution of status, jobs, and money; ideology; or current crises of humanity as interpreted by the mass media or the next-door neighbour. All require attention. Problems are, however, distinct from choices, and they may not be resolved when choices are made.
2 *Solutions*: A solution is somebody's product. A computer is not just a solution to a problem in payroll management, discovered when needed. It is an answer actively looking for a question. The creation of need is not solely a curiosity of the market in consumer products; it is a general phenomenon of processes of choice. Despite the dictum that you cannot find the answer until you have formulated the question, you often do not know the question in organizational problem solving until you know the answer.
3 *Participants*: Participants come and go. Since every entrance is an exit somewhere else, the distribution of 'entrances' depends on the attributes of the choice being left as much as it does on the attributes of the new choice. Substantial variation in participation stems from other demands on the participants' time (rather than from features of the decision under study).
4 *Choice opportunities*: These are occasions when an organization is expected to produce behaviour that can be called a decision. Opportunities arise regularly and any organization has ways of declaring an occasion for

choice. Contracts must be signed; people hired, promoted, or fired; money spent; and responsibilities allocated.

They summarize the process as follows:

> The garbage can process, as it has been observed, is one in which problems, solutions and participants move from one choice opportunity to another in such way that the nature of the choice, the time it takes, and the problems it solves all depend on a relatively complicated intermeshing of the mix of choices available at any one time, the mix of problems that have access to the organisation, the mix of solutions looking for problems, and the outside demands on the decision makers.
>
> (March and Olsen, 1976)

The concept of the garbage can is linked to another concept which has become popular in the recent literature on organizations, presumably because it resonates with the experience of theorists and participants (and theorists-as-participants, for it must be remembered that organization theorists usually work in organizations). This is the concept of *organized anarchy*. Weiner writes:

> In these conceptions an organised anarchy is an organisation typified by unclear goals, poorly understood technology, and variable participation.
>
> (Weiner, in March and Olsen, 1976)

The above summary of some of the elements in March's approach to organization is necessarily concentrated and the reader should read March and Olsen's collection for an elaboration and for an account of case studies which explore organizational decision-making with the aid of these concepts, case studies which deal mainly with educational settings of different kinds. Some critics of March claim that he has overemphasized the degree of ambiguity and anarchy in organizations. Against this, it must be said that March does not wholly throw out the baby with the bath water. He believes that rationality is present in organizational decision-making but simply notes that organizational choices get made sometimes in rather odd ways and always in conditions much more complex and adventitious than conventional theory allows. As such, it is an attractive and prima facie compelling view of organizations. Against this necessarily condensed theoretical background we can now consider some aspects of school decision-making.

The succession of goals

This phenomenon has long had a place in the literature on organizations. However, it has usually been applied to organizations which survive by moving successively from one goal to another as each is fulfilled, or as particular goals become less significant for the supporting environment. The classic case in the literature is the American Infantile Paralysis Association which, as the cause for which it was founded ceased to be important when the incidence of infantile paralysis dramatically decreased, moved on to other charitable concerns (Sills, 1957). However, the 'succession of goals' concept has not been generally applied to 'domesticated' organizations, nor has it been informed by the insights of March and colleagues into organizational choice.

A school can be said to be characterized by a 'succession of goals'. As was noted in the previous section, schools have a very broad set of agreed goals which, whilst they are expressed at the most general level, are uncontroversial and schools can always claim to be pursuing these generalized goals as, indeed, they are. The issue of the succession of goals comes at the point where schools convert these goals into *commitments* (Corwin 1965), and make choices between the alternatives which are competing for attention at any given time. March's approach takes over when it becomes a question of determining by what process particular goals become salient and what factors lead to choices being made. There are enormous conceptual difficulties in such an enterprise, not least in defining what is an *issue*. The possible elements in what might be said to constitute an issue are its significance for the effectiveness of the school, the intensity of feelings amongst the staff, the number and hierarchical status of staff engaged in the making of choices, and the expectations of outsiders. Each of these is capable of independent variation. Thus one need not elaborate the difficulties entailed in understanding the ebb and flow of issues. There are very few studies of what can be termed 'the natural history of issues' from which generalizations, if such there are, can be drawn. The methodological problems involved in such a study need not be elaborated. Unless a researcher was immersed in a school over a long period of time and able to detect the first showings of what was to become an issue, studies would need to become *post hoc* with all the attendant problems of recall and reinterpretation by participants.

There are thus very few case studies of the natural history of an issue in schools, but one exception is Christensen's (1976) study of a Danish free school in which three apparently unequivocal decisions were made: to establish a 'Society of Friends of the School', to change the school to a non-graded pattern of organization for instruction, and to rehire a teacher who had been dismissed. Yet none of these decisions was implemented. In order to explain this rather surprising fact he calls upon the 'garbage can' model and makes the following points: that the *outcome* of a decision is often less important than the *process*, that implementation is in the hands of people who have the resources but who might not share the attitudes of the decision-making group. ('Votes count but resources decide': Rokkan, 1968.) The high level of attention to the making of a decision may not be sustained through to its implementation, and, finally, the fact that other problems come to absorb the allocation of the organization as new crises arise.

The unpredictable character of the natural history of issues in schools arises because they have the following characteristics:

1 The diffuseness and diversity of goals means that only a very limited number can have the attention of the school at any time.
2 The diversity of goals means that issues will arise from a variety of sources, e.g. LEA requirements, the imperatives of a national report or the report of an HMI visit, parental pressures, adventitious issues arising accidentally (perhaps literally arising from an accident), the head's identification of important issues, the emergence of an issue from a staff analysis of problems and needs, the persistence of an individual member of staff in pursuit of an interest which may sometimes take on the character of an *idée fixe*.
3 The ambiguous nature of the decision-making system of the school in which the head has a high degree of authority but generally establishes some pattern for involving colleagues. Since teacher involvement in consultation is voluntary, participation will be variable. There might be a high initial involvement which drops away as the daily imperatives of teaching reassert themselves, and as teachers 'discover' that their personal interests are not involved. On the other hand, there might be a limited initial involvement which grows as teachers recognize the significance of the issue. Or this might be an in-and-out involvement with a consequent loss of continuity and the introduction of new opinions, or the affirmation of new interests over time.
4 There is, as Christensen noted, often a division between those who decide upon a choice and those with executive power. It is usually the head who has the executive power and there may be a disjunction between decision and implementation (see Bailey, 1982).
5 The loosely coupled nature of the school means that although the head, as chief executive, can implement some decisions which have obvious school-wide and structural consequences, there are other decisions, usually affecting classroom practice, which are less easily implemented. A choice is made, but nothing happens. This is a situation of 'innovation without change'. There is a symbolic acceptance of a decision but practice remains the same.

Conclusion

One volume of Isaiah Berlin's collected writings is entitled *Against the Current* (1979). The 'current' is the developing belief in the rationality, or the promise of rationality, in human affairs with the growing application to these affairs of the procedures of the natural sciences. The papers in that volume celebrate those writers who have perceived the inherent limits to scientific rationality and have stressed the idiosyncratic, adventitious, unpredictable and intractable nature of human action. The rationalistic 'current' has dominated management theory and, with some exceptions and until recently, organization theory. Yet anyone who observes organizations closely, or who tries to run an organization, is aware of their less-than-rational, even chaotic, nature and the unpredictable pebbles which derail the best-laid plans. The less-than-rational nature of policy-making and implementation even at the highest levels has been revealed in Allison's (1971) study of the Cuban missile crisis, and the comments by Zbigniew Brezinski, President Carter's adviser on national security, that history is the reflection of continuing chaos rather than consciously formulated policies (Urban, 1981). Of the less lethal level of the educational system Kogan (1975) has written that it is 'pluralistic, incremental and reactive'. And life in schools is certainly no more rational than in the educational system as a whole.

This chapter has explored the aleatory aspects of the school as an organization by pursuing two themes. One was the slippery concept of *organizational goal*. Although most schools will certainly move in some broad direction, the notion of a set of goals to which all the components are geared fails to correspond to the reality which is that in so far as a school has specific goals these will emerge from the interplay of interests within the school. A second was the inescapable limits to the particular kind of means-ends rationality which pervades the natural sciences in the contexts of social affairs. The limits arise from the fact that there are competing rationalities which are the outcome of different interests, the cognitive limits to rationality which arise because not all possibilities can be conceived in the planning process, and logical limits to rationality which arise because individual rationality can engender collective irrationality. These limitations were illuminated by reference to the work of March and others who have written 'against the current' in organization theory.

This rationality-questioning perspective raises a problem for those who run organizations and the management theory which is designed to guide their efforts. To *understand* organizations may be to detract from the task of *running* them. However, as noted, the work of Simon, March and Lindblom does not characterize organizations as wholly, or even mainly, irrational. They are probably more rational than they are adventitious and the quest for rational procedures is not misplaced. However, organizational pathos will remain and rationalistic approaches will always be blown off course by the contingent, the unexpected and the irrational.

References

Allison, G. T. (1971) *Essence of Decision: Exploring the Cuban Missile Crisis*, Boston, Mass., Little, Brown.

Bailey, A. J. (1982) 'The question of legitimation: a response to Eric Hoyle', *Educational Management*, **10**(2), 99–105.

Berlin, I. (1979) *Against the Current*, London, Hogarth Press.

Braybrooke, D. and Lindblom, C. E. (1963) *A Strategy of Decision*, New York, Free Press.

Carlson, D. (1974) 'Environmental constraints and educational consequences: the public school and its clients', in D. E. Griffiths (ed.) *Behavioural Science and Educational Administration*, 63rd NSSE Yearbook, Chicago, Ill., University of Chicago Press.

Christensen, S. (1976) 'Decision-making and socialization' in J. G. March and J. P. Olsen (eds) *Ambiguity and Choice in Organisations*, Bergen, Universitetforlaget,

Clark, B. R. (1960) *The Open Door College*, New York, McGraw-Hill.

Corwin, R. G. (1965) *A Sociology of Education*, New York, Appleton-Century-Croft.

Dahl, R. A. and Lindblom, C. E. (1953) *Politics, Economics and Welfare*, New York, Harper & Row.

DES (1977) *Education in Schools: A Consultative Document*, Cmnd 6869, London, HMSO.

Elster, J. (1978) *Logic and Society*, New York, Wiley.

Elster, J. (1979) *Ullysses and the Siren*, Cambridge, Cambridge University Press.

Gross, E. (1969) 'The definition of organizational goals', *British Journal of Sociology*, **20**, 277–94.

Hirschman, A. O. (1978) *Exit, Voice and Loyalty*, Cambridge, Mass., Harvard University Press.

Hirschman, A. O. (1981) *Essays in Trespassing: Economic Politics and Beyond*, Cambridge, Mass., Harvard University Press.

Kogan, M. (1975) *Educational Policy Making*, London, Allen & Unwin.

Lindblom, C. E. (1959) 'The science of muddling through', *Public Administration Review*, **19**.

Lindblom, C. E. (1966) *The Intelligence of Democracy*, New York, Free Press.

Lindblom, C. E. (1968) *The Policy-Making Process*, Englewood Cliffs, NJ, Prentice-Hall.

March, J. G. and Olsen, J. P. (1976) (eds) *Ambiguity and Choice in Organisations*, Bergen, Universitetforlaget.

March, J. G. and Simon, H. A. (1958) *Organisations*, New York, Wiley.

Musgrove, F. (1971) *Patterns of Power and Authority in English Education*, London, Methuen.

Olson, M. (1965) *The Logic of Collective Action*, Cambridge, Mass., Harvard University Press.

Perrow, C. (1968) 'Organizational goals', in *International Encyclopaedia of the Social Sciences*, London, Macmillan.

Rokkan, S. (1968) 'Norway: numerical democracy and corporate pluralism', in R. A. Dahl, (ed.) *Political Opportunities in Western Democracies*, New Haven, Conn., Yale University Press.

Schon, D. (1971) *Beyond the Stable State*, Harmondsworth, Penguin.

Sills, D. L. (1957) *The Volunteers*, New York, Free Press.

Simmel, G. (1968) *The Conflict in Modern Culture and Other Essays*, New York, Teachers College Press.

Simon, H. (1964) *Administrative Behaviour: A Study of Decision-Making Processes in Administrative Organization*, 2nd edn, New York, Collier-Macmillan.

Swidler, A. (1979) *Organization without Authority*, Cambridge, Mass., Harvard University Press.

Urban, G. (1981) 'The perils of foreign policy: a conversation with Dr. Zbigniew Brezinski', *Encounter*, May, **98**, 12–30.

11

Managing curriculum change

Michael Fullan

The purpose of studying the dynamics of curriculum change is to make the change process more explicit. This means identifying the key factors related to success, developing insights into the change process, and developing action programmes.

Background

Studies of educational change have moved through several phases. In the 1960s research concentrated on tracing the adoption of innovations, for instance how many new schemes were actually in use in schools. It is obvious now, but it was not at that time that such research information was of limited value. For one thing, adoption by organizations tells us almost nothing about how individual members feel or act. For another, reported use by individuals does not indicate whether an innovation is actually in use, let alone the quality of use.

We do not need to dwell on the reasons why researchers and policy-makers were content to stop with adoption. Perhaps it relates to the symbolic value of having 'appeared' to change by launching a major reform effort; or to the naive optimism of the 1950s and early 1960s; or to the possibility that people were fully occupied with developing innovations and policies with little energy and resources for follow-through; or more basically to the fact that initiating projects is much more glamorous and visible than the time-consuming, laborious front-line work of implementing an innovation project; or more charitably to the possibility that worrying about implementation and actual use was a natural outgrowth of earlier adoption efforts that came with time.

Whatever the case, it was not until 1971 that the first works appeared analysing problems of implementing educational innovations (Sarason, 1971; Gross *et al.*, 1971).

The 1970s were concerned with classroom practice and essentially resulted in documenting failure (see Fullan and Pomfret, 1977 for a review). We learned more about what not to do than anything else (don't ignore local needs; don't introduce complex, vague innovations; don't ignore training needs; don't ignore local leaders and opinion makers, etc.).

The 1980s were concerned with identifying and analysing success and effectiveness in educational settings. Research provided some evidence on the factors related to success. Depending on the study, the latter were defined in terms of increases in student achievement, degree of institutionalization, or in more intermediate terms such as teaching skills, teacher change, teacher commitment.

We are now embarking on a new phase which can be called the management of change (or more accurately the management of change for achieving successful outcomes). At first glance one might think that the earlier descriptions of what constitutes success would have solved the management of change problem. But 'explanations' of situations are not the same as 'solutions' in new situations, although they can help. Our future efforts will need to concentrate on managing change and developing strategies for making it happen.

Six basic observations about curriculum change

The six observations described in this section are ways of thinking or insights into the phenomenon of educational change that should give us pause for thought and provide important orientations prior to launching into any particular change project.

Brute sanity

The problem of brute sanity was identified by George Bernard Shaw when he observed that 'reformers have the idea that change can be achieved by brute sanity'. The tendency towards brute sanity on the part of change initiators or planners is natural. What could be more rational than advocating a change which one believes in and may be in a position to introduce? The use of sheer argument and sheer authority can get a change 'on the books', but it is, of course, not a very effective strategy for implementing change. Research has demonstrated that persistence, patience and attention to detail in putting something into practice is critical. Brute sanity is the tendency to overlook the complexity and detailed processes and procedures required, in favour of more obvious matters of stressing goals, the importance of the problem and the grand plan. Brute sanity over-promises, over-rationalizes and

consequently results in unfulfilled dreams and frustrations which discourage people from sustaining their efforts and from taking on future
change projects.

Overload

The overload of change projects on implementers is well known and there are
frequently conflicting priorities on the agenda. One could say that the
initiation of change projects represents a mixture of political and educational
merit. As such, (a) too many projects are launched, (b) implementation is
often attempted too early, i.e. the political process often outstrips the
educational development process, (c) overly ambitious projects are adopted,
and (d) simultaneous multiple projects are introduced in an unco-ordinated
way. The basic observation is: 'just because a change project is on the books
does not mean that it should or could be implemented'. No theory or strategy
can do the impossible, and the impossible in this case is to implement
everything that is supposed to be implemented.

Implementing the implementation plan

Many people have responded to the research of the 1970s, which documented
implementation problems, by developing elaborate implementation plans
designed to take into account factors known to affect success. This seems
sensible enough on the surface but ironically has led to the problem of 'how
do I implement the implementation plan?' It is useful to recognize that
implementation plans, when they are first introduced, are *innovations* as much
as, if not more than, curriculum innovations. Everything we know about the
dos and don'ts of implementing curriculum innovations must be applied to
the problem of developing implementation plans.

Content versus process

It is also helpful to distinguish between the content of change and the process
of change and to realize that each represents distinct bodies of knowledge and
expertise and each needs an appropriate implementation strategy. They are
independent in the sense that it is possible to have expertise in one and not the
other. It is possible, in other words, to be highly knowledgeable about a
particular curriculum or curriculum development programme but yet be a
disaster in working with others to implement it. Indeed, those most committed to a particular innovation may be least effective in working with
others to bring about the change. Both elements of expertise must be present
and integrated in any given change project.

Pressure and support

Research in recent years suggests that effective change, even if voluntarily
pursued, rarely happens unless there is a combination of pressure and

support. These are two important balancing mechanisms and success is usually accompanied by both. The positive role of pressure in change has been neglected until recently. Support without pressure can waste resources; pressure without support creates alienation (see Fullan, 1985).

Change = learning

Successful change, or successful implementation, is none other than learning, but it is the adults in the system who are learning along with or more so than the students. Thus, anything we know about how adults learn and under what conditions they are most likely to learn is useful for designing and carrying out strategies for implementation.

What is implementation?

Implementation means curriculum change. For teachers in classrooms, new materials are important, but are ineffective by themselves. Change also involves new behaviours and practices, and ultimately new beliefs and understandings. It involves changes in what people know and assume.

It is possible to obtain some degree of change through policy decision and the initial process of getting new structures and materials in place, but this represents the more obvious, structural aspects of change in comparison with the new skills and understandings required of front-line implementers. In the absence of the latter, only superficial change is achieved. The effectiveness of a change project stands or falls with the extent to which front-line implementers use new practices with degrees of mastery, commitment and understanding.

Factors related to successful change

These can be grouped within the three broad project phases of initiation, implementation, and institutionalization.

Initiation factors

There are four requirements

1 educational need should be linked to an agenda of political (high-profile) need
2 a clear model should exist for the proposed change
3 there needs to be a strong advocate for the change
4 there should be an early active initiation establishing initial commitment, as an elaborate planning stage is wasteful of energy.

Implementation factors

Some critical needs include

1 careful orchestration: implementation requires the clear direction of many players; a group is needed to oversee the implementation plan and carry it through
2 the correct alchemy of pressure and support
3 early rewards for implementers
4 ongoing INSET, to maintain commitment as behaviours often change before beliefs.

Institutionalization factors

An innovation will be more successful if

1 it becomes embedded into the fabric of everyday practice
2 it is clearly linked to classroom practice
3 it is in widespread use across several classrooms and schools
4 it is not contending with conflicting priorities
5 it is subject to continuing INSET for new staff, to consolidate commitment.

Implications for action

I would offer finally the following eight basic guidelines or insights:

1 effective entrepreneurs exploit multiple innovations
2 overcome the 'if only . . .' problem, e.g. 'If only more heads were curriculum leaders . . .'; 'If only the government would stop introducing so many policies . . .'
3 manage multiple innovations: 'Do two well and the others as well as possible'
4 get better at implementation planning – more by doing than planning; start small but think big
5 beware of implementation dip, i.e. the risk of temporary de-skilling as innovators learn new skills
6 remember that research shows behaviour changes first and changes in belief follow
7 recognize that project leaders need to have a vision of content and process and the relationship between the two which will promote change; to have a vision of content change without a vision of process change is an example of 'brute sanity'
8 acknowledge the importance of ownership and commitment and that ownership is a process where commitment is increasingly acquired.

Conclusion

The process of curriculum change is complex and the search to understand it continues. If the teachers are to be convinced, those in authority positions in LEAs and schools must believe and understand the change sufficiently to convey its meaning. The psychiatrist Ronald Laing has captured the essence of this in one of his poems:

> There is something I don't know
>   that I am supposed to know.
> I don't know *what* it is I don't know,
>   and yet am supposed to know,
> and I feel I look stupid
>   if I seem both not to know it
>   and not know *what* it is I don't know.
> Therefore I pretend I know it.
>   This is nerve-racking
>   since I don't know what I must pretend to know.
> Therefore I pretend to know everything.
>
>   (Laing, 1970)

References

Fullan, M. (1985) 'Change processes and strategies at the local level', *Elementary School Journal*, **85**(3), 391–421.

Fullan, M. and Pomfret, A. (1977) 'Research on curriculum and instruction implementation', *Review of Educational Research*, **47**(1), 335–97.

Gross, N., Giaquinta, J. and Bernstein, M. (1971) *Implementing Organizational Innovations: a Sociological Analysis of Planned Educational Change*, New York, Basic Books.

Laing, R. D. (1970) *Knots*, London, Tavistock.

Sarason, S. (1971) *The Culture of the School and the Problem of Change*, Boston, Mass., Allyn & Bacon.

Section III

Practices

12

TVEI: curriculum issues and staff perspectives

Douglas Barnes, George Johnson, Steven Jordan, David Layton, Peter Medway and David Yeomans

Curriculum organization at school level: patterns of accommodation and the grouping of students

In our interim report (Barnes *et al.*, 1987, pp. 7–23), we used the categories, first suggested by Murray Saunders (1986), of *containment*, *accommodation* and *adaptive extension* to classify schools' responses to the Technical and Vocational Education Initiative (TVEI). We summarized these as follows:

1 Adaptive extension
   The school utilises TVEI as an opportunity to review and reshape the whole 14–18 curriculum.
2 Accommodation
   The school organizes a TVEI scheme with innovative elements but effects a compromise between TVEI goals and the claims of existing curricular arrangements.
3 Containment
   The effects of TVEI funding are almost entirely confined and absorbed by the school's existing practices which resist change.

We found that of the first twelve schools visited seven had contained TVEI, five had accommodated the initiative and there were no examples of adaptive extension. Of the remaining fourteen schools eight (A, D, L, P, S, X, Y, Z) had contained TVEI, five had accommodated it (G, J, M, N, V) and there was one example of adaptive extension (F). Thus the final distribution for the 26 schools is:

Containment	15 schools
Accommodation	10 schools
Adaptive extension	1 school

This confirms our impression, reported previously, that the majority of the schools have not undertaken radical changes across the curriculum.

Interpretation of this finding has, of course, to be made cautiously. Given that the initiative was a pilot experiment which concentrated on a particular cohort of pupils only, schools could legitimately argue that a radical reshaping of the total 14–18 curriculum was an extravagant response.

A second potentially significant dimension of the way in which schools have responded to TVEI is whether they have decided to separate TVEI students from the others for their TVEI lessons or have chosen to integrate the two groups. We found that fifteen of the schools had mixed groups of TVEI and non-TVEI students taking TVEI designated courses. Twelve of the schools had discrete TVEI groups (school I had discrete groups in the fifth year and mixed groups in the fourth year). Table 12.1 combines the discrete/mixed dimension with the containment/accommodation/adaptive extension dimension.

We can now use the table to describe briefly the responses to TVEI made by the schools.

Box 1

This represents the most common responses to TVEI. These schools have used the initiative to add new subjects to their options list and to enhance some existing subjects. The basic core plus options structure of the curriculum remains unchanged. It is often an explicit aim of senior management in these schools that TVEI and TVEI students should not be seen as separate from the rest of the school, hence the decision to open the TVEI courses to all the fourth year and fifth year students. TVEI students are often only identified for monitoring purposes. Students do not opt for TVEI, they opt for subjects which may result in them becoming designated TVEI students. In some of the schools, however, TVEI students may have been on residentials or have had separate arrangements for work experience.

Table 12.1

	Contained	Accommodated	Extended
Discrete	I^5,K,X, Z,W,S 2	B,R,O N,J,V 3	
Mixed	H,E,U,I^4,C P,A,L Y,D 1	T,Q M,G 4	F 5

Box 2

In this group of schools the core plus options structure is retained. Students are, however, required to opt for a distinct TVEI package which often includes some form of TVEI core. The result is that there is a discrete group of TVEI students.

Box 3

In this group of schools the TVEI curriculum has various novel features. In school B this was the Project Unit, in school R the system of workshops and assignments, in school J the modularization of the curriculum and in school V the establishment of consortium arrangements which led to TVEI being taught by a team of central teachers. In all cases, however, since the TVEI curriculum was provided to a discrete group of students who had opted for TVEI, influence on the mainstream curriculum was limited.

Box 4

Here again TVEI has led to the introduction of significant curriculum innovations. These included: in school T the spread of information technology (IT), profiling and counselling across the curriculum; major changes in the timetable in school Q; and modularization in schools M and G. In these schools there were opportunities for non-TVEI students to participate in parts of the TVEI curriculum.

Box 5

Only school F fell into this category. In this school a decision has been taken to modularize a large part of the 14–16 curriculum and a large proportion of fourth and fifth year students were involved in the modular courses.

Over half the schools, then, have adopted a contained version of TVEI. In these schools the initiative has not been allowed to substantially change the structure of the fourth and fifth year curriculum. We wish to make it clear that this does not necessarily reflect on the quality of the classroom experiences. We have seen a great deal of impressive teaching in individual subjects in these schools but this work has been carried on within a conventional subject-based 30–40 period per week curriculum structure.

There is some evidence that schools have felt more freedom to experiment where the TVEI students are a discrete group. The project unit in school B, the system of assignments and workshops in school R and the flexible modular structure in school J were among the most innovative approaches to curriculum organization and all were available only to TVEI students. A further advantage of this approach is that it makes possible the emergence of a distinctive team of TVEI teachers with its own ethos and common approach to teaching. Such teams were a strong feature of TVEI in schools B and R. However, this still leaves the task of extending such approaches to the rest of the 14–16 curriculum. In all three schools at the time of our visits little progress had been made in this direction and the mainstream curricula had scarcely been influenced by TVEI developments.

Five schools (F, G, K, Q, T) had embarked on changes which affected TVEI and non-TVEI students but in most cases these changes were less radical than those attempted in schools B, J. and R. In schools T and Q, despite the changes noted above, TVEI had not made a great impact upon the rest of the curriculum. In schools F and M, TVEI had encouraged the modularization of part of the 14–16 curriculum, this process having gone much further in school F than in school M. In both cases, however, the way in which the modular system was organized limited the extent to which there was a real change in the nature of the students' experience. Students were required to follow the courses they had chosen for two years and complete all the modules, the main change from conventional two year courses being that the content had been divided into free-standing units and shorter term learning objectives were spelled out to the students.

In school G a more flexible modular system had been established. Students took four compulsory modules in the fourth year and were then able to choose four further modules in the fifth year. This modular course was open to all fourth year students. There was also a clear intention in this school to extend the modular approach to other areas of the curriculum.

Modularization of the curriculum

Considerable interest has been expressed in the development of modular curricula. Five of the schools in our sample (F, G, J, M, N) have responded to TVEI by modularizing parts of their 14–16 curriculum. In this section we examine the rationales which have been given for modularization, the forms which it has taken and the costs and benefits which have arisen.

The structure of the modular curriculum

We do not offer any pre-emptive definition of modularization; rather we shall describe the operationalization of the concept in the five schools which claimed to have modularized parts of their 14–16 curriculum. It is *their* interpretations of a modular curriculum which will be presented here.

The length of modules varied between ten and eighteen weeks. In schools F, M and N once students had opted for a particular course they had to complete all the modules; mixing of modules from different courses was not allowed or was strongly discouraged (we heard of only one student in the three schools who had been allowed to mix modules). In these three schools modularization had resulted in the courses being broken up into smaller free-standing units. The intention was that these small units would have shorter term learning objectives and that this approach would help to motivate the students. The structure in schools G and J was considerably more flexible. In school J, 28 modules were offered; each student had to complete thirteen. There were two compulsory modules, but students could choose widely for their remaining eleven. Modules had to be clustered into groups of five for certification purposes and certain combinations were disallowed. Despite this the scheme was very flexible. The module on information processing, for example, could be used in five of the nine certification clusters as could the word processing modules. In school G students took four compulsory modules in the fourth year but in the fifth year they chose a further four from the 22 on offer although here also students had to choose combinations which could be certified.

Rationales for Modularization

Modularization was said to greatly increase the motivation of the students. Here are just a few of the opinions expressed to us:

> Tremendous motivator of lower ability kids, may encourage them to carry on (with school).
> (Head, school N)

> Kids don't get bored with modules.
> (Teacher, school N)

> Modules more intense (than two year course) due to time constraints and that is a motivating factor. They take it a bit more seriously than they do the two year course.
> (Teacher, school J)

> It (the modular system) has advantages, the 16 week deadline is very stimulating. It has a sense of urgency.
> (Teacher, school M)

This increased motivation was linked to the setting of short-term objectives and the intensity of the teaching approach.

It was also claimed that modularization promoted changes in teaching style. The school co-ordinator in school J explained that:

> What we want to be distinctive about the modules is the active-based learning that gives them choice and responsibility, changes in teaching style, content, retraining teachers, developing relationships with pupils.

The head of school G argued that:

> Teachers *have* to identify learning objectives in modules so teachers know *why* they're teaching them.

In school F the head suggested that modularization had led to courses which were concept and process, rather than content, orientated. The rewriting of courses which modularization had necessitated had allowed teachers to rethink and bring syllabuses up to date. The claim that modular courses placed greater emphasis on concept and process was not always supported by teachers as we shall see below.

Modules were also linked with the development of continuous assessment. The modular courses did not have two year terminal exams, and this again was said to be a motivating factor as well as being a fairer method of assessment. Modularization was also said to make it easier to move to criterion-referenced assessment.

A further advantage claimed for the modular system was that it provided for balance, breadth and relevance. Students were able to taste modules from a wide range of subject disciplines and this would give a better basis for choice at sixteen. As one teacher said, 'the two year option choices are like joining the army, once you're in you can't get out'.

This argument only applied in schools G and J where students had some choice within the modular system. Modularization could also help to combat gender stereotyping. As was noted earlier, in school G all students had to take modules in community studies, technology, business studies and information technology; in school J there were compulsory modules in product development and computer literacy. In effect these schools had extended the compulsory core for those students opting for the modular courses. It was also hoped that students would be more adventurous in choosing modules if they knew they could always move into another area after, at most, a term. There was some evidence in school J that this had happened with some girls being prepared to try modules in electronics and technology although few of them pursued these subjects in later modules.

Assessment in modular systems

This was a major source of concern in the schools. In school N the modular courses had not been accepted by the examination board in May of the first year. In all five schools there had been a considerable amount of negotiation with the boards. This proved particularly difficult where there were proposals for the mixing of modules in cross-curricular courses. In schools M and N the uncertainties over certification had, in part, led the schools to discourage mixing of modules. In the project of which school J is part a deputy head had been seconded for a year to negotiate with the exam board and this perhaps accounted for the success of this project in achieving a flexible modular structure. While it was accepted that the boards had tried to be helpful there was a feeling that they were not geared up to deal with the assessment of modular courses. Moderators of one board were said to be more interested in product than process and the same board had been 'tardy' in agreeing to the modular scheme in which school G participated. The head of school F said of the boards:

> Boards are not staffed by innovators, they're staffed by administrators.

Problems of modular systems

In each of the five schools the modules had been written by groups of teachers. The staff involved had found this a stimulating and valuable experience. However it had also made very great demands on their time and caused a lot of stress. There was pressure to keep 'pumping stuff out' and this might be 'all right for five years but what about the next 35?' one teacher asked. The coursework and end of module tests associated with the assessment of modules also increased the pressure on teachers and some teachers were concerned that the amount of work associated with the assessment of modules might make the whole system unworkable.

A teacher in school J complained that 'too much time was spent on assessment' and that this was 'horrendous on project work'. This problem of time-consuming assessment practices had been exacerbated by GCSE with its increased emphasis on coursework and practical assessment. A teacher in school G explained the problems:

> GCSE assessment and practical work involves observing pupils working – how do you do that with 28 at the same time and ensure safety?

Another commonly noted problem was the overloading of modules with content. This was mentioned in all five schools and was often accompanied by complaints that the modules were too short to cover all the work. Thus it can be seen that some modules stressed content rather than process or concepts as was claimed.

Some teachers, particularly in science, were concerned that modular courses would not give a sound foundation for those wishing to go on to A-level physics, chemistry or biology. Their argument was that students would be able to mix the sciences and so not get sufficient background in any of them.

For the most part the modular systems were accommodated within conventional timetable structures, although in school J half day blocks had been created for the modules. The decision not to combine modularization with a restructuring of the timetable was a weakness for a teacher in school F:

> I'm not running a truly modular curriculum because we have not broken the timetable. As long as that continues we're not running a modular course, we just have modular assessment of parts of the course.

This teacher's argument was that since the structure of the timetable remained unchanged there had also been no major change in the students' overall curricular experience; the students' day continued to be broken up into a series of forty minute, relatively disconnected, lessons.

We felt that there was a tendency among some TVEI leaders, heads and teachers, to assume that because modularization had taken place changes in pedagogy, content and assessment techniques would follow. This is not necessarily the case. Controlled pedagogy is just as likely to take place in modules as in conventional courses. Modularity does not necessarily lead to greater realism or to assessments which reflect a wider range of skills, knowledge, attitudes and personal qualities. We suggest [. . .] that modularization also makes integration of curriculum content difficult to achieve. These issues remain to be tackled. Yet as a teacher in school F told us:

> We're under no pressure to change what we do except to modularize.

We tend to agree with the project co-ordinator who said that:

> I don't think there is anything intrinsically worthwhile about modularization, it's a fairly neutral device, it is only a device for using time more constructively, I suspect.

and

> Modules in themselves are not going to change the learning process.

The disappearance or subordination of subjects

We investigated the extent to which the introduction of new subjects and the enhancement of existing subjects as a result of TVEI had affected the options offered to the students in the fourth and fifth years. Had any subjects disappeared from the curriculum or been significantly subordinated as a result of the changes which TVEI had brought in the 14–16 curriculum?

It is clear from the data that in many schools subjects had disappeared or attracted fewer students. Subjects affected included: commerce, woodwork, metalwork, geology, child care, traffic studies, geography, history, biology, Latin and RE. However the fact that these changes *coincided* with the introduction of TVEI does not allow us to say that they were *caused* wholly or in part by the initiative; often TVEI had accelerated changes in the patterns of option choice which were already in train. Other changes in the fourth and fifth year curriculum of the schools can clearly be attributed to TVEI. Some courses disappeared because they had been directly replaced by TVEI courses, for example the replacement of engineering science and economics by technology and business studies in school X or non-examination technology and electronics by electronics technology in school P. In schools D, H, K and Z the introduction of a TVEI core had meant that TVEI students lost time for PE and games. Careers was also affected in schools B, D and Q. Some claims were made that TVEI distorted class sizes and staffing elsewhere in the curriculum. In school U the Head of Science claimed that TVEI had made the policy of 20 per cent science for all more difficult to achieve by tying up teachers with small groups of TVEI students, and in school O groups in mathematics, English and science were said to be larger because of TVEI. Our data do not allow us to verify these claims. It is perhaps significant that some teachers and students blamed TVEI for changes for which the initiative was not responsible. In school Q, for example, students complained that they could not go to college to do typing and building studies because of TVEI. This was not true. These changes had come about because of the introduction of a course for the less able introduced independently of TVEI.

Changes in the lower school curriculum

Care must again be taken in establishing causal links between the introduction of changes in the lower school curriculum and TVEI. Indeed in general terms mono-causal explanations for curriculum changes are likely to be over simplified.

However, it is clear that in several schools (I, K, T, and X) TVEI had contributed significantly to the introduction or expansion of information technology in the lower school. This had been made possible by the expansion of computing facilities as a result of TVEI. In schools K, W and X there had also been an extension of technology into the lower school. There seems to be a growing awareness that the teaching of technology needs to start lower down the school if fourth and fifth year technology is to be made more effective.

Not all changes in the lower school curriculum were seen as positive. In school Q we were told that performing arts in the second year had become 'just book reading' because of TVEI. In school M the commitments of teachers to TVEI had resulted in a part-time teacher being employed to teach lower school science and in most schools there must have been some redistribution of teachers among classes although our data allow us to say little on this.

Resources

Schools were anxious that wherever possible TVEI resources were also used for non-TVEI lessons. Not only would this enhance teaching and learning in those lessons but, it was hoped, it would reduce resentment among non-TVEI staff at the scale of TVEI resourcing. As we shall see in the next section non-TVEI teachers were often quick to draw comparisons between the resources available through TVEI and those which they had received for their subjects. As was indicated in the previous section such changes as had taken place in the lower school curriculum in the schools had often come about as a result of TVEI resources.

Teachers expressed some concerns about the resource implications of TVEI. Several non-TVEI teachers were worried that when TVEI funding ended the maintenance of expensive subjects such as technology and computing, which had been expanded or introduced under TVEI, would affect the distribution of school capitation money to the detriment of non-TVEI subjects.

Some LEAs, in an attempt to ameliorate divisions between schools in and out of TVEI, had allocated all their funds for curriculum development to non-TVEI schools. The effect of this was that non-TVEI departments in TVEI schools were finding it impossible to obtain any money at all for curriculum development.

Teachers' responses to TVEI

The potential 'enclave' effects of an educational experiment such as TVEI on teachers and other staff within schools and projects have been succinctly expressed in Saunders' triad of management responses to TVEI (Saunders 1986). [. . .] We shall here focus on the generalized implications of the initiative within the broader context of the school as a community. That is, we will be concerned [. . .] to outline a spectrum of effects on both TVEI and non-TVEI teachers within the 26 schools.

One of the most obvious and visible aspects of the introduction of TVEI into schools was the reduction of class sizes. In eight of the schools, the fact that TVEI finance was used to reduce group sizes generated a mixed response from teachers both inside and outside TVEI. In all the schools, TVEI teachers commented favourably on having smaller groups to teach. This was particularly the case with technology and PSE [personal and social education] teachers who felt that the success of their teaching strategies depended very much on group size. One only needs to comprehend the complexities of technology project work with, for example, a group of 25–30 (or more) to grasp the nature of the problem which teachers were referring to here. However, the fact that TVEI teachers had smaller groups sometimes had consequences for colleagues outside TVEI. In cases where there was a clearly defined cohort of students, taught in classes of smaller size than usual, non-TVEI teachers might have to contend with larger classes, a situation which caused resentment. Teacher shortages in certain subjects could be an exacerbating factor, as might a decision to use funding for equipment rather than teaching staff. On the other side of this coin is the phenomenon of non-viable student groups outside TVEI and disappearing subjects, on which we have already commented.

Teachers also compared the relatively lavish resourcing of TVEI courses with that of non-TVEI courses. For example an English teacher in school A speaking of a TVEI resourced media studies course said that:

> Last year media studies obtained more resources for 27 children than English for 1200 children. That is ridiculous.

In addition to this uneven distribution of resources between the subjects, he also claimed that whereas there was provision made for INSET on TVEI courses, none at all had been made for English. A similar situation emerged in school O, where a considerable sum of money had been spent on purchasing four CNC lathes for technology classes but where in the science department, particularly in physics, equipment was becoming obsolete or was in short supply. The combined factors of smaller class sizes and privileged resourcing for TVEI in these schools was therefore the source and topic of some degree of tension between TVEI and non-TVEI staff.

Another issue that was a source of potential friction between TVEI and non-TVEI staff could be traced to TVEI extra-curricular activities for students and INSET for staff: both required cover from either full-time staff or supply teachers. This was a topic that featured prominently in at least seven schools. In school Q for example, non-TVEI staff commented on the fact that TVEI students 'were always out of school' engaging in surveys, residentials, or work experience. This led to some anxiety in 'academic' subjects such as English and mathematics, where teachers felt that TVEI students were missing out on large sections of the syllabus and would therefore have to 'catch up'. As a consequence of these activities and TVEI INSET, cover often had to be provided for classes. This gave rise to two related issues: that of cover itself and the quality of it. Teachers in these seven schools commented on the *extent* to which cover was required for TVEI classes from non-TVEI teachers, and secondly, that such cover in terms of its *quality*, particularly if it was supply cover, was often reduced to child-minding. TVEI was seen in these circumstances by non-TVEI teachers as being not only over-funded and privileged, but also parasitical on the school as a whole. It was drawing away much needed teacher time and finance from the general school curriculum. For TVEI teachers this was also a problem. In school M, a TVEI teacher stated that:

> There's a tension between my role as a teacher and a curriculum developer. My teaching has gone to pot . . .

In school C, a TVEI business studies teacher felt that 'I'm more marketable' as a result of TVEI but that TVEI was also 'A load of bloody hassle'. What both these teachers felt acutely, was that because of the extra time they had to devote to curriculum development as a result of being involved in TVEI, their non-TVEI teaching had been adversely affected. [. . .]

The fact that TVEI required extra time and attention from school staff within TVEI was particularly felt by school co-ordinators. Their position best exemplifies this issue of the contradictory demands placed on TVEI teachers in general: that is, at one level they are expected to pioneer and be responsible for the implementation and development of a broad range of new teaching practices and subject content, while also performing their existing teaching and administrative duties within the context of the school as a whole. In order that this could be achieved effectively, most school co-ordinators were on a senior scale or deputy head appointment. This was in recognition of the fact that TVEI, being a major curriculum development, required someone of seniority in the school to over-see it (the only exception here being school B). In school Z, an assistant co-ordinator had been appointed in support of the school co-ordinator, the holder of that post being already a senior teacher with responsibility for developing new GCSE Technology courses within the school. However, school O illustrated the problems which senior staff in schools who were given the role of school co-ordinator faced. The policy of the LEA in which school O was situated was to appoint deputy heads to the role of school co-ordinator (without any remuneration) and as a consequence 'overload' them. The deputy head here felt that because of the already demanding position he was in – 'going to meetings most evenings of the week' – he could not effectively deal with TVEI. As he put it, he felt 'remote from the chalkface'. In school C, the school co-ordinator, who was also director of studies, complained that despite the effort he put into TVEI curriculum development, he felt 'very bitter about the effect it's had on me' and that 'TVEI has done nothing for me at all'. In the project in which school S was situated, the school co-ordinator had been virtually ostracized by senior management within the school. In fact within the project as a whole, the extra pattern of management organization which TVEI had brought with it was generally viewed with some suspicion by other senior staff and management. It would seem appropriate to conclude that school co-ordinators must be given responsibility, authority and remuneration for their work in developing TVEI and where this is not adequately allocated, it might adversely affect TVEI curriculum development.

The fact that TVEI has brought with it not only resources to the classroom and encouraged major curriculum development, but also opened up a potential career route for teachers in terms of promotion, has, as the head of school K said, been 'very, very significant', or, as the head of school N put it, 'it's been a God-send'. The fact that heads of these schools have in most instances been able to offer extra scale points to induce staff to participate in TVEI curriculum development has been a very positive enabling factor in getting TVEI started within schools. We have already noted that this can, potentially, have negative side-effects in creating a TVEI enclave. It can also lead to what the school co-ordinator in school O described to us as 'poaching'. Given that TVEI has established a career route within schools, particularly amongst technology, electronics and IT staff, schools such as school O have found themselves in the position where staff have rapidly advanced their careers within the school as a result of TVEI, been offered a more senior position elsewhere, and left. This clash of career development, being offered more and better opportunities in a different position and school, and a teacher's loyalty to a school has been the cause of some friction within at least half the schools we visited, and indeed was probably more generalized than this finding suggests.

To conclude this section on teachers' attitudes towards TVEI, it is important to mention teachers' perception of the political factors which they saw surrounding the introduction of TVEI. In eight schools, teachers made reference to the haste with which TVEI was introduced. This was particularly resented by school co-ordinators, and senior management who were responsible for buying materials and equipment. Teachers felt that more time should have been allowed for consultation, dissemination of the principles on which TVEI was based as a curriculum initiative, resource selection and allocation, and staff INSET. Many of these teachers felt that the rush to establish TVEI had its cost in the quality and structure of provision made for students. The haste with which TVEI was implemented within these schools also appeared to affect communications, particularly between TVEI schools in a project and between TVEI and non-TVEI staff.

In half the schools we visited some staff viewed TVEI as a specifically vocational *training* initiative and *not* as being educational. This was a concern held particularly by non-TVEI staff where they counterpoised TVEI with liberal education: that is, they viewed TVEI's vocational emphasis as being a threat to liberal traditions and values in schools and especially the comprehensive principle. For example, the head of languages in school G criticized TVEI's vocational orientation because it had, by virtue of this fact, devalued the aesthetic, literary and creative aspects of the curriculum. The hidden curriculum for him and the head of school U was that humanities and the liberal-comprehensive ideal of developing the total attributes of the individual were to be subordinated to a narrowly technical and vocational curriculum producing equally narrow minded students. To this extent, teachers who expressed this opinion in schools perceived TVEI as producing an imbalance in the curriculum. However, it was common in the same schools to be told that although MSC provided the finance and framework for TVEI, many of the aims and objectives of TVEI had already been practised by teachers within schools for years. There was nothing 'new' about TVEI in this sense, they argued; it was merely TVEI taking credit for what they had been doing for several years, or what they had wanted to do but did not have the money or resources to do.

Conclusion

In this chapter we have examined various aspects of the introduction of TVEI in the 26 schools. We have attempted to discover what effects TVEI has had on the organization of the curriculum and on staff. [. . .]

Involvement in TVEI has revitalized many teachers giving them opportunities to teach in new ways, participate in curriculum development and improve their professional knowledge and skill through INSET. The workload has been heavy, the rewards have sometimes seemed small and issues such as the provision of adequate and suitable supply cover remain to be tackled. Nevertheless, most teachers have thrown themselves into TVEI with gusto.

These are very considerable benefits, but there have been costs as well. For far too many teachers their introduction to TVEI was to an initiative, often imposed on the school, which had to be accommodated within a short space of time. First impressions are important and for many teachers their first impressions of TVEI were of a rushed and poorly managed scheme. As Pamela Young has pointed out:

> Thus once the decision was made [to adopt TVEI] things happened quickly – too quickly for effective implementation. Or, more precisely, planning for implementation was not recognised as an important component requiring more advanced attention.
>
> (Young, 1986, p. 60)

There is also much evidence that non-TVEI teachers and students have resented the additional resources with which TVEI students and teachers have been favoured. Many heads have attempted to minimize these enclave effects by spreading TVEI resources widely within their schools but even where this policy has been followed differentials have remained between areas of the curriculum.

There are two responses to complaints about the divisiveness of TVEI. First, it must be remembered that TVEI was a pilot scheme and this implies that a group of schools and students will be singled out for special attention. To attack this is to attack the very notion of a pilot. Second, TVEI did not create struggles for resources and status in schools. Such struggles are in the nature of organizational life. What TVEI has done in some schools has been to provide more resources and improve the status of traditionally low-status subjects such as craft, design and technology (CDT), business studies, catering and child care.

[. . .]

The data have confirmed our impression, reported in our interim reports (Barnes *et al.* 1987), that most schools have not engaged in major changes in the structure of their curriculum as a result of TVEI. Over half of the schools have contained TVEI within their existing structures. Let us again remember that TVEI was a pilot scheme affecting only a minority of fourth and fifth year students. It has perhaps been unrealistic to expect many schools to go through a major curriculum upheaval under these circumstances. Despite this a number of schools have experimented with new ways of organizing the 14–16 curriculum and there is evidence that many of these experiments have taken root. In particular there have been a number of examples of schools developing modular approaches. Modular systems have appeared to increase motivation among students and in some schools offer considerably greater choice to students than does the conventional two year options system. But it is important to remember that there is no necessary connection between the structure of the curriculum and the quality of teaching and learning experiences. Modular systems, block timetables and consortium arrangements may make certain teaching and learning situations easier to achieve but they do not guarantee that changes in content, pedagogy and assessment occur.

References

Barnes, D., Johnson, G., Jordan, S., Layton, D., Medway, P. and Yeomans, D. (1987) *The TVEI Curriculum 14–16. An Interim Report Based on Case Studies in Twelve Schools.* London, Manpower Services Commission.

Saunders, M. (1986) 'The innovative enclave: unintended effects of TVEI implementation', in R. Fiddy and I. Stronach (eds) *TVEI Working Papers 1.* Norwich, CARE, University of East Anglia.

Young, P. (1986) 'An example of the management of change', in C. McCabe (ed.) *TVEI: The Organization of the Early Years of the Technical and Vocational Education Initiative.* Clevedon, Multilingual Matters.

13

The management of pastoral care: a qualitative perspective

Peter Ribbins

The 'conventional wisdom' and its alternatives

Much of the earliest literature on 'pastoral care' dating from the 1960s and early 1970s was dominated by practising managers within secondary schools who sought general principles based upon their own experience. From the work of Blackburn (1975), Haigh (1975), Marland (1974) and others, it is possible to identify what came to be called a 'conventional wisdom' in which the development of institutionalized pastoral care in the comprehensive school was seen as unproblematic and as having thoroughly worthwhile consequences for the individual, the school and for society as a whole. (For a summary of this view see Best and Ribbins, 1985.)

In the later 1970s this view began to be challenged by Best *et al.* (1977; 1980), Lang (1977) and others. [. . . They] questioned whether the wholly favourable impression of pastoral care presented by the conventional wisdom squared all that well with their own experiences as teachers or as teachers of teachers. On the basis of this experience they proposed explanations of the growth and functioning of pastoral care structures and processes which were much more sceptical and which had much more to do with the needs of teachers than with those of pupils (see Best and Ribbins, 1985).

Furthermore, [they] argued that the conventional wisdom failed to take account of the actual meanings which people in schools attach to what normally counted as 'pastoral care', and also failed to take account of the motives and interests of the different groups involved in the creation and operation of pastoral care structures. These, it was suggested, could be explored by focusing on the kinds of things which constituted problems for the relevant groups involved and by using qualitative methods of investigation.

This has meant looking at the perspectives and styles which teachers adopt to the pastoral dimension of their roles, how they perceive and enact those roles, and how they interpret and work the structures and processes through which institutionalized pastoral care is delivered. [. . .]

The organization and management of pastoral care

I should like to illustrate the use of a qualitative approach to investigation by examining two related issues which have major implications for the management of pastoral care and which have received a good deal of attention – the first is concerned with structure (the 'pastoral–academic split'), and the second with process (the organization of the system of pupil referral within secondary schools). In doing this I shall draw mainly upon evidence from the case of Rivendell school, supplemented as necessary with, examples taken from Revelstone school. Before I turn to this perhaps I should say something about the two schools. They are both fairly large (1,200+) co-educational, 11–18 comprehensive schools located in the south-east and the Midlands respectively.

The dangers of institutionalizing artificial distinctions between the curricular and non-curricular aspects of the school worried a number of teachers at all the schools I have researched. This is a concern which has been the subject of a growing debate within the literature on the issue of the 'pastoral–academic split' (Best and Ribbins, 1983). At Rivendell various strategies were used by different heads to minimize the possible detrimental effects of such a split. The first head, 'Mr Barber', sought to implement a policy of curriculum development justified in terms of the school's fundamental task to educate the 'whole child'. Since this was central to his thinking, the objectives of pastoral care were broadly conceived as a concern for the total welfare of the child and, as such, not in any real sense seen as separate from the kind of total experience the curriculum ought to provide. To achieve this, pastoral, academic and behavioural responsibilities were combined in the same people:

> Heads of House were also Heads of Subject Departments and also had responsibility for a particular year located in a particular area of the building. Major responsibilities for all aspects of the child's welfare were thus concentrated in the hands of a small number of senior staff. Although a formal division existed in the separation of Houses from subject departments, there were strong connections between the two, with staff from the same subject departments being generally members of the same House. Moreover, the forms (tutor groups) were also the teaching groups, and this was justified in terms of making the pastoral and academic an undivided whole. . . . In these ways the Head claimed to create an organic unity.
>
> (Best *et al.*, 1983: 113)

Under the second head, 'Mr Sewell', a policy of rationalization of the organic structure, which was perceived as unclear and unspecified, led to the setting up of a highly complex structure (see Best *et al.*, 1983: 34, 35). In a sense, a 'dual academic and pastoral system' had been institutionalized but within a structure which contained four or even five substructures of authority and differentiation of task within the school. A curricular structure of eight faculties and heads of faculty and some twenty subject departments each with its head of subject, and a non-curricular system of schools-within-schools (lower, upper and sixth with a head and assistant head of lower and upper school and a head of sixth), four houses (each with its head and assistant head of house) and of five years (each with its head of year). Taken separately, each of these structures could be defended on the grounds that it catered for a particular type of pupil need and dealt with a particular type of problem. Problems of the provision and organization of learning situations were essentially a faculty and departmental responsibility, problems of a 'pastoral' nature were the main province of the houses, problems of general control and discipline were the defining task of the schools-within-schools, and problems of 'academic progress' were the particular task of the years. In theory any problem with which a class-teacher or a form tutor could not deal could be referred to the appropriate faculty/department head, house head/assistant house head, head of school/assistant head of school, or year head. As we remarked at the time

> It is fairly easy to think of a justification for such a complex and highly sophisticated set of structures. It can be argued that, together, they represent all the major aspects of the teacher's role as an imparter of knowledge, a supporter and counsellor of children with personal and academic problems, a disciplinarian and custodian of children, a monitor of educational progress, and, finally, as an administrator. The rationale for the system, as more than one teacher remarked, was that it constituted a 'net through which no problem could fall'.
>
> (Best *et al.*, 1983: 46)

Such remarks had considerable rhetorical force, but there were also those who felt that all was not well with the net, particularly in regard to what came to be thought of as the 'dual' structure of years and houses. In particular, many teachers were uncertain about what was involved in the role of the year head and doubted the validity of the distinction between the 'pastoral' concerns of the houses and the 'academic' concerns of the years.

Another reason for lack of confidence in the 'net' was the apparent absence of any systematic relationship between the curricular structure of faculties or departments and the 'non-curricular' systems of houses and years. Except in relatively minor ways, house heads and year heads both seemed to regard the content and organization of the curriculum and its pedagogy as something separate and beyond their legitimate concern or influence. Conversely, some of the faculty heads were amongst the most dismissive critics of the 'dual' structure of houses and years, and of what they saw as the 'burgeoning bureaucracy of pastoral care'. Three main sets of related criticisms emerged. The first of these questioned the relevance, even the reality, of the distinctions the system seemed to entail between 'pastoral', 'academic' and 'disciplinary' problems. Those who took this line, commonly argued, for example, that disciplinary problems could stem from academic ones, or from genuinely pastoral ones, such as family difficulties, while academic performance could be adversely affected by personal problems or disciplinary problems. Ironically, these kinds of views were also likely to be expressed by those who had been appointed to posts of responsibility as house heads, year heads or heads of school:

> Although I am more on the academic side, I don't believe you can distinguish between academic and pastoral, although I have been told that I should.
>
> (head of year)

> The academic problem should go to the form teacher, then the year head. If it is a behaviour problem, then it goes to the head of house, or the assistant head of house. It's very difficult, a behaviour problem may stem from an academic problem or a pastoral problem so that the year staff may pass it on to the house staff, or they may get together on it.
>
> (head of lower school)

The second kind of criticism followed from the first. Thus it was said that, if the sort of overlaps identified above do exist and if it is very difficult to distinguish these problems from each other, this must make for serious difficulties for heads of house and heads of year, and for subject teachers and for form tutors attempting to use the system. The 'dual system' of houses and years was an especial source of confusion and even quite senior and experienced staff sometimes seemed to founder in what was widely seen to be a situation rife with the possibility of demarcation disputes and problems of procedure and protocol as the following remarks from three quite experienced staff show:

> It clashes too much having a dual system. Both positions, that is head of year and head of house, are weakened by the existence of the other. It is not so much that they are in competition, but that there are problems of who you should go to . . .

> I certainly feel that at times it's clumsy, having two alternative systems of pastoral care/discipline, in that it's quite conceivable you tread on somebody's corns because you didn't refer them to them, and you referred them to somebody else.

> Having a vertical and a horizontal system is a mistake and sometimes people get caught between the two. Sometimes people don't know whether to go to the head of house or the head of year.

These kinds of difficulties could be especially serious for the inexperienced teacher, particularly if they were allocated to a year or a house where the pastoral leader was not prepared to make much effort to help them to settle in.

The third set of criticisms concerned the sheer scale of the structural hierarchies to be found at Rivendell – several staff described the school as a 'bureaucratic nightmare'. For some this was true of the structure of the school as a whole, others felt that this was also true of the curricular structure of faculties and subject departments but the greatest number reserved their most forceful comments for the 'dual system' within the non-curricular structure. This was said to create imbalances between subordinate and superordinate positions, foul-ups in communications and referrals, as well as the kinds of problems of role definition and of role conflict discussed above. The following comment by a senior member of staff may be taken to represent a widely held view:

> There are too many chiefs to the point of having no indians. It should not be necessary to have more than 20 people in positions of authority (within the non-curricular structure), and in some schools it is starting to look like everybody is . . . they cease to be teachers and become bureaucrats. Whether you do it vertically or horizontally, it needs to be clear cut. For example, eight or ten people as pastoral heads and deputies, whether as year heads or house heads wouldn't matter much.

As one might expect, many staff began to bypass the formal system or to 'work it' in ways that met their own perceived needs but which had little to do with officially designated procedures as such. As one probationary teacher said of the non-curricular structure:

> I have a pretty decent idea of the outline but some of the intricacies are not too clear to me. I find that I know who to go to to get something done but I don't know their titles and precise positions. I've got enough idea to know who deals with what sort of problem. For example, for class problems I go to the head of house, for discipline problems I go to the form tutor, or, more usually, to the head of that section of the school.

However, simplicity is no absolute guarantee that staff will not try to ignore formal systems when it suits them to do so. They did at Revelstone, where the pastoral system was much simpler. This was admitted by both junior and senior staff, particularly with reference to the 'official' system of referral to which we shall return shortly.

For some staff, the fact that formal structures and processes were sometimes circumvented simply did not matter very much. Rather, they believed that, since all systems were always more or less imperfect, what really matters is the attitudes and commitments of the people who work them. However, for others, the problems that result from intrinsically unsatisfactory systems cannot be so easily discounted. For example, one of the deputy heads at Rivendell took the view that if the pastoral system was being regularly bypassed this did not demonstrate that no system could work, rather what was necessary was that the system itself should be changed. Finally, many staff at Rivendell seemed to believe that much that was worthwhile in both the curricular and the non-curricular activities of the school happened as much in spite of as because of the structures which had been institutionalized there. Some of these spoke of the dangers of setting up artificial distinctions in the organization of the school:

> The main effect of having a horizontal system of years as well as the house system was to create a grey area, such that when there is praise to be given both heads of year and house staff can claim the kudos, but when there are problems both may be able to deny responsibility.

Clearly all was not well with the non-curricular net through which 'no problems could fall'. Regardless of the best intentions of teachers, some pupils and their problems got lost within these grey areas:

> The school's idea of a cross-structure of houses and years is that there is a net to catch people, but in fact things tend to get overlooked. Each person thinks someone else is taking care of it.

A further change of head, 'Mr Lucas', brought further sweeping changes. The discredited 'tripartite' system of houses, years and schools was replaced with a pastoral structure based upon a 'lower school', 'middle school' and 'upper school', each with its own head and assistant head of school. Role descriptions for these staff were set out in a staff handbook, and seemed very much a combination of the duties expected of the heads of house, school and year in the past. The role description for heads of subject departments was laid out in great detail whereas that for heads of faculty was very brief indeed. This, along with the promise that the faculty/department structure would be examined and if necessary revised, signalled a further rationalization in which the subject heads of department would be given greater prominence within the curricular structure and a consequent phasing out of the role of the faculty heads. The motives for these changes can be interpreted in different ways. Their effect was to create structures within the school which were both administratively more simple and which enabled tighter hierarchic control. As Mr Lucas put it:

> The structure has to be much more clearly set out and much simpler. The responsibilities people have must be more clearly set out and the sanctions that can be applied by different people in different positions have to be much more clearly specified.

But these were not the only justifications he offered for the new system which he had implemented. He also claimed to justify it in terms of the contribution it made to overcoming the 'pastoral–academic split' which he felt had been institutionalized under Sewell. As one senior member of staff remarked:

> The head's view, which I don't completely share, is that if you are going to overcome the dichotomy between academic and pastoral care you have to emphasize the academic people as being pastoral. The head of department now has a dual role which reduces the academic–pastoral split, therefore the heads of department underpin the heads of school.

This 'enhanced' role for the head of subject department could be seen in the part they were to play in a new process of referral which he introduced at the time (Figure 13.1). Although Mr Lucas defended the changes he had made in terms of the contribution which they made to overcoming the 'pastoral–academic split', the 'pastoral' aspect he seems to have emphasized has much to do with 'discipline'. This interpretation was shared by a number of senior staff, not all of whom were hostile to the new system. Thus one commented 'in terms of pastoral, in Mr Lucas's terms, read disciplinary'; and another, a former head of house and a head of school in the new system, when asked what part he saw pastoral care as playing within the school replied, 'Being a buffer state, a discipline state. Pastoral care is another word for discipline'. A head of department, describing what the new system could mean for him, and in particular its referral aspect, put it bluntly:

> [It] puts a premium on incompetence. For example these [referring to a bundle of referral slips] are the forms I have had from one particular teacher this week. Instead of creating his own discipline he has referred to me. The onus of forcing discipline falls on me. . . . What is happening is that the weak teacher is pushing his problems of discipline on to the head of department.

At Rivendell, and to a greater extent at Revelstone, the issue of the 'pastoral–academic split' has given rise to significant conflict between the curricular and the non-curricular systems and their respective subject heads and pastoral leaders. With a pastoral structure of four houses, each with a head and assistant head of house, and an academic structure of subject departments, with one or two quasi faculties such as science (which does not operate as a faculty) and design studies (which does), Revelstone has possessed for a number of years the kind of managerial and professional system at which the latest regime at Rivendell seems to be aiming.

Both house and subject department structures at Revelstone can be traced back to its grammar school origins but as one of the deputies points out:

> Well, of course, in the grammar school days there were houses but they were very much used for sporting and other competitive activities. . . . When we went comprehensive the whole structure of the house system was strengthened . . . by the time I came (in 1969) the 'dual-management system' had been set up. I think there was a quite considerable amount of friction between heads of department, who were well established in the grammar school, and this new system.

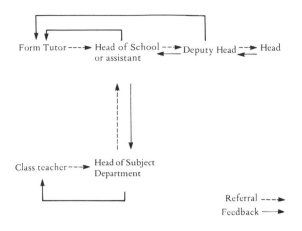

Source: Best *et al.* 1983: 51

Figure 13.1   The new referral process

This was much as the head remembered things. He also recalled an earlier experience:

> When I was at . . . we had enormous arguments between the heads of department and the heads of house as to who was running the show, was the tail wagging the dog? This kind of thing . . . and when I came here there was clearly some bitter feeling between the two.

In the years since then some of these problems, he felt, had to some extent been resolved or, at least, diminished. Thus although the houses 'were given very much greater importance when the comprehensive system came in', since then 'perhaps the emphasis has changed slightly. I have shifted things back a little towards the heads of department because I think the house heads were tending to be regarded as the only people who could keep the place together'. Furthermore,

> I have set things out fairly clearly as to who does what. . . . I have not been aware that there has been a major split. . . . I do not accept that any head of department, as such, does not have any pastoral responsibility. What these may be is not so easy to define. But most heads of department at some time are going to be tutors of certain groups for which they are responsible to a head of house. By the same token every house [head] is responsible to some head of department for his academic work.

For all these reasons he felt that he could 'assume that most of the antipathies which were there at the beginning are not there now. This is not to say that every now and again something does not surface'.

Not all staff share his optimism. One head of house rejected the idea that the house system had ever been in the ascendent. Rather, at Revelstone:

> We put the pastoral side as of less importance than the academic . . . the academic is the strong side of the school and the pastoral side is of less importance. It's the weaker side. Up until the present time this has been agreed upon but there is a wind of change taking place and people are beginning to realize that there are more and more problems.

While he rejected the idea that a significant 'pastoral–academic split' existed at the school, he did think that some of the heads of department did take the view that the school put too much emphasis on pastoral care:

> But those very same people are the first to come running for help . . . [some] are hostile because they can't see any immediate results . . . somebody comes to me and says that little Billy has not been doing any homework this term and what am I going to do about it? Next week they find that the boy is still not doing homework and are critical. They expect immediate action and because it does not happen they assume the system is not working. Also, a lot of them are against pastoral care because they don't want to do it themselves.

Some heads of department were, indeed, very critical of aspects of the house system. As one put it:

> I feel that the pastoral system is weak at this school and it has no reason to be. It is very heavy on scale points, there is a scale four and a scale three in charge of every house. . . . Which in a school of 1,200 kids is far too many. . . . I don't feel that the second houseperson is necessary. I think there is only one strong house [head] . . . he will act on what is told to him. The other three are weak. I have taken discipline problems to them and have realized that the way they have dealt with it is far milder than the way that I have dealt with it before I took it to them. In that case you rarely go back. You need to feel that 'when I have exhausted my resources', I can go on to them. They are the bigger guns . . . there are serious holes in the pastoral structure, consequently there is a tendency for staff to hop over them and go straight to the deputies.

Similar points were made by other staff at Revelstone:

> The most effective houses are 'Milton' followed by 'Keats'. . . . They both have strong house staff who are helpful and support you if you have a discipline problem. . . . The others are less useful.

Such references to pastoral leaders as being more or less 'strong' or 'mild' in the way in which they deal with problems of discipline referred to them, as 'big guns' of the final resort, and to their 'usefulness' or 'helpfulness' as agents of control as the criteria for judging their 'effectiveness' are all characteristic of the discipline-centred perspective. Although more staff at Revelstone were likely to adopt such an attitude than at Rivendell, they were certainly not absent from the latter:

> As far as I can see, there is little in the way of distinguishing features between [the house structure and the year structure]. In individual cases the head of house may be stronger than the head of year, so you go to the former. At least this arrangement gives you two bites at the cherry: if one doesn't pay off the other does.

> When a teacher needs an ultimate deterrent they send the child to me. If it is a serious problem . . . I make contact immediately with the parents. In such cases I contact the house head to put together information on the case. . . . I have a thirty-year reputation as a disciplinarian, known to be firm and fair. The children know it's a 'fair cop'.
>
> (assistant head of upper school)

The last remark shows that some pastoral leaders also shared such attitudes to their responsibilities. These comments quoted from the staff at the two schools lead us to a problem which can be stated as two questions. First, 'What is pastoral care?' Second, 'What do the staff of particular schools actually mean by pastoral care and how do they enact those meanings?' As we have seen from the cases of Rivendell and Revelstone there are no simple answers to these questions. This is a hard but crucial lesson for those concerned with the management of pastoral care. But it is one they must take seriously.

How can research help the pastoral manager?

As a prescription for what 'pastoral care' ought to be, I have a great deal of sympathy for the kinds of views expressed by the authors of the 'conventional wisdom'. But I am less happy about some of the assumptions they make when they turn to the management of the pastoral care. To put it simply, they all too often start from the wrong place. For an example of this we may turn to Keith Blackburn's (1983) fine and often useful treatise on the role of the pastoral leader. In his introduction he writes 'I have assumed throughout that the school has a developed idea of what will be achieved through its pastoral structures, and that those who hold a post of responsibility have in fact real areas of responsibility and leadership within the school' (1983: 1). The cases of Rivendell, Revelstone, and of other in-depth studies in schools (see 'Bishop McGregor', Burgess, 1983; 'Marshland Castle', Lang, 1982; 'Deanswater', Ribbins and Ribbins, 1986; 'Oakfield', Woods, 1983) all suggest that these are just the kinds of assumptions that ought not to be made.

To summarize, systematic research by 'professional researchers' and by 'practitioners as researchers' calls into question many of the central tenets of the 'conventional wisdom' in so far as these:

1 consider pastoral care as one aspect of the teacher's role on the tacit assumption that teachers are, or ought to be, 'child centred' in all aspects of their role – some clearly are not;
2 fail to take account of the meanings which teachers give to 'pastoral care', the construction they put on formal pastoral structures and processes and their responsibilities within these, and the extent to which the perspectives, styles and ideologies they adopt are essentially 'teacher centred' rather than 'child centred';
3 ignore the importance of teachers' own interests as instructors, disciplinarians and administrators in the perspectives and styles they adopt towards pastoral purposes, systems and practices;
4 ignore the problem of institutionalizing something which may have quite different meanings for different teachers and groups of teachers in the same school.

This last is very much a key idea of the conventional wisdom, that the absence of some kind of formal structure for the provision of 'pastoral care' leaves it to 'blind chance and sentiment'. In short, as Marland (1974) puts it, 'it is really a truism of school planning that what you want to happen must be institutionalised'. This is a popular idea; but what was it which was actually institutionalized at the schools listed above? What, for example, had Rivendell institutionalized? What was written in the staff handbook and in other official documents, and what staff said on public occasions looked a lot like the things to be found in the conventional wisdom. But from our observations and from the things teachers at the school told us, we concluded that:

1 only two of the houses worked really effectively;
2 the role of the head of year was nowhere clearly specified and most teachers were pretty uncertain about what they were expected to do;
3 teachers were therefore frequently uncertain as to whom they should go, or to whom they should refer children with problems;
4 problems of protocol resulted;
5 many teachers used the system for passing on their own problems, particularly as a means of buttressing their own discipline;
6 many teachers complained of communications problems and others that the system was so complicated that some children fell through the net anyway;
7 the form periods were often not used for pastoral care;
8 the 'induction programme' was inadequate and largely served purposes not too obviously connected with the needs of children;
9 there was nothing remotely like a pastoral curriculum;
10 teachers often evaluated the system as an unsatisfactory use of scarce

establishment points, an administrative nightmare, or an ineffectual
disciplinary machine;

11 finally, when the system was 'rationalized' the rationale for the reorganization seemed to have little to do with the advantages and disadvantages
of alternative systems for the care of children.

We concluded that there was some truth in our own conception of pastoral
care systems as having as much to do with the problems of teachers as
disciplinarians and as administrators, as with the needs and interests of pupils.

This does not mean that the teachers at Rivendell did not care about
children. Many of them did – some superbly! But some of them saw 'caring'
through formal-traditional eyes as instructors and disciplinarians. Yet others,
and these teachers are quite numerous at Rivendell (and elsewhere), are so
preoccupied with their own problems of classroom survival that they seem to
have little time or energy left over to think about the individual problems of
identity, adjustment and happiness of their pupils.

Finally, what passed for the institutionalization of pastoral care in the
form of a highly elaborate 'net' through which no problem could fall, turned
out to be a bureaucratic nightmare and an ineffective control hierarchy. When
the system was drastically rationalized and simplified it did probably become
a more efficient disciplinary instrument but at the cost of being even less
successful at meeting the caring needs of children. It is not that there were no
caring teachers at Rivendell; rather it is the case that such caring teachers were
often caring *despite* the established systems. None the less, in the case of two
of the houses and, perhaps, two of the years, the structure did provide a
framework in which some effective caring was facilitated. To some extent, it
also facilitated the activities of a wonderfully effective school counsellor,
although, in his case, much of his success had little to do with the system
itself. Finally, the shortfall between the stated objectives of the conventional
wisdom – reproduced by senior staff on public occasions and written up in the
official documents of the school – and actual practice were considerable. In
regard to this school at any rate, the conventional wisdom is used, to a
significant extent, for rhetorical purposes.

[. . .]

The following proposals are intended to suggest possible strategies
which those seeking to improve the organization and management of
pastoral care might consider rather than a detailed recipe appropriate to all
needs and circumstances. These suggestions are designed to achieve two
main outcomes:

1 To ensure that as many members of the teaching staff as reasonably
possible reach a common understanding of the nature of pastoral care and
of how it relates to the other facets of a school's provision;

2 To ensure that such an understanding is translated into effective practice
through the setting up of appropriate organizational and managerial
arrangements.

The Rivendell experience shows clearly that 'without a substantial degree of consensus about what it is that both people and structures are supposed to be doing the opportunities for inefficiency, misunderstanding, tension, conflict, and personal antagonism are enormous' (Best *et al.*, 1983: 282). Once some agreement on this has been achieved it is necessary to deliver this through structures appropriate to such purposes. Unnecessary complexity may be a barrier but one should not be fooled into thinking that complexity alone was the cause of Rivendell's problems. 'Rather, the system was mystifying and counter-productive because it was created in the absence of a clear understanding of precisely how different aspects of the school were to operate' (Best *et al.*, 1983: 282).

Improving the character of pastoral provision will raise different problems in different schools and in different contexts. The plan of attack, for example, of the senior staff of a new school might be both different and easier than those in a long established school. With these qualifications in mind, the following sequence of seven phases for the improvement of the management of pastoral care is proposed:

1 An initial and substantial period of discussion and consultation involving as many staff as possible aimed at achieving as high a level of consensus as practicable as to what pastoral care is and how it ought to be achieved.
2 In such planning or reorganizing of the pastoral provision of a school it is necessary to consult and listen carefully to the views of individual teachers and groups of teachers in order to be clear about what they expect and want from the various facets of the school's organization.
3 Those concerned with the management of pastoral care at the level of the school as a whole, and to some extent with the management of pastoral divisions as well, might find it helpful to compile a list of what it is they want their pastoral care provision to achieve, and also a second list of what it is that other teachers expect the pastoral system to do for them.
4 A great deal of thought needs to be given to the geographical and social conditions of the school, and to the relationships between teachers and teachers and between teachers and pupils in the setting up of appropriate pastoral structures and systems. Hard decisions will also be needed in determining the scope and scale of the changes to be attempted.
5 Change for the sake of change has little to recommend it. Those who seek to improve the provision of an existing or established pastoral system at the level of the school as a whole or of some part of it should undertake a careful evaluation of what already exists. At the level of the whole school this may entail examining a wide range of its pastoral, academic, disciplinary and administrative arrangements. Such an evaluation would take as its point of departure the recognition of the fact that aims and functions are not the same thing. The prospective innovator would need both to assess existing arrangements in terms of stated objectives and to establish as precisely as

possible what functions these existing arrangements are performing as a prelude to any worthwhile change.

6 Once decisions are made about the kinds of changes which are necessary the system to be aimed for should be the simplest which will achieve the stated objectives. But however 'simple' it is, it must not be assumed that teachers or pupils will necessarily understand it. Effort will have to be put in to ensure that this happens.

7 Finally, schools need to devise some strategy for ongoing evaluation. Successful achievement of some of the earlier phases are a necessary prelude to this exercise. Thus if a clear understanding of what is being attempted under the heading of pastoral care, some statement of specific objectives however difficult it is to give them expression, and some set of agreed performance indicators do not exist it is hard to see what useful purposes would be served by such an evaluation or by what criteria it should be accomplished. Without these things, of course, the existence of effective and worthwhile pastoral structures and systems within a school would be a matter of chance and good fortune.

References

Best, R. and Ribbins, P. (1983) 'Rethinking the pastoral–academic split', *Pastoral Care in Education*, **1**(1); 11–18.

Best, R. and Ribbins, P. (1985) 'Research in education: pastoral care in the comprehensive school' (unpublished paper).

Best, R., Jarvis, C. and Ribbins, P. (1977) 'Pastoral care: concept and process', *British Journal of Education Studies*, **25**(2), 124–35.

Best, R., Jarvis, C. and Ribbins, P. (1980) *Perspectives on Pastoral Care*, London, Heinemann.

Best, R., Ribbins, P., Jarvis, C. and Oddy, D. (1983) *Education and Care*, London, Heinemann.

Blackburn, K. (1975) *The Tutor*, London, Heinemann.

Blackburn, K. (1983) *Head of House/Head of Year*, Oxford, Blackwell.

Burgess, R. (1983) *Experiencing Comprehensive Education*, London, Methuen.

Haigh, G. (1975) *Pastoral Care*, London, Pitman.

Lang, P. (1977) 'It's easier to punish us in small groups', *Times Educational Supplement*, 6 May, p. 17.

Lang, P. (1982) 'Pastoral care: concern or contradiction?', MA thesis (unpublished), University of Warwick.

Marland, M. (1974) *Pastoral Care*, London, Heinemann.

Ribbins, P. and Ribbins, P. (1986) 'Developing a design for living course at 'Deanswater' Comprehensive School', *Pastoral Care in Education*, **4**(1), 23–37.

Woods, E. (1983) 'The structure and practice of pastoral care at Oakfield School', M.Ed. dissertation (unpublished), University of Birmingham.

14

Towards a collegiate approach to curriculum management in primary and middle schools

Mike Wallace

The purpose of this chapter is to explore how the process of management development may assist the professional staff of primary and middle schools in moving towards collegiate management of the curriculum. It is argued that HMI and other informed professionals have put forward a model of good management practice which appears not to have been implemented in many schools because it contains certain contradictions. Some ways are suggested of facilitating its implementation.

The official model of good practice

In England and Wales during recent years the way in which professional staff in schools organize the curriculum has been subjected to the criticism of HMI, the DES, the Welsh Office and other informed groups within the education service. Implicit within the plethora of policy statements, surveys, inquiries and inspection reports lies a model of good management practice. Evidence of the 'official' model is contained in positive statements and may be inferred from criticisms expressed about schools. A broadly consistent view is set out in, for example, major national surveys conducted by HMI (DES, 1978; 1979; 1982a; 1983a; 1985a; Welsh Office, 1978); HMI inspection reports published since 1983 and their summaries (DES, 1984a; 1984b; 1985b); other surveys and occasional papers by HMI (e.g. DES, 1977; 1980a; 1982b; Welsh Office, 1984; 1985); official publications informed by HMI reports (e.g. DES, 1980b; 1981; 1983b; 1985c; 1986); the reports of national (Bullock, 1975; Cockcroft, 1982) and local committees of inquiry (e.g. ILEA, 1984; 1985); and the working papers of the Schools Council (1981; 1983). In essence, good curriculum management is seen as a process where all professional staff participate actively in negotiating an agreed curriculum and contribute jointly to planning, implementing and evaluating its delivery (including evaluating and giving feedback upon each other's performance as managers and class-teachers). Where the model is implemented, it is held to be a contributory factor in ensuring that pupils receive a desirable, consistent and progressive educational experience.

The model is to some extent consistent with the principles of 'collegial authority', defined by Lortie (1964) as the form of authority in which professional equals govern their affairs through democratic procedures. According to the sources mentioned, managerial roles and tasks should be shared out among professional colleagues who work collaboratively through various consultation procedures. While a management hierarchy exists, [. . .] there is a degree of overlap between the spheres of responsibility which is very different from the models of 'line-management' prevalent outside education (e.g. Handy, 1981).

The greatest overlap between responsibilities occurs in primary and middle schools, where most teachers operate in a range of curriculum areas where they are not designated as a specialist or expert, most significantly in their role as teachers responsible for a class. This arrangement of over-lapping responsibilities may be interpreted as approximating to a model of management based on principles of collegiality.

Figure 14.1 is a simple framework for analysing the official interpreta-tion of good practice. Pupil learning is influenced by individual teachers' classroom performance in delivering the curriculum within the climate of the school. The latter term refers to the general conditions surrounding learning which reflect the values of the various groups of people within the school as expressed in, for example, expectations about pupil behaviour (inside and outside the classroom) and about levels of achievement. Teachers' actions are influenced, in turn, by how all members of the professional staff organize themselves so as to bring about effective teaching within a climate supportive of learning. Organization is achieved through management tasks performed by individuals occupying various roles. Incumbents of particular roles are expected to act in certain ways in carrying out tasks associated with the areas of school life for which they are responsible. The key role which affects management of the curriculum is that of the headteacher, who is legally responsible for the day-to-day work of the school. Heads' behaviour in retaining or sharing the tasks of curriculum management has a bearing upon colleagues' performance of their roles. As the 'gatekeepers' of their schools, heads respond to various external influences, most immediately through the governors. Influence runs in two directions since the response of pupils and of heads and teachers in their class-room management roles has a bearing upon the actions of others at each level.

In the official documents good practice is seen to be based upon the clear differentiation of roles within the professional staff. Individuals occupy two or more roles, some of which, such as the leader of a group of classes, appear

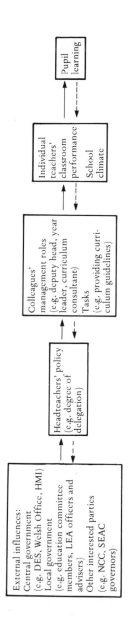

Figure 14.1   Management of the curriculum at school level

Table 14.1 Roles, curriculum responsibilities and associated tasks

Role	Curriculum responsibility	Major task area
Headteacher	Overall responsibility for curriculum management	Consulting with colleagues Developing staff through structure of delegated responsibilities Clarifying roles and tasks through job descriptions Managing the staff development policy Evaluating pupils' progress and the work of professional staff
Deputy headteacher	Leading staff in formulation of curriculum policy	Arranging for curriculum planning Supporting curriculum consultants Devising timetable
Leader of groups of classes	Co-ordinating day-to-day work of a group of classes	Co-ordinating teaching within and between year groups Liaising with other schools
Teacher/ tutor	Induction of probationary teachers and oversight of staff development	Guiding probationary teachers within curriculum policies Managing staff development policy
Curriculum consultant	Oversight throughout the school for an area of the curriculum	Planning a programme of work Consulting colleagues during planning Organizing study groups Initiating dialogue during implementation Giving demonstration lessons and working alongside colleagues Procuring resources Observing classes or analysing test results and evaluating colleagues' work Arranging school-based INSET Liaising with other schools
General class or specialist teacher	Teaching the agreed curriculum	Working according to guidelines Using agreed resources Contributing to planning and consultation procedure Evaluating pupils' progress

only in larger schools. Each role carries responsibilities associated with the curriculum, achieved through specific tasks. These tasks are held to contain both a content dimension, in so far as individuals should engage in certain activities, and a process dimension – an idea of how the activities should be carried out using certain skills. The roles, responsibilities and tasks outlined in Table 14.1 are mentioned in one or more of the official guidelines; there appear to be no major inconsistencies between statements in different documents. Particular importance is attached to the contribution of curriculum consultants as subject specialists or advisers to their colleagues.

A gulf between the model and reality

There is ample evidence quoted within the documents mentioned and available from other sources (e.g. Bornett, 1980; Rushby and Richards, 1982; Williams, 1982; PSRDG, 1983; Rodger, 1983; Campbell, 1984; Robinson, 1983; ILEA, 1986) to suggest that, in perhaps the majority of primary and middle schools, the model has not been fully implemented. Some incumbents of each role are criticized in this literature: heads often fail to: delegate management responsibility, set up procedures for curriculum planning or give colleagues enough time to carry out their delegated management activities. Deputy heads are frequently excluded from sharing the overall management of the school, to the detriment of those who are preparing for future headship. Leaders of groups of classes may be unclear how their sphere of influence articulates with that of curriculum consultants. The latter are rarely given the support necessary to enable them to take the initiative in supporting their colleagues. Many class-teachers lack the expertise necessary to teach a broad curriculum effectively. Many heads do not delegate enough and their colleagues do not engage in the process of communication implied by the collegiate model of curriculum management.

HMI reports indicate that it is possible to implement the model and research (ILEA 1986) suggests that it is associated with effective pupil learning. If we accept the plausibility of the model, it is important to ask why it has consistently proved difficult to implement.

Unpacking collegiate management

From a management perspective, it is possible to identify within the model several tensions or contradictions related to the way the professional staff are expected to organize themselves so as to manage the curriculum effectively. 'Good practice' is more complex than it might initially appear.

First, there is considerable overlap between the curriculum responsibilities accorded to the various roles. All members of professional staff (except perhaps probationary teachers) are expected to carry out at least two roles, one or more of which entails influencing the work of colleagues. For example, the House of Commons Education, Science and Arts Committee (1986) recommends that the requirement for heads to teach pupils should be established in legislation and suggests that most heads should act as co-ordinator for one aspect of the school's work. If the logic of the model is carried through, conflict may arise between overlapping responsibilities carried out by different people (or occasionally by the same person). Where consensus exists over the shape of the curriculum, such tensions will not be apparent; but when people hold different views, the issue arises over who has the right to define what should actually take place during the processes of planning, implementation and evaluation. It is widely recognized in middle schools that those with 'horizontal' responsibility for a year group and those with 'vertical' responsibility for an area of the curriculum throughout the school must negotiate the degree of influence each is to hold over the curriculum, occasionally giving rise to conflict (e.g. Bornett, 1980).

Second, potential tension is also embedded in the relationship between the roles of curriculum consultant and class-teacher. Many teachers expect a high degree of autonomy over the delivery of the curriculum in their classrooms, yet their professional judgement may conflict with that of the consultant. Campbell (1984: 353) gives an example of a curriculum con-sultant responsible for language who experienced strain in her role because she perceived that working alongside colleagues, advising them and moni-toring the progress of the curriculum policy throughout the school would be perceived by her colleagues as 'inspecting' the quality of their response to the language policy. She preferred to avoid potential conflict by waiting for staff to seek advice.

Third, it is only since the revised salary scales were introduced in the Teachers' Pay and Conditions Act of 1987 that the salary structure has come to reflect the management structure of schools (Wallace, 1986a). Prior to that, the number of posts available that carried salary scale 2 or above was dictated by the size of the school and the age range of the pupils. The number of these posts did not necessarily coincide with the school's management structure. Consequently, 'anomalies' were common: for example, Jefferson (1984) mentions several cases of joint curriculum responsibility including a situation where curriculum development in mathematics was shared between two teachers, one on scale 1 and the other on scale 3. In smaller schools, teachers often have more than one responsibility in order to cover curriculum and organizational areas. The salary structure has been revised but most of the roles set out in Table 14.1 continue to exist. Many 'middle management' roles fall to teachers on the main salary scale, only some of whom receive an incentive allowance.

Fourth, in the literature there are few if any accounts of tension between the headteachers (or deputies) in their class-teaching roles and curriculum consultants or leaders of groups of classes. Yet according to the logic of the model, when headteachers are undertaking their regular class-teaching they come under the jurisdiction of the curriculum consultant for the area in which they are teaching, and in larger schools they may also be working with pupils within the influence of the leader of those classes. It is possible that in small schools some of the heads' teaching lies within the sphere of influence of teachers on the main scale who are acting as curriculum consultants. According to the official model, these teachers might be recently trained and well versed in new ideas on curriculum content and pedagogy. Are such teachers likely to feel comfortable in asking to observe heads' classwork so as to evaluate their teaching performance? The model may not have been implemented in many cases because the hierarchy of curriculum influence contradicts the formal hierarchy supported in recent years by differential salaries.

Fifth, problems related to overlapping roles are expressed in the associated tasks: the boundaries of responsibilities must be negotiated at the level of quite detailed activities. For instance, according to the official model, curriculum consultants are expected to procure resources for their colleagues to use. It is debatable who is to prepare resources once they have arrived in school.

Sixth, the task of evaluating the curriculum is potentially highly sensitive. Some years ago, HMI stated that holders of posts of special responsibility should assess the effectiveness of the guidance and resources they provide, and this may involve visiting other classes in the school to see the work in progress (DES, 1978). Many teachers do not find this task amenable – whether as curriculum consultants (PSRDG, 1983; Rodger, 1983) or as year leaders (Robinson, 1983). It is not clear how many headteachers observe, evaluate, and give feedback to colleagues. Such action may be seen to transgress teachers' rightful classroom autonomy as professionals. Yet unless steps are taken to discover whether an agreed curriculum has been implemented in the way that was intended by the person responsible, or whether there have been unanticipated consequences, there is no guarantee that curriculum guidelines will actually influence practice.

Finally, it is apparent that achievement of the tasks of curriculum management recognized within the official model requires a considerable amount of time to be set aside during the school day. HMI has noted this necessity on many occasions (e.g. DES, 1986). Assigning time depends upon various factors including headteachers' and colleagues' perception of the need, staffing levels which are influenced by national and local government policies, and LEA policies for provision of supply cover. Southworth (1985) points out that many primary school heads are frequently forced to act as supply teachers, to the detriment of the management aspects of their work. Some proponents of the official model may not have understood the amount of time needed to manage the curriculum management process – the dialogue required to plan, negotiate, introduce, implement and evaluate what, for the staff of many schools, is a new way of working together, contradicting many deeply ingrained habits and deeply held beliefs, according to a sophisticated and complex model.

In sum, the new way of working presupposed in the model appears often to have been implemented at a superficial level. In many schools the professional staff appears to go through the motions of collegiate management without integrating the full implications of the model into everyday practice – a situation of innovation without change. Many heads seem to make what Lortie (1969) calls 'low constraint decisions': it is tacitly accepted that colleagues have considerable choice in practice over the extent to which they implement formally agreed policies, and it is mutually understood that there will be no follow-up to check that decisions are actually put into effect. Moreover, there are different zones where those with formal authority to make decisions are perceived to have the necessary power in practice. It is generally accepted that curriculum consultants may produce guidelines and procure resources, but monitoring colleagues' work and commenting upon their pedagogy tends to lie outside their decision-making zone. Through reliance on low-constraint decisions and variable zoning, decision-makers avoid the vulnerability which could stem from colleagues' reactions in sensitive areas.

Collegiate management: nightmare or worthwhile innovation?

To many managers outside education, the collegiate model would probably appear to be a nightmare – too many overlapping fingers in the management pie! But shared management accords with the value of collaboration associated with teaching as a profession (Hoyle, 1975), although collegiality is limited by heads' legal authority for the work of their schools and differential salaries currently awarded for senior levels of management responsibility (Hoyle, 1986). There is evidence, largely from North America, that schools which practise a broadly collegiate style of management are effective in implementing all kinds of curriculum and organizational innovations. On the basis of a synthesis of the literature, Fullan (1985: 400–4) has identified four factors that underlie successful school improvement efforts:

1 a feel for the complexity, turbulence and demands of the improvement process on the part of the leadership
2 an explicit guiding value system which favours collegiality, clear rules, genuine caring about individuals and commitment to examination of detail
3 intense interaction and communication which provide positive pressure and support and give rise to new understanding
4 collaborative planning and implementation within schools and among those involved in their support.

These factors have much in common with the collaborative process by which the incumbents of various roles are expected to achieve their tasks within the official conception of collegiate management outlined in earlier sections of this chapter.

If the model is broadly accepted in principle as a means of improving pupil learning through a process which accords with professional values, we may usefully explore further how schools which do not practise collegiate management might work towards that aim. It seems that each person involved must come to understand what is entailed, know how to perform the necessary tasks with skill and tact, value collegiality and develop a positive attitude towards learning to work in this way. As Fullan (1982) identified, attitude change is particularly difficult to bring about. These analytic categories of conceptual knowledge, skills, values and attitude cannot, in the view of the present writer, be tackled sequentially in reality. Activities may, however, focus upon particular aspects of necessary knowledge, skills, values or attitudes while implicitly helping to develop others. From personal experience it seems valuable for staff to develop together:

1 awareness of individuals' educational values
2 acceptance of the need to agree upon school aims
3 clarity about rights, responsibilities and their boundaries in respect of each other
4 acceptance that people are likely to have different, and possibly conflicting, interests
5 understanding that different perceptions of the same situation are likely to exist – no one has a monopoly on truth
6 acceptance of the need therefore to give and receive constructive evaluation and feedback
7 specific skills needed to carry out tasks effectively
8 mutual trust and respect
9 willingness to give and take in order to achieve consensus or to implement an agreed compromise once majority agreement has been obtained.

The implementation strategy for the development implied by this innovation is likely to take a long time, since the people involved, the challenges they face and the experience upon which they draw are continually changing. It would be unwise to regard the model as a 'blueprint for perfection' as experience suggests that any innovation becomes modified in the light of the implementation attempt through mutual adaptation (Dalin and Rust, 1983). The model is merely what the term 'model' implies – a simplified vision which gives us something to aim for.

Management development

A strategy that may support the joint development process is conceived by the National Development Centre for School Management Training as 'management development', or that part of staff development concerned with those who have, or aspire towards management responsibility. In essence, it is 'the process whereby the management function of an organization becomes performed with increasing effectiveness' (Bolam, 1986: 261). This definition implies that individual 'manager development' is organized so that, over time, those with or aspiring towards management responsibility develop in such a way that the organization as a whole develops. In order to ensure that co-ordinated management development takes place it is necessary for each school to develop a management development policy and associated programme of activities as part of its concern for staff development. A review of individual needs is conducted, through appraisal interviews or a staff questionnaire, for example. These needs are balanced with group and school-wide needs, identified by the headteacher or by participative means such as a school self-evaluation exercise. Once priorities are established, suitable activities are selected, implemented and evaluated, leading to the identification of new needs. Within the wide range of activities more or less closely related to the normal job available (see Wallace, 1986b) there are several which seem to be particularly appropriate for promoting a collegiate approach to curriculum management, including:

1 an exercise in role, responsibility and task clarification through negotiation of job descriptions
2 training in specific skills, such as active listening, counselling and assertiveness
3 practice in carrying out structured classroom observation and review procedures
4 a team-building exercise to help staff members to articulate their views and feelings and to promote mutual trust
5 school-based, in-service workshops organized by curriculum consultants
6 opportunities to try out other roles in the school (see Wallace 1985)
7 self-development exercises designed to raise individuals' awareness of their personal values and their assumptions about colleagues
8 development of critical friendships for mutual and confidential support
9 shadowing exercises involving observing colleagues and giving feedback upon their management performance
10 techniques such as brainstorming or the use of flipcharts which encourage participation in meetings
11 evaluation of staff meetings
12 school-wide monitoring of the use of each person's time
13 organization development activities to improve the school's ability for problem-solving (e.g. Schmuck and Runkel, 1985).

For management development to be effective in all schools within an LEA, it is necessary for the needs identified by schools to be matched with those relating to the LEA's policy. LEA policies may include curriculum initiatives such as home language teaching or equal opportunities in physical education whose implementation must be managed by staff in schools. They may also refer directly to management concerns: forming clusters of primary schools or the preparation of deputy heads for a possible headship, for example. Therefore, it is also necessary for a management development policy and programme for schools to be developed at LEA level within its framework for staff development. Management development needs of school staff must be identified in relation to LEA policies and according to groups at similar points in their career across the teaching force, such as newly appointed headteachers. Surveys of LEA advisers' informed opinion, questionnaires sent to schools or the development of a data base containing details of teachers' individual career stages throughout the LEA are among the methods that may be employed to identify these needs. The LEA's management development policy and a programme may be articulated with that of the schools through a consultative process such as a scheme of bids for support or a joint committee representing schools and the LEA so that priorities for meeting needs may be established and activities designed within available resources, implemented and evaluated (see McMahon and Bolam, 1987).

One priority for LEAs may be to promote a collegiate approach to curriculum management in primary and middle schools. It will be necessary to identify the needs of individuals, groups and whole schools across the LEA by the various means outlined and to develop a suitable programme of activities, possibly including financial support for the school-based activities listed earlier. LEAs are required by central government to articulate a policy and programme of in-service training for their teaching force (DES, 1985b). Management development forms a part of that policy and programme within the framework of the LEA training grants arrangements.

[. . .] The House of Commons Education, Science and Arts Committee recommended that there should be additional primary teachers to enable schools to benefit both from additional curriculum expertise and from more flexible staffing with more teachers than registration classes. LEA arrangements for in-service training coupled with the influx of extra teachers if these were to materialize would provide a golden opportunity for LEAs to promote collegiate management in primary and middle schools. We are in a period of rapid change as the government implements its radical programme for educational reform. Heads and staff have to manage the implementation of multiple innovations – from a national curriculum with regular testing, through new conditions of service to local financial management in larger schools. Since each of these innovations has implications for managing the curriculum in schools in the primary sector, the government's programme suggests that developing collegiality as a means of managing change is now a matter of urgency.

References

Bolam, R. (1986) 'The National Development Centre for School Management Training', in E. Hoyle and A. McMahon (eds) *The Management of Schools*, London, Kogan Page.

Bornett, C. (1980) 'Staffing in middle schools: the roots and routes of hierarchy', in A. Hargreaves and L. Tickle (eds) *Middle Schools*, London, Harper & Row.

Bullock, Sir A. (1975) *A Language for Life*, Report of a Committee of Inquiry chaired by Sir Alan Bullock, London, HMSO.

Campbell, R. J. (1984) 'In-school development: the role of the curriculum post-holder', *School Organization*, **4**(4), 345–57.

Cockroft, W. H. (1982) *Mathematics Counts*, Report of a Committee of Inquiry chaired by Sir William Cockcroft, London, HMSO.

Dalin, P. and Rust, V. (1983) *Can Schools Learn?*, Windsor, NFER–Nelson.

DES (1977) *Ten Good Schools: A Secondary School Enquiry*, London, HMSO.

DES (1978) *Primary Education in England*, London, HMSO.

DES (1979) *Aspects of Secondary Education in England*, London, HMSO.

DES (1980a) *A View of the Curriculum*, HMI series: Matters for Discussion, London, HMSO.

DES (1980b) *A Framework for the School Curriculum*, London, HMSO.

DES (1981) *The School Curriculum*, London, HMSO.

DES (1982a) *Education 5 to 9: An Illustrative Survey of 80 First Schools in England*, London, HMSO.

DES (1982b) *The New Teacher in School*, London, HMSO.

DES (1983a) *9–13 Middle Schools*, London, HMSO.

DES (1983b) *Teaching Quality*, London, HMSO.

DES (1984a) *Education Observed*, London, DES.

DES (1984b) *Education Observed 2*, London, DES.

DES (1985a) *Education 8–12 in Combined and Middle Schools*, London, HMSO.

DES (1985b) *Education Observed 3*, London, DES.

DES (1985c) *Better Schools*, Cmnd 9469, London, HMSO.

DES (1986) *Report by Her Majesty's Inspectors on the Effects of Local Authority Expenditure Policies on Education Provision in England – 1985*, London, DES.

Fullan, M. (1982) 'Research into educational innovation', in H. L. Gray (ed.) *The Management of Educational Institutions*, Lewes, Falmer Press.

Fullan, M. (1985) 'Change processes and strategies at the local level', *Elementary School Journal*, **85**(3), 391–421.

Handy, C. (1981) *Understanding Organizations*, 2nd edn, Harmondsworth, Penguin.

House of Commons Education, Science and Arts Committee (1986) *Achievement in Primary Schools*, London, HMSO.

Hoyle, E. (1975) 'Professionality, professionalism and control in teaching', in V. Houghton, R. McHugh and C. Morgan (eds) *Management in Education*, London, Ward Lock Educational.

Hoyle, E. (1986) *The Politics of School Management*, London, Hodder & Stoughton.

ILEA (1984) *Improving Secondary Schools*, Report of the Committee of Inquiry chaired by D. Hargreaves, London, Inner London Education Authority.

ILEA (1985) *Improving Primary Schools*, Report of the Committee of Inquiry chaired by N. Thomas, London, Inner London Education Authority.

ILEA (1986) *The Junior School Project*, Summary of Main Report, London, Inner London Education Authority Research and Statistics Branch.

Jefferson, C. (1984) 'The responsibility of scale post holder primary-schools', in L. Watson (ed.) *Aspects of Primary School Management*, Education Management Department, Sheffield Polytechnic.

Lortie, D. (1964) 'The teacher and team teaching', in J. Shaplin and H. Olds (eds) *Team Teaching*, New York, Harper & Row.

Lortie, D. (1969) 'The balance of control and autonomy in elementary school teaching', A. Etzioni (ed.) *The Semi-Professions and their Organization*, New York, Free Press.

McMahon, A. and Bolam, R. (1987) *School Management Development: A Handbook for LEAs*, Bristol, NDC.

PSRDG (1983) *Curriculum Responsibility and the Use of Teacher Expertise in the Primary School: Five Studies*, Birmingham, Primary Schools Research and Development Group, University of Birmingham.

Robinson, M. (1983) 'The role of the year leader: an analysis of the perceptions of year leaders and deputy heads in 8–12 middle schools', *School Organization*, 3(4), 333–44.

Rodger, I. (1983) *Teachers with Posts of Responsibility in Primary Schools*, Durham, University of Durham.

Rushby, T. and Richards, C. (1982) 'Staff development in primary schools', *Educational Management and Administration*, 10(3), 223–31.

Schmuck, R. and Runkel, P. (1985) *The Third Handbook of Organization Development in Schools*, Palo Alto, Calif., Mayfield.

Schools Council (1981) *The Practical Curriculum*, London, Methuen.

Schools Council (1983) *Primary Practice*, London, Methuen.

Southworth, G. (1985) 'The headteacher as supply teacher', *Education*, 1 March: 189.

Wallace, M. (1985) 'Promoting careers through management development', *Education 3–13*, 13(2) 12–16.

Wallace, M. (1986a) 'The rise of scale posts as a management hierarchy in schools', *Educational Management and Administration*, 14(3), 203–12.

Wallace, M. (1986b) *A Directory of Management Development Activities and Resources*, Bristol, National Development Centre for School Management Training.

Welsh Office (1978) *Primary Education in Wales*, Cardiff, Welsh Office.

Welsh Office (1984) *Departmental Organization in Secondary Schools*, Cardiff, Welsh Office.

Welsh Office (1985) *Leadership in Primary Schools*, Cardiff, Welsh Office.

Williams, A. (1982) 'Physical education in the junior school', *Education 3–13*, 10(2) 36–40.

15

The micro-politics of the school: baronial politics

Stephen Ball

Baronial politics

In the middle ages the conflicts between English barons were essentially concerned with two matters: wealth and power. In the school the concerns and interests of academic and pastoral barons are fundamentally the same: allocations from the budget, both in terms of capitation moneys and in relation to appointments, timetable time and control of territory (teaching rooms, offices, special facilities), and influence over school policies. Clearly, to a great extent, in the micro-political process these concerns are inseparable: 'If politics is regarded as conflict over whose preferences are to prevail in the determination of policy, then the budget records the outcomes of this struggle' (Wildavsky, 1968: 192).

[. . .]

Here I want to deal with the disputes and struggles between subject departments, particularly in and around the concomitant issues of resource allocation and departmental status.

In the secondary school, leaving aside the pastoral-care structure, subject departments are usually the most significant organizational divisions between teachers as colleagues. On the one hand, the department provides and maintains a special sense of identity for the teacher: it can be a basis for communality. 'The pedagogic subject department forms an epistemic and spatial boundary-maintaining community that its members share as an experience of being a common "kind" of teacher' (Smetherham, 1979: 1), they share a speciality. On the other hand, as I have indicated, the department is the basis for special interests and internecine competition; it is a political coalition:

definitions of centrality and marginality arise through the super-imposition of departmental boundaries on speciality boundaries. One of the significant consequences of this is a budgetary separation which creates competitive groups. Boundaries are rationalized through decisions taken about what is central and what is peripheral as they are exemplified in allocation of time, money, and staff and even students.

(Esland, 1971: 106)

Thus budgets forge and perpetuate (and occasionally change) a pattern of status and a distribution of influence. The competition between departments is a competition between unequals. Relative status and influence become embedded in the curriculum structure of the school and more immediately in the timetable. (Once established, this fixed structure is difficult to alter, either by outside agencies or internal interest groups.) In practice the 'voice' of any particular department, both in relation to policy issues and/or resource decision-making, is effectively limited by whether it is expanding, remaining static or on the defensive.

The specific distribution of the strong baronies and weak baronies will differ between institutions and will change over time; it is the outcome of ongoing conflicts and rivalries. None the less there are typical patterns, and clearly the expectations of influential outside audiences do enhance the claims made by certain subjects and detract from those of others. Richardson gives a flavour of strengths and weaknesses in her account of Nailsea Comprehensive:

> Two of the most persistent images that I carried . . . concerned the modern languages and science departments on the one side and the geography and history departments on the other. The former I saw as the 'giant' departments which seemed able to make their own con-ditions regardless of changes elsewhere in the system – almost, at times, to be holding the staff up to ransom. In contrast to my impression of power and independence in these areas, the departments of geography and history seemed to me to be suffering more than any others (except perhaps classics) from the problems of encroachment, erosion and loss of wholeness.

(Richardson, 1973: 90)

The metaphor of baronial politics seems particularly apt in this case. As Richardson expresses the situation at Nailsea, it is the curriculum that is at stake. With curriculum control comes influence and control over resources; without it there is political impotence. In addition, the strength of modern languages and science also raises the question of the state of their mutual relations as well as their disposition towards weaker departments:

> Were their departments allies, rivals, or equally powerful independent forces in the school? Both were staffed almost entirely by specialist teachers; neither did any appreciable sharing of personnel with other

departments; both insisted, or appeared to insist, on finer setting by ability throughout the school than any other departments did; both were concerned with the development of new methods of teaching that involved the purchase, control and maintenance of expensive technical equipment.

(Richardson, 1973: 92)

However, as Richardson goes on to point out, there were occasions when the giants clashed, but these clashes did little to weaken their entrenched positions. It was the geography and history departments that seemed to be continually losing out in the battle for resources and control over the timetable:

I began to think of geography as a department that was trapped – or perhaps suspended – between the arts and the sciences, having allegiances to both sides and a visible link with both sides through geology, but fearing encroachment from the arts side because of the uncertainty about where the subject was rooted. In the recurring discussions about the humanities course, geography was always linked (uneasily perhaps) with history, as mathematics seemed, in the recurring discussions about mixed-ability grouping, to be uneasily linked with science.

If I saw geography as an area that was being crushed between opposing forces or being stretched in opposite directions, I saw history as an area that felt itself to be shrinking. The encroachments on its territory from humanities in the lower school, from social studies in the middle school, from general studies in the upper school, and perhaps also to a lesser extent from ancient history through classics, had to do partly with the loss of recently acquired subject matter, even of new approaches first worked out in terms of history, and partly with a loss of contact with younger children.

(Richardson, 1973: 95–6)

Several processes affecting the status and political 'voice' of subject departments are evident in the examples drawn from Richardson's study. It is apparent that the fortunes of certain departments are rising while others are in decline. In some areas, like humanities, new empires are being carved out. In others, like history, declarations of independence are undermining status claims which previously seemed inviolate. In the first case, smaller, weaker subjects areas are being swallowed up in expanding conglomerates. In the second, smaller subjects are emerging as separate entities to make their own claims for time, territory, money and personnel.

The impetus for the emergence of new subjects can take several different forms but is inevitably surrounded by political struggle and intrigue. In some cases the arrival of a new subject, and its struggle for departmental status, is shortlived. Goodson (1987) provides one example in his examination of the birth pangs of European studies. The 'subject', such as it was, developed from a combination of idealism, what Bucher and Strauss refer to as a sense of mission, in this case the creation of European consciousness among British school-children, and pragmatism, 'as a vehicle for motivating the less able in languages lessons' (1961: 9). In schools it was the latter that was the main driving force; Goodson (1987) quotes a number of examples, among them:

> Well you see . . . I think as far as we are concerned this was a conscious turning away from what was beginning to develop and then people were starting to say 'what are we going to do with the youngsters who are not learning French or German?' . . . From the point of view of timetable convenience they ought to be doing something associated . . . 'let them learn about Germany, you know and what you have for tea in Brussels or something' . . . we were so frightened that this was what European studies was going to become, some sort of dustbin . . . I think we have consciously turned away from that and although we haven't got to lose sight of it eventually, I think we've got to come back to terms with this after we've done the other things. . . . I think we've got to go ahead from our middle school into our sixth form first and get that thing right and get the subject established with status . . . then we may be able to add on these less able youngsters.
>
> Well, when I became Head of Humanities they also made me Head of European Studies . . . which had been taught on and off for several years to the 'dumbos' in languages. . . . So I organised a meeting to discuss it as a subject – only the young assistant teachers were interested. I went to the Head and asked for money. I was given £150.
>
> (Goodson, 1987: 215)

Here we have both the strengths and weaknesses of an assertive claimant for subject status. On the one hand, European studies teachers can claim to be heard and make demands on school resources in so far as they take responsibility for problematic groups of pupils, the less able. On the other hand, one crucial measure of subject status is taken from access to the most able pupils, particularly in the establishment of sixth-form A-level courses. Here European studies has a problem. The first teacher clearly recognizes this and is suggesting a strategy which will distance the 'subject' from its less able clients and go instead for recruits in the sixth form. But this is exactly the sort of strategy that is likely to meet with opposition from other subjects. To capture sixth-formers for European studies means luring them away from other subject choices. This threatens access to sought-after teaching allocations, capitation, status and perhaps chances of promotion within other departments. The second quotation also suggests contradictory pressures and possibilities. The interest of young teachers can provide important inputs of energy and commitment necessary for the development of new ideas and materials. However, these teachers lack institutional status; there may be considerable political disadvantage as a result of this and not having friends in high places. None the less, from the point of view of the young adherents, a new 'subject' area can offer the potential of career enhancement and increased promotion possibilities, although these possibilities clearly rest upon the successful establishment of that 'subject'. Again Goodson provides a clear example of the problems:

> I'm very disillusioned about my future. Well it hasn't given me a future after five years so I can't see that it will suddenly give me a future in the next few years. I don't think I could have done much more than I have done. I got involved with the County syllabus, had a lot of contacts with the European Resources Centre, one thing and another, and I thought this can only be of benefit to my career. But it's been going on and I've been doing things and doing things and it's done me no good whatsoever. You know I'm still where I was when I came here seven years ago. I just don't know really . . . obviously I've become disillusioned, disheartened.
>
> (Goodson, 1987: 17)

This teacher clearly sees his career tied closely to the development of his subject. The success of work put in is measured in terms of creating a 'future'. To a great extent the teacher is the subject. Their fortunes are inextricably linked.

The conflict potential posed by the rise of a new 'subject' like European studies is increased further if claims are made which actually involve encroachment into the subject matter of other departments. This is often a problem for the 'subjects' which, like European studies, have an interdisciplinary orientation. Much of the failure of interdisciplinarity in the 1960s and 1970s can be accounted for in terms of micro-political resistance. While in content and pedagogical terms interdisciplinary work makes perfect sense, in micro-political terms it looks like empire-building, and it is rational for those who see their interests threatened to resist, to defend their patch. Again Goodson's European studies teachers recognized the problems:

> In a place like this departments are huge and they like to keep their legality. It's [i.e. the construction of a new subject] all a problem of trying to cross barriers which have been there for a long time. However well you get on with people it's still a thought in the back of their mind that their empire could be chipped away at. Interdisciplinary studies are always going to be in that situation.
>
> (Goodson, 1987: 220)

When attempts are made to separate off a new subject from its parent discipline – European studies from languages, drama from English, humanities from history – there are material interests at stake. The new boundaries involve a new distribution of resources – someone gets more and someone else less. Many a proposed innovation has floundered upon the opposition of potential losers in subject restructuring. Change cannot usefully be examined without attention to institutional micro-politics.

When structural change does occur the new divisions are quickly reinforced by new allegiances. New identities are forged:

> What ties a man more closely to one member of his profession may alienate him from another: when his group develops a unique mission, he may no longer share a mission with others in the same profession.
>
> (Bucher and Strauss, 1961: 227)

Where relationships between teachers are poor almost any attempt at innovation can be seen in terms of the political motivations or career aspirations of the instigators. One of the headteachers I interviewed described a group of teachers who had pressed for the school to become involved in PGCE work with the nearby university as 'suffering from frustrated ambition'.

European studies provides one example of a 'failed' innovation, a 'subject' which, with a few exceptions, was unable to establish itself as an independent department with its own resources and career structure. In contrast, classics provides a case where a once great subject has declined and virtually disappeared from the timetables of most comprehensive schools. Stray (1985) offers a case study of the declining fortunes of classics in Llangarr Comprehensive. The department and its teachers experienced a series of setbacks during the 1970s, which marked a gradual loss of political credibility and status for the subject. The first blow came when Latin was made optional:

> In the head of departments' meeting . . . the head confronted us with a sheet of paper which showed the options . . . we were horrified to see that Latin had been put against History. Whereas at present in the third form it was a class subject for the top two classes.
>
> (Stray, 1985: 39)

Such a change has both practical and symbolic implications. Symbolically, it indicates the removal of Latin from the assured status position of being a compulsory subject, a crushing blow. Access to pupil numbers is threatened and valued teaching, to the top classes, is at risk. Politically, two points are significant: first, the lack of consultation – the department was faced with a *fait accompli*; second, the inability of the department to mount a serious defence or call upon support from colleagues in other departments. The classics teachers were soon to find themselves further beleaguered. To add insult to injury, the reorganization of the option system also redefined classical studies as a subject for the less able, for those pupils who were prevented from continuing with French or Welsh:

> We get the poorer children, the difficult children. Now in a sense you may say this is justice, since we've had the cream in the past . . . but by virtue of the choice, the pupils we're getting, they're the rejects.
>
> (Stray, 1985: 216)

As noted already, a critical indicator of the status of a subject is the status of those it teaches. Once again the fortunes of the subject must be associated with the career opportunities of the teachers. The classicists began to find themselves under pressure in this regard from unsympathetic colleagues:

> One remarked that there were 'several people who don't see why a subject they think is on the decline should have two graded posts'; points are taken away from their own departments such as . . . practical subjects. They see themselves as more relevant to the comprehensive set-up than Classics.
>
> (Stray, 1985: 41)

Stray notes that the rivalry over promotion in Llangarr became ingrained in the micro-political processes of the school. The processes of influence were through these informal channels discussed above:

> The merger of the three different staffs and the tensions caused by 'overpointing' and the scarcity of promotions, in particular, discouraged open discussion; instead points were made via sarcastic jokes, the mutter in the corridor, separate trips into the 'administrative suite'.
>
> (Stray, 1985: 42)

Classics was often the subject and butt of these informal pressures and behind-the-scenes manoeuvrings. It was clearly a subject on the slide. There were few collegial scruples preventing the subject from being kicked when it was down. By 1974 Stray notes that 'The Llangarr classicists had thus suffered successive dislodgements towards an uncertain and marginal position. Underlying this process was a shift in the relations, and relative power, of the knowledge, occupation and organization systems' (Stray, 1985: 44).

In many schools both classics and European studies teachers have found themselves locked into a rather precarious and often unrewarding existence on the periphery of the curriculum. Their 'missions' (Bucher and Strauss, 1961) have failed and in the battle for institutional status they have been, for the present at least, routed. Falling rolls, a teacher who leaves, or any other contingency might extinguish the subject entirely. But clearly, in contrast, some new 'subjects' do make it, do establish themselves as secure and (relatively) permanent, taken-for-granted parts of the school curriculum.

Here again we must recognize that the rise and fall of subjects and departments is not solely dependent upon the outcomes of micro-political manoeuvring. The impact of changing patterns of external legitimation is also significant, Reid makes the point that

> For while it may appear that the professionals have power to determine what is taught (at school, district or national level, depending on the country in question), their scope is limited by the fact that only those forms and activities which have significance for external publics can, in the long run, survive.
>
> (Reid, 1984: 68)

While I would accept this statement in general terms, I would still want to argue that the legitimation of external publics is essentially a constraint upon or opportunity for the interest-groups and coalitions at work in the school. These constraints and opportunities are mediated through the micro-politics of the institution.

The impressive growth of computer studies is a good example. The high level of public awareness of 'high-technology', the massive infusion of government support and moneys, and programmes to get computers into every school during the 1980s provided a powerful base for the take-off in computing courses. Certainly in some schools, departments of computer studies emerged, in others such initiatives remain under the auspices of the mathematics departments. In some schools battle ensued to ensure that computing is seen to be relevant across a range of subjects; in others it is a specialist subject in its own right; in still others the impact of new technology has been minimal. The differences between schools can be explored and explained in terms of micro-political factors. The control of expensive, high-status hardware is at stake. So too are the reputations and futures of departments. The ability to respond to and cope with the new technologies may be critical in the long-term survival of certain subjects. This is not simply a matter of responding effectively but being seen to be able to respond. Once again it must be said that new curriculum initiatives like computing or TVEI or CPVE provide new career avenues; they also threatened established patterns of preferment. Indeed, a whole range of scarce and valued resources are subject to renegotiation. New skills are in demand, older skills are threatened with extinction. Interestingly, newer, younger teachers may be better trained and prepared, while others, keen to exploit the new opportunities, may turn to in-service courses. Awareness of new developments and up-to-date contacts, especially those which might provide equipment or money, are themselves important resources in the ebb and flow of status and influence.

External legitimation, or delegitimation, is just one factor at work in affecting the standing of departments and teachers. Innovations can be stifled by established interests or 'knowledgeable' young teachers may find themselves being sponsored by older, more influential colleagues. Outcomes, in terms of curriculum change cannot be assumed to be the result of rational, bureaucratic procedures. The departmental barons will not concede control easily. To a great extent, change or resistance to change will depend upon the relative influence of protagonists over organizational decision-making.

Influence at court

The complex political calculus which underpins the actual distribution of status, and resources, in the school is by no means easy to unpick. One way to begin is by examination of those cases which fall outside the typical pattern.

For example, where mathematics, science or English departments have failed to achieve status and resource preferment, or where departments like drama, CDT or music have done so.

Oak Farm Comprehensive (Ball and Lacey, 1980) provides a case of the former kind. Here the English department is to be found in a marginal position. The head of department explained his predicament:

> We have three full-time English teachers including myself. . . . So that at the moment we have ten people who are teaching partly in the department or wholly. I've been fighting for more full-time English specialists since I've been here. We ranged from 22 teaching English, for a while it was 17, now it's 10.
>
> (Ball and Lacey, 1980: 42)

Despite the improvements, the head of department faces a difficult situation: he is unable to draw upon the support of a group of teachers committed fully to the English department in any negotiations over resources. Indeed, the status of English as a department in its own right is questionable. Most of his staff have major commitments elsewhere:

> it involved one trying to bring as much pressure as possible to bear on the Head and Deputy Head and other influential people in the school to make them see that English was being too much fragmented. And the most important subject, at least I consider it so. . . . I know that every teacher is a teacher of English, the old tag, but it doesn't work out that way.
>
> (Ball and Lacey, 1980: 158)

The head of department seems to acknowledge his own lack of influence in the school and the failure among those who have influence to recognize his case as valid. English has failed to acquire the infrastructural base which accompanies and underpins subject status:

> It's only for three years that I've had a second in charge. It was thought that there were other priorities. And also physical things like an office. Which is quite a sore point, it hasn't been recognised in that way. But this was determined not so much by a positive opposition but by the circumstances which prevail in the school which make it difficult. I just asked in this financial year that some provision be made whereby I could get a base to work from, but although it appeared on the list of requests, when it was sorted into priorities, it missed the priorities and was shelved again.
>
> (Ball and Lacey, 1980: 159)

Without a group of specialist teachers English cannot establish its credibility and assert demands for resources and facilities. There is a vicious circle. While the head of English continues to have no influence over the definition of new appointments, there is little possibility of such specialists being appointed.

English will continue to be regarded as something that anyone can teach. Once established in the culture and history of the institution, collective assumptions of this kind are difficult to break down. As the head of department sees it, the preferences and background of the headteacher are crucial factors at work here:

> it so largely depends on the background and previous careers of Headmasters. My present Headmaster has done quite a lot since he's been here for the science department; which is a good thing. But I feel that English is not recognised as firmly and as widely as it ought to be.
>
> (Ball and Lacey, 1980: 159)

In the same vein, St John Brooks (1983) provides as account of an English department in a Bristol comprehensive which as a result of ideological differences with the headteacher is also excluded from influence over school policy. Indeed, to a great extent the department was unwilling to engage with the accepted procedures of debate and policy-making.

> The department as a whole could not defend their position in a manner comprehensible or acceptable to most of the other teachers, especially the Headmaster. By rejecting the bureaucratic world of institutions and the realm of public argument and debate, along with the kind of justification it demands, such romantic individuals or groups are destined to remain forever marginal.
>
> (St John Brooks, 1983: 56)

By opting out of school micro-politics, the department marginalized itself and put itself under pressure. Sponsorship by the head can clearly do much to advance the position of a department both in terms of status and resources. An antagonistic head can make life very difficult. The relationship between headteacher and head of department will to a great extent rely on mutual obligation. The head will expect efficiency or loyalty or both, in return for continued support. This relationship will thus depend not only upon the *quality* of personal relationships, but also upon a matching of styles and some sharing of goals and ideologies. However, this is not the only relationship to be attended to: the head of department must face in three directions, towards the headteacher and senior management and a concern with whole-school policy, towards the interpersonal arena of departmental relationships and the specific policy interests of the department, and across towards other heads of department as colleagues with shared problems or competing interests. Taafe quotes a head of creative arts from a London comprehensive on the qualities of a head of faculty required by his headteacher:

> To be a senior head you must be very flexible and devious. Flexible to fit in with the headmaster, back off if necessary. Devious, to get your faculty to do what the headmaster wants.
>
> (Taafe, 1980: 23)

Careful tending of their patch, positive support from colleagues and positive indicators of department success can put the head of department in a powerful political position. In some cases, from the headteacher's point of view, heads of department can become too powerful. From Taafe's study again, the head of mathematics explains:

> If you look at the staff overall, forgetting creative arts for the moment, you will not find any large departments. I think this is a conscious effort on the part of the Head to break down influential bodies on the staff. Certainly maths has no influence.
>
> (Taafe, 1980: 39)

The head of languages takes up the point:

> Look at Science, you have specialists there, it is probably the largest department in the school. The last Head of Department was very strong, utterly ruthless, out for what he could get for his department. Science was a potent influence in the school. I don't think the Head liked it. Look at the new appointment, he's wet, the exact opposite. The result is science now is not an influential body.
>
> (Taafe, 1980: 40)

Two major themes of the analysis emerge here. One is the role of influence: here we see the problematic nature of *too much* influence, at least as far as the head is concerned. The other is the crucial importance of control of appointments and promotions: heads can do a great deal to bolster their position politically by the appointments that they make. However, it should not be assumed that it is the headteacher who is always successful in power struggles with departments. Latus offers the following account of ground gained by a head of department against opposition from 'the hierarchy':

> The English department is led by an academically strong Head of Department who in addition to taking over in difficult circumstances also had to assert his authority over his own specialism. This involved challenging the deputy headmaster, a member of the department, who was exercising positional power and thus depriving Mr Jenks [the HOD] of authority and status. In ousting his rival Mr Jenks also secured hitherto unknown autonomy for the department and this in turn led to gains on other fronts e.g. the right to be present at departmental appointments, and also a policy change: English specialists are appointed rather than general subject teachers offering some English.
>
> (Latus, 1977: 36)

Here the head of department gained ground in exactly those areas which proved so intractable for the head of English at Oak Farm.

The political role of the head of department is clearly significant not only in relations with the head but also in dealings with their own department members. If the heads of department are unable to produce and maintain at least an outward display of unity and coherence within their departments, then it becomes extremely difficult to mount a convincing case for new initiatives, additional resources or changes to the timetable. Both ideological and interpersonal tensions can arise to undermine the unity of a department, and heads of department find themselves more or less able to deal with the difficulties which ensue. (See Jago, 1983: ch. 8, for a discussion of leadership problems in subject departments.) If strong heads of department can create problems, so too can weak ones. If matters threaten major disruption, then the headteacher may step in.

Meadows (1981) describes a situation at Millrace Comprehensive where an existing head of department is eased out of her position and replaced, through a series of manoeuvres carefully managed by members of the department and the headteacher. Clearly, the head of department was not well regarded by her colleagues:

> Mary Standen gave the impression of perpetual bewilderment. She had a narrow, Scots', rigorous view . . . but she was out of her depth. Her qualities just weren't right. . . . The department was put in charge of an incompetent. (Colleague 1)
>
> (Meadows, 1981: 14)

> At the interviews some were even worse and so she got the job. She was administratively conscientious, but never well organized. She tended to listen to the last person, therefore the department's autonomy went. (Colleague 2)
>
> (Meadows, 1981: 14)

The members of department attempted their own solution to the problems created for them. Informal arrangements, a negotiated order of sorts, were brought into play to fill and to circumvent the formal vacuum:

> things tended to get done via the back door . . . she was prepared to let me get on, but I was a senior teacher in her eyes. She was very conscious of protocol. But she wouldn't give Victor responsibility for the middle school course. So, last year, the conspirators explored ways of moving things along. Victor produced a job description. It accepted Mary's nominal control, but the responsibility for English was split between different people. The head accepted the job description. (Colleague 1)
>
> (Meadows, 1981: 14–15)

With the retirement of the school librarian, despite the appointment of a temporary replacement, the head saw a solution to the English department difficulties:

> He saw the situation and worked out a way of getting a new head of department. He created a department – Library and Resources – and moved Mary Standen into it. (Colleague 3)
>
> (Meadows, 1981: 16)

The temporary incumbent was understandably not pleased: she had believed that the head had promised the permanent library post to her.

> Abruptly he pushed Mary Standen sideways into my job. He took five minutes to tell me. I was shocked but I went back and argued with him for half-an-hour. I told him he was unfair. He is incapable of running a school. He has no feelings. He will walk over people. (Colleague 4)
>
> (Meadows, 1981: 16)

Once again the interplay between institutional politics and individual careers is in evidence. Political solutions tend to dispense advantage to some and disadvantage to others.

What I have been attempting here is to establish some of those factors which enter into the making and breaking of departmental reputations and subject status, concentrating on the degree of influence that may be available to a department in varying circumstances. Certainly, however, as the case of classics illustrates, there are a number of objective indicators which enter into the appraisal of any department. The inability to attract option choices, a poor teaching or disciplinary record and poor examination results will, over time, undermine the position of even the most well entrenched subject. This is evident in the following interview extract where a headteacher explains his view of the mathematics department in his school:

> Their track record now is one which says 'No I'm not going to do this'. In the summer they wanted to have single-sex maths. Well, I said no to that. I had already given them £2,000 above their normal capitation to invest in SMILE. So they had this heavy investment in SMILE and immediately, within one year, they wanted to move on to something else. The difficult thing is why is it that the English results are good and the maths results are so appalling. It's roughly 10 per cent O-level in mathematics and 58 per cent in English, across the fifth-year group. It must be to do with the teaching, and with the organization. Now, the maths department has a problem because of the head of maths.

In the contemporary jargon, heads of departments are 'middle managers', with all the implications of 'line' responsibility that that suggests. It may be that baronial politics and the feudal relationships through which they have worked are being replaced by the bureaucratic procedures and relationships of management theory. On the other hand, the pristine language of management may only serve to obscure the real struggles over policy and budgets – who gets what, when and how?

[. . .]

References

Ball, S. J. and Lacey, C. (1980) 'Subject disciplines and the opportunity for group action: a measured critique of subject sub-cultures', in P. E. Woods (ed.) *Teacher Strategies*, London, Croom Helm.

Bucher, R. and Strauss, A. (1961) 'Professions in process', *American Journal of Sociology*, 66, January: 325–34.

Esland, G. (1971) 'Teaching and learning as the organization of knowledge', in M. F. D. Young (ed.) *Knowledge and Control*, London, Collier-Macmillan.

Goodson, I. F. (1987) *The Making of Curriculum: Essays in the Social History of Education*, Lewes, Falmer Press.

Jago, W. (1983) 'Teachers at work: a study of individual and role in school', unpublished Ph.D. thesis, Falmer, University of Sussex, Education Area.

Latus, E. (1977) 'Seatown High School', unpublished MA project in Education, Falmer, University of Sussex, Education Area.

Meadows, E. (1981) 'Politics and personalities', unpublished MA project in Education, Institutional Profile, Falmer, University of Sussex, Education Area.

Reid, W. A. (1984) 'Curricular topics as institutional categories', in I. F. Goodson and S. J. Ball (eds) *Defining the Curriculum: Histories and Ethnographies*, Lewes, Falmer Press.

Richardson, E. (1973) *The Teacher, the School and the Task of Management*, London, Heinemann.

St John Brooks, C. (1983) 'English: a curriculum for personal development?', in M. Hammersley and A. Hargreaves (eds) *Curriculum Practice: Some Sociological Case Studies*, Lewes, Falmer Press.

Smetherham, D. (1979) 'Identifying strategies', paper given at SSRC-funded conference, 'Teacher and Pupil Strategies', Oxford, September.

Stray, C. (1985) 'From monopoly to marginality: classics in English education since 1800', in I. F. Goodson (ed.) *Social Histories of the Secondary Curriculum*, Lewes, Falmer Press.

Taafe, R. (1980) 'Charisma and collegiate: conflict or harmony?' Unpublished MA minor project in education, Education Area, University of Sussex.

Wildavsky, A. (1968) 'Budgeting as a political process', in D. Sills (ed.) *International Encyclopaedia of the Social Sciences*, 2, 192–9, New York, Cromwell, Collier Macmillan.

Author index

Subject index